THIS GENERATION

Volume I

NOTE

This work will be completed in two
volumes; the second will be ready
this autumn.

THE THREE MONARCHS OF THE TWENTIETH CENTURY

THIS GENERATION

A HISTORY OF
GREAT BRITAIN AND IRELAND
FROM 1900 TO 1926

by

Thomas Cox Meech

VOLUME I
1900—1914

CHATTO & WINDUS
97 & 99 ST. MARTIN'S LANE
LONDON

FIRST PUBLISHED 1927

PREFACE

The aim of this work is the presentation of a faithful picture of Great Britain and Ireland during the first quarter of the twentieth century in a narrative which may be interesting to readers of all ages and in every walk of life.

The greater proportion of the incidents are described from personal knowledge. By kind permission of the Publishers the writer has received considerable assistance from the Annual Register in checking the sequence of events.

With the courteous assent of the Editors and Publishers the Encyclopædia Britannica has been consulted, and valuable help obtained, for the purpose of linking and verifying certain historical details.

It has been thought desirable to quote certain individual pronouncements and important passages from the official verbatim reports of Parliamentary debates.

T. C. M.

THE TEMPLE,
   LONDON.

CONTENTS

ILLUSTRATIONS

THIS GENERATION

*

Chapter 1

AT THE DAWN

THE driver on the dickey of the hansom cab reined in his horse smartly.

The Constable's uplifted hand enforced the Sessional Order from the House of Commons to the Commissioner of Police:

> That the passages through the streets to this House be kept free and open and that no obstruction be permitted to hinder the passage of Members to and from this House.

A neatly built, well knit man slowly crossed the street in front of the halted traffic. His head slightly forward he glanced at the watching crowd through a single eyeglass and passed beyond the big iron gates with the confident step of one for whom the fierce light that beats upon a statesman has no embarrassment.

The new century was at the dawn. The hansom cab was the swiftest public vehicle on the London streets. Mr. Joseph Chamberlain was the most conspicuous figure in public life. Day after day as he walked through Whitehall from the Colonial Office little knots of people gathered on the pavements outside the House of Commons—the infallible indication that Parliament is unusually interesting. The old century now gliding into history was leaving a legacy of turmoil arising out of the long controversy between British statesmen and the Boers or farmers dwelling in the Transvaal and Orange Free State Republics founded by Dutch settlers in South Africa. The discovery of gold and precious stones and the consequent rush of immigrants had brought exclusive old-world pastoralism into conflict with commercialism. Discussions and abortive negotiations as to the rights of

British "Outlanders" and the extent of British powers of
suzerainty had developed into war.

The campaign that was to have been over—officially—
months ago was dragging on and on. Business men said it
"held things up". Bands of Boers, with their matchless
capacity for moving rapidly from point to point ; aided by
their superior knowledge of a country in which the regulation
tactics of orthodox warfare proved useless; were still inflicting
serious damage on the British positions and continuously
evading capture. The exploits of General de Wet, the most
elusive leader of these galloping troops, had become notorious
throughout the civilised world. Britishers travelling abroad
were asked "When will you catch de Wet?"

The British people, willing to take most things in good
humour up to a point, smiled philosophically at a cartoon
which depicted two leading statesmen as very old and
decrepit men still assuring each other that de Wet would be
captured very soon. There was, however, a limit to this
tranquil acceptance of facts. We were entering upon one of
those periods inseparable from all wars when a cloud of
pessimism descends upon the popular mind. The situation
was weighed and found wanting by the armchair critics of
the clubs. The drawing-rooms were unusually unhappy.
The oracles of the saloon bars were profoundly eloquent.
That greatest of all exponents of public opinion; now, alas,
gone without leaving a successor—the driver of the old horse
bus—assured favoured passengers on the box seat that
something would have to be done about it.

It was strictly a military matter, but by all the traditions of
the British constitution the Prime Minister and the Ministers
selected by him as heads of the great Departments of State
were directly responsible. The British Public claimed its
inalienable right to put everything down to the Government.

There were people who said the war might have been
avoided and that peace should be made immediately. These
persons were called "Pro-Boers"—the most violent term of
abuse the tongue of conventional man could name.

The man in the street looked to "Joe". As Secretary of State for the Colonies he was directly identified with the policy of the Government in South Africa. Was he going to put things right?

No man knew better than Mr. Chamberlain that this question was on the lips or in the minds of the men and women lined up outside the gates of the broad Palace Yard that separates the House of Commons from the hum of the busy streets.

At the south-west corner of the Yard the Colonial Secretary entered the imposing buildings by a private door reserved for Members of the Government, and passed on to the special retiring room set apart for him as a Minister, where his Secretaries were waiting with latest information as to the feeling in the House. From thence along the silent corridors, through the door behind the Speaker's Chair, he entered the Debating Chamber.

For a quarter-of-a-century he had been a Member of the House of Commons and every nook was familiar. Possibly he had by this time forgotten that first inevitable impression of mingled surprise and disappointment at the smallness of the Chamber, and the austere simplicity of the long wooden benches upholstered in green leather upon which great men sat cheek by jowl. He realised no doubt that the House is a debating and deliberative assembly—not a platform for oratorical demonstrations.

In the full-bottomed wig and flowing robes of the centuries the Speaker—so designated because he does not speak save as the official spokesman of the whole House—presided with the impressive dignity of moral authority. To the right of his Chair stretched the Treasury Bench, occupied exclusively by Members of the Government.

For generations the country had lived politically under the two-party system. The influence of leadership in the latter half of the nineteenth century under Lord Beaconsfield and Mr. Gladstone still remained. These two born captains of multitudes had so thoroughly ranged their countrymen behind them in one camp or the other that as Gilbert and Sullivan in their inimitable comic opera "Iolanthe" truthfully recorded:—

> Every boy and every gal
> That's born into the world alive
> Is either a little Liber-al
> Or else a little Conservat-ive!

The Conservatives, anxious to "leave well alone", were assumed to regard change as undesirable until proved necessary. The Liberals were understood to anticipate change, and claimed by so doing to avoid the risk of waiting till necessity became danger.

These broad interpretations included various grades of thought. There were "progressive Conservatives" and also old-fashioned "Tories"—the designation borne by the century-ago Party of which the Conservatives were the historical descendents. The "Whigs"—forbears of the Liberals and old-time opponents of the Tories—were almost forgotten, though the term was occasionally applied to a cautious Liberal as distinguishing him from the Radical—or advanced Member of the Liberal Party.

The Marquis of Salisbury had succeeded Lord Beaconsfield. The Liberal Unionists—men who had been followers of Mr. Gladstone but left him in 1886 when he made Home Rule and a separate Parliament for Ireland an essential part of Liberal policy—had their own organisation of which Mr. Chamberlain was a leading Member, but in effect they were at one with the Conservatives. Lord Rosebery had succeeded Mr. Gladstone as Leader of the Liberal Party but had retired, and the Liberals were now led by Sir Henry Campbell-Bannerman.

For all practical parliamentary purposes the old century closed with a clean-cut division between two Parties in Great Britain.

From the south and west of Ireland some eighty representatives had come to Westminster year in and year out under protest. As Irish Nationalists they pledged themselves to accept no Office in the British—or, as they described it, the English—Parliament. Their one mission was to demand in season and out of season the restoration of the Irish Parliament that existed before the Act of Union between Great Britain and Ireland—which Act they repudiated, declaring it to be contrary to the wishes of the vast majority of the Irish people. Led by Mr. John Redmond, a member of one of the old county families of Ireland, an orator with the qualities of a statesman, they included members of the Irish aristocracy like Sir Thomas Esmonde, professional men such as Mr. John Dillon, a doctor, Mr. Tim Healy, a successful barrister, litterateurs and journalists like Mr. T. P. O'Connor, farmers and peasants.

The Conservatives were returned at a General Election in the autumn of 1900 by a crushing majority over both the Liberals and the Irish Nationalists for a second period of Office after having been in power from 1895. According to constitutional usage their Leader was Prime Minister and selected from his own Party the other Ministers collectively known to praise or blame as "the Government".

Mr. Joseph Chamberlain took his place on the Treasury Bench beside Mr. Arthur (afterwards Lord) Balfour, Leader of the Conservative Party in the House of Commons and thus Leader of the House; outwardly a dreamy philosopher lolling upon his hips with his feet resting against the long table—actually the most nimble mind in the assembly. On the other side of the table Sir Henry Campbell-Bannerman sat between Sir William Harcourt—a link with the great past of nineteenth century oratory—and Mr. Asquith (afterwards The Earl of Oxford), the concise logical debater of the newer school. According to parliamentary usage, Sir Henry led the Opposition—the recognised critics of the Government.

Behind their respective leaders, in the places above the gangway which cuts through the middle of the long green benches on either side, sat the unswerving Party supporters. The younger and more independent men of both Parties took their places below the respective gangways.

From the Government side there were some murmurs of unrest—more in sorrow than in anger. The Liberals above the gangway were watchful, but inclined to dwell on matters of detail. From the benches below the gangway on the Opposition side the criticism took the form of direct frontal attack, open and avowed. Foremost in these vigorous tactics was a dark-haired, round-faced, genial young man who occupied the corner seat of the second bench and slashed the Government with all the fiery eloquence of the Cymric Celt. This Hotspur of young Liberalism was known at Westminster—and far beyond—as David Lloyd George, the Welsh pro-Boer.

The Irish Nationalists, also bitterly opposed to the war, sat immediately behind Mr. Lloyd George—" permanently anchored in opposition", as Mr. Redmond once observed.

Such was the composition of the House of Commons—the Chamber of representatives elected by the voters in the towns and counties. Majorities here might come and go. In another Chamber on the opposite side of the building, beautifully decorated with symbols of ancient tradition and the effigies of great men in history, the Peers of the Realm, occupying their seats by hereditary right or special creation independently of the chances and fortunes of elections, were led by the Marquis of Salisbury.

As a peer Lord Salisbury was ineligible for election to the House of Commons and was thus remote from the Debates in that Assembly. He belonged to the patrician order of Prime Ministers. His massive frame, flowing beard and dome-like forehead inspired a simple faith in the solidarity of the existing order of society. That floating mass of opinion which takes no deep interest in Party fortunes and by its very mobility decides the issue, held a single-hearted belief that the great brain which must be at work in that wise head—allied to Mr. Chamberlain's "pushfulness"— would bring the old country through in God's good time.

Within the British Empire the bonds of sympathy between the various self-governing communities were growing stronger and stronger as the threads of the legal ties grew finer and

finer. On January 1st, 1901, Australia formally became one
large Commonwealth. The task of linking up the six
Australian Colonies into one Federal Union—a Dominion with
complete self-government extending over a whole Continent—
had long occupied the minds of great thinkers and workers
in Australia and in Great Britain. Mr. Edmund Barton, an
Australian born, was the first Prime Minister of the Commonwealth, and a Cabinet was formed to represent the various
Colonies—now known as States—each of which still preserved
its individual constitutional liberties.

This was destined to be the concluding Imperial achievement of a glorious reign. Queen Victoria had summoned
fifteen Parliaments extending over sixty-four years; her
death on the 22nd January, 1901,—the peaceful passing from
ripened years to rest—touched the hearts of a homely people.
The wonderfully impressive tribute by the Marquis of
Salisbury in the House of Lords after long years of service
to the Great Queen was as the soul-searching note of a
powerful minute bell. The Prime Minister was the most
venerable figure in the world of statesmanship. His speech
marked the end of an epoch.

It was left to Mr. Balfour in the House of Commons, after
expressing deep reverence for the dead Monarch, to herald
the new reign in recognition of the all-mastering human fact
that the world is for the living.

Chapter 2

RETROSPECTION AND ANTICIPATION

AT the end of the Victorian era the chronicler of that day
gazed back over a marvellous period of ever-increasing
change and ever-increasing prosperity during which an old
had been transformed to a new Society.

Man was moulding the forces of nature to his will. Steam
and electricity had commenced to revolutionise travel and
manufacture. Social relations had grown more elastic. The

outposts of an age-worn citadel had surrendered. The presence of Peers of the Realm on Boards of Directors under the application of the Limited Liability Company Acts forecasted the slow decline of ancient prejudice. In the great novel "Lorna Doone", it will be remembered, the lordly and law-abiding relative of the robber band of outlawed gentry on Exmoor indulgently assured his cousin: "Trade alone can spoil our blood". That spirit lived long after the later Stuart period of which the words were written, as shown by the mid-Victorian sentiment immortalised by Charles Dickens, who in "Bleak House" describes the consternation of Sir Leicester Dedlock when the Ironmaster dared to draw a parallel between the Dedlock ancestral home and a factory. All this was changing in the restless transition of national life.

The new order was as yet only at the initial stages. Business at the close of the century was still conducted in the main by "private enterprise"—a term ultimately used in a much wider meaning than that which it is here intended to convey. The High Street grocer was the rule; the branch of the "multiple" shop the exception. Well-informed public spirited tradesmen, generation succeeding generation, controlled local affairs. Factories in the industrial districts were owned by private firms or conducted by companies in which the family of the original founders held the dominating interest. An ideal description of such an establishment was given many years later in a reminiscent speech by a distinguished Statesman who had been an active partner in the concern:

It was a place where I knew and had known from childhood every man on the ground, a place where I was able to talk with the men not only about the troubles in the works but troubles at home; where strikes and lock-outs were unknown. It was a place where the fathers and grandfathers of the men then working there had worked, and where their sons went automatically into the business. It was also a place where nobody ever " got the sack ".

In such places fortunes had been made and families destined to occupy high positions in public life and in Society had been founded. Human feeling was allied to efficiency.

The firms with no strikes or lock-outs, it should be stated, were not entirely representative in that respect. Shortly before the end of the century there had been a long and bitter struggle between employers and wage-earners in the engineering trade. Industrial troubles had existed throughout the rise and progress of the industrial system, but there were many firms and many trades which could point to long records of peace.

Keen observers detected the signs of new conditions. Rumours of great combinations came from America. British undertakings began to link up for convenience in working. Men predicted—some in trepidation, some with philosophic complacency—the trend of business towards amalgamations arising out of a driving force that compelled people to combine for competition and for protection against competition.

The domestic habits and customs of the people then, as in every age, were "not what they used to be". Pessimists assured each other in vague terms that the rising generation was neither so well-behaved nor so respectful to its elders as it ought to be; that the people of that day were a sad contrast to the people of some unspecified former period; that things were going from bad to worse and nobody could say "what the country was coming to". On the other hand optimists observed a change for the good, and publicists of big repute recorded an improvement in morals and in manners. Young minds—unable to judge from personal knowledge between the contending sages—could only concentrate upon the future and hope for the best.

Wherever facts and figures were available they were on the side of the optimists. It was general ground that there had been a remarkable decrease in the habit of over-drinking among the upper and middle classes in these Islands since Byron, with his painful cynicism, wrote "Man being reasonable must get drunk". The example extended to persons in less prosperous circumstances and statistics proved that crime had materially diminished.

The general character of public amusements showed an improvement. This was indicated by a comparison between the new type of popular entertainment and the very few survivals of the once-popular music halls where alcoholic refreshment stood on a ledge in front of every seat and the clinking of drinking vessels competed in noise with the crude inanities of the red-nosed comedian.

The "New Woman" was endeavouring to assert herself. Economic conditions were already demanding a wider scope of occupation. Factory work had afforded an outlet for the weekly wage-earner. Shops provided employment for a certain number but promotion was limited. Managerial posts were mainly held by men. Broadly speaking the ambitious girl had a choice—or a chance—between teaching, for which many of them were unsuited; nursing, for which many were unfitted; or marriage. Business houses and Government Departments were timidly admitting girls to minor appointments. The lady secretary was seldom met, and then only in literary circles. The lady doctor was heard of but would hardly be called a "general" practitioner. For a very big proportion of middle-class young women life was a vocationless struggle with genteel poverty in overcrowded villas. It was quite clear that an alteration was bound to come. Among the well-to-do classes women were also growing tired of Victorian conditions. A tendency to join in outdoor sports on the same terms as men was exhibiting itself, but—apart from the hunting field—this had not yet become general. Ladies of fashion were passing through an uncertain stage between the boredom of drawing-room life and some as yet undefinable mental and physical activities. Meantime it was recorded that card playing among the classes which constituted Society was an absorbing occupation. One well-known authority wrote:

It may be doubted whether Englishwomen of that order ever indulged in games of cards before quite as freely and with as much devotion to the pastime as they are doing in England at the present day.

It was at that juncture that the cigarette invaded feminine circles. Writing of the "spread of the smoking habit among Englishwomen in Society", Mr. Justin McCarthy the cultured nineteenth century Historian observed:

> Only the other day, it seems, when no English women of education and respectability ever thought of imitating their fathers, their brothers, or their husbands in the smoking habit.

Among "fast" women the cigarette was not unknown and was supposed to have been adopted from Southern European customs. All of a sudden—so it appeared to the Historian watching the development of the new century—ladies of fashion were reported to be taking an occasional cigarette "for their nerves". Then it speedily became a pastime, but the custom was strictly confined to private houses. It was never seen in public places and was as yet practically unknown outside what was called the "smart set".

It should also be mentioned that men who closely studied social conditions observed an expanding and deepening interest on the part of the public—and by people in "Society"—in the homes and lives of the poor. The housing conditions in the large towns and industrial districts as well as in the agricultural areas were a serious problem. Private charity did much to alleviate suffering, but it could not solve the ever-growing question of decent houses for decent people. One of the most embarrassing legacies from the past was the system—or lack of system—under which habitations had been erected for the working population. Rows of houses were thrown up without any regard to town planning. In many instances they were built "back to back" without any "through" ventilation on either side. The builders of small dwellings, even in the little towns, where there was plenty of space, had a habit of crowding them together in cramped courts off the main streets with the front doors and windows looking into narrow passages where the sun rarely penetrated.

In some of the mining districts the conditions were even worse than in the towns. Pits had been sunk which might or might not be "worked out" in a few years and primitive huts had been erected in a temporary fashion. The years had gone on; the huts still remained. They were remote from main drainage, and harrowing descriptions were written from time to time of the insanitary environment. Material prosperity during the rapid growth of trade and commerce, of which the new generation were reaping the reward, was counterbalanced in no small measure by social errors committed from lack of thought and not from lack of heart.

The death of Sir Walter Besant early in the new century recalled the fact that writers and social reformers had continued the work of Charles Dickens who in his day stirred the public conscience. Walter Besant's book "All Sorts and Conditions of Men" had stimulated interest in London's East End condition, and, as a consequence, the "People's Palace" in the Mile End Road was established. Another book that had created considerable enthusiasm was Richard Whiting's "No. 5 John Street" which vividly described the existence of workers in slumland. The stage, too, was doing its part. Mr. Charles (afterwards Sir Charles) Hawtrey in "A Message from Mars" preached the doctrines of altruism with huge success. The general trend of thought was towards a sympathetic view of life.

The broad outlook was promising. The everyday person believed in the good times ahead if only the war would come to an end.

Chapter 3

THE NEW PARLIAMENT. SAD NEWS

AN auburn-haired youth one evening very early in the new year hovered within the entrance of the House of Commons like a bird seeking a favourable landing.

Members had heard that a son of Lord Randolph Churchill, a Conservative leader of the "eighteen eighties", was among the young men returned at the General Election.   His family were direct descendants of John Churchill, the great Duke of Marlborough, and his God-parents had named him Winston after John's father—Sir Winston Churchill, a prominent Dorsetshire Royalist Squire who held out against the Cromwellians in the great Civil War, and was driven for shelter across the Border a few miles into Devon, but afterwards sat as Member of Parliament for Weymouth and Lyme Regis in turn.

The new Winston was now one of the representatives for Oldham.   He had already gone through thrilling experiences as a soldier in Cuba, Tirah and the Sudan.   He had also served as a special war correspondent in South Africa, and the subject immediately under discussion had a special attraction for him.   The Government were being attacked on their South African policy.

The King, in accordance with his prerogative, had summoned Parliament and duly opened the 1901 Session with all the old-time ceremonial—the procession through the streets, the assembly in the House of Lords, the peeresses and peers in their robes occupying the red benches; while the Members of the House of Commons stood behind their Speaker at the end of the Chamber, their presence having been required for the purpose of hearing the King's speech. During the latter years of Queen Victoria's reign the fatigue of this function had been avoided.   The duty of reading the speech was performed by Royal Commission and the text distributed beforehand to the newspapers.   King Edward revived the stately function and read the speech himself from the Throne.

It was the duty of both Houses to vote an Address thanking His Majesty for his gracious speech from the Throne, but since, under our Constitution, the words of the speech are drafted by the Government as a forecast of the policy to be pursued by them during the forthcoming parliamentary year, opponents of the Government were entitled to move amendments expressing regret that His Majesty's Ministers had not advised him more wisely.   Governments have fallen on adverse votes upon such amendments. This Government, backed by a big majority, met their critics without fear of consequences.

Mr. Lloyd George vigorously denounced their policy in South Africa. He contended that such terms should be given to the Boers as would bring the war to an end.

During this onslaught Mr. Winston Churchill, by the courtesy of an old Member of the House, had secured the corner seat of the second bench on the Government side—an ideal vantage point for a maiden speech. Mr. Lloyd George, observing that Mr. Churchill had got into position, said he would not prolong his own argument, as he understood that a new Member whom the House would desire to hear intended to take part in the Debate.

When Mr. Churchill rose, the indicators, which by electrical contrivance spell out the name of the Member addressing the House, informed the men in the writing rooms, smoke room and library that one of the most interesting of their recruits was on his feet. The opening sentences suggested that the new Member was unlikely to suffer from lack of confidence.

"If I were a Boer I hope I should be fighting in the field," said Mr. Churchill at one point and this burst of candour was cheered in all parts of the House. He earnestly hoped that whenever these brave and unhappy men prepared to recognise that their small independence must be merged in the larger liabilities of the British Empire there would be a full guarantee for their property and religion; an assurance of equal rights; a promise of representative institutions; and last of all, but not least of all, what the British Army would most readily accord to a brave and enduring foe—all the honours of war.

"If," Mr. Churchill continued, "the Boers remain deaf to the voice of reason and blind to the hand of friendship: if they refuse all overtures and disdain all terms then, while we cannot help admiring their determination and endurance, we can only hope that our own race in pursuit of what they feel to be a righteous cause will show determination as strong and endurance as lasting."

Concluding his speech, the son of the Conservative statesman, looking round at the crowded benches, thanked the
House for this gratifying reception and modestly attributed
it to "a splendid memory which many honourable Members
still preserve".

It was quite evident that a great family tradition was
renewed.   In certain quarters it was prophetically observed
that in the course of history Winston would not be known as
the son of Randolph but Randolph as the father of Winston.

The Debate meantime pursued its course.   When the time
was ripe for a Government reply Mr. Joseph Chamberlain
rose slowly opposite one of the two brass-bound despatch
boxes containing certain official documents which stand on
either side of the Table and provide a convenient ledge for
manuscript points when Ministers or Opposition Leaders
address the House.

The Colonial Secretary began on a note which from another
man would have been inaudible.   So extraordinary was the
carrying power of his balanced musical voice that every
syllable could be heard from the far corner of the Gallery.
As usual, Mr. Chamberlain scarcely spoke a single sentence
above his ordinary tone.   The striking characteristic of his
speeches was that he never shouted.   There was keen
thrusting force behind each crisp, telling phrase.   Defending
the policy of the Government, he proceeded on the principle
that attack is the most effective defence and swung the current
of the Debate round by sheer weight of individuality till his
accusers became the accused.

Subsequently in the same Debate Mr. Asquith deprecated
the epithet "pro-Boers" but indicated that he did not concur
with the tone of the attack made upon the Government by
Mr. Lloyd George.

The Debate typified the position of Parties, more particularly in the Liberal ranks, some of whom were represented
by Mr. Asquith and some by Mr. Lloyd George.   Although
Lord Rosebery, Mr. Gladstone's immediate successor, had
retired from the Leadership, there were movements to bring

him back by those Liberals who gave a general support to the Government upon the South African problem. Sir Henry Campbell-Bannerman, as the recognised Leader, endeavoured to hold the balance between the different sections, but was assumed to lean towards what was described as the "pro-Boer" position. Mr. John Morley (afterwards Lord Morley), the scholar and statesman, was frankly anti-war.

Those Members of the Party who followed Lord Rosebery and Mr. Asquith were known as Liberal Imperialists or, more familiarly, "Lib Imps". Mr. Asquith disclaimed this title or any hyphenated description of Liberalism, but the designation was the popular colloquial term. The "Lib Imps" dined together on several occasions and discussed the situation. Other dinners were held by the "pro-Boers". It was announced that a state of "war to the knife and fork" had been declared.

It has always been an accepted principle of British parliamentary life that for effective work there must be an efficient Opposition; critical, watchful and tireless—a disciplinary check upon, and a salutary spur to, the Government of the day.

Statesmen in the past have laid it down that the first duty of an Opposition is to oppose. The Liberals were not sufficiently agreed for this essential task. The Irish Nationalists began to take upon themselves the spade work of Opposition. As a consequence, Ireland made the pace, and in pursuance of this purpose a wild Irish demonstration arose out of the special right and jealously guarded privilege of the House of Commons to vote the necessary supplies of money to the Government.

In the early part of the year estimates of the needed expenditure are presented by each Department. These are discussed in the first instance in "Committee of Supply".—The whole House resolves itself into a Committee for this purpose with the Speaker out of the Chair and the Deputy Speaker, in his capacity as Chairman of Committees, sitting at the Table. The Estimates having been passed in Committee are "reported" to the House with the Speaker in the Chair, re-discussed if necessary, and, after the formula "The House doth agree", the money is at last placed at the disposal of the Government.

The Services must have funds to go on with while the Estimates are passing through these stages, and, according to custom, the Government asks for a "Vote on Account".

In this instance they asked for a vote of seventeen millions to be applied for various purposes, and the House went into Committee to discuss it. It so happened that one topic affecting Secondary Education had become very pressing, and the Debate on this part of the vote went on till midnight, when, according to the rules in force at that period, the House should automatically adjourn. It was within the prerogative of the Government to claim to move that the main question—embodying the whole vote—be put. Mr. Balfour exercised this right, and immediately the Irish Nationalist Members protested vehemently that there were Irish votes in the seventeen millions upon which they wished to speak.

It was then a fixed rule that when a motion was put to the vote the House must be cleared for the division. A short period was allowed while the strident notes of many bells pierced every corner of the building, and if a Member desired to remain neutral he must escape into some other part of the precincts during these few minutes. When the bells ceased ringing the outer doors were shut. Every Member then in the Chamber must go into the "Aye" Lobby, which runs parallel with the House to the right of the Chair, or the "No" Lobby to the left, and be counted by the Division Clerks, who tick off the names of the Members as they pass through a turnstile at the Lobby doors.

An Irish Member rose to a point of order. The Chairman ruled that the House must clear for the Division.

The Irish Members remained in their seats shouting and gesticulating and declaring that "not an Irish voice had been heard".

"I must ask honourable Members to be kind enough to proceed to the Division Lobbies," said the Chairman after another pause. A storm of protest and defiance was the

B

only response. The Chairman sent for the Speaker and reported to him that certain Members had defied the Chair and had declined to proceed to the Division Lobbies. The Speaker asked did they still persist in their refusal, and they promptly indicated that they did. In accordance with precedent the Speaker referred to each of them and in the ancient formula announced "I name the honourable Members for wilfully obstructing the business of the House and disregarding the authority of the Chair".

Mr. Balfour, as Leader of the House, immediately rose and said "I move that these gentlemen be suspended from the service of the House". In the general whirl of excitement the Irish Members allowed this Motion to be carried without a division, and the Members named thus came under the then existing rule of banishment from the precincts of the House for a week if this were the Member's first offence, a fortnight if the second and a month if there were more than two previous offences.

Up leapt Mr. Michael Flavin, a "six-footer" from the countryside. In a ringing voice he shouted "Mr. Speaker, you have named me and I refuse to leave the House".

This was the signal for a general chorus of similar declarations. The Speaker reminded the honourable Members that sufficient force would be requisitioned if necessary. The Serjeant-at-Arms, the dignified official in Court dress and sword who sits facing the Speaker at the opposite end of the Chamber and is in control of all officials and matters affecting law and order within the precincts, was directed to "remove the honourable Members". He touched each one on the shoulder, thus applying "constructive force". The Members clung to their seats. Attendants who act under the authority of the Serjeant-at-Arms were brought in, but failed to dislodge the "constructive trespassers".

A force of the Metropolitan Police are always on duty in and about the courtyards of the House. By order of the Speaker they were summoned to the assistance of the Serjeant-at-Arms. One by one the protesting Members

" A DIVISION "

(*for which even the Irı-Mochael Fl-v-n and Co. will quit the House*).

" The mhost injhoyable noight oi iver spint! "—*Mr. M-ch-l J-s-ph Fl-v-n*.

IRISH MEMBERS CARRIED OUT OF THE HOUSE OF COMMONS

By permission of the proprietors of " Punch "

were lifted shoulder high. A middle-aged gentleman who had been induced to join with the boys shouted, as he was swung aloft in brawny arms, "God save Ireland". Physical pressure re-awakened the activities of an old enemy. In the strong grip of the law the pangs of slumbering gout in the region of the ankle were revived. The victim shouted in his anguish "Oh, me poor feet!". Patriotism re-asserted itself a moment later and in a still louder voice the champion of the Green Isle shrieked "God save Ireland!". Again his aching feet advanced their claims and, ringing the changes between "God save Ireland" and "Oh, me poor feet", he went forth to the outer world in solemn procession—his country and his personal extremities alternately sharing the fullness of his commiseration.

In the course of a subsequent debate on a proposal to strengthen the rules against disorder Mr. John Redmond asserted that he and other members had left the House under the impression that the vote would not be concluded that night. He further contended that the incident only showed that for Irish members the glories and traditions of that House had no meaning and went on to say:

> So long as we are forced to come to this House to endeavour in the midst of a foreign majority to transact our Irish business we will use every form of this House, every right, every privilege, every power which membership of this House gives us just as it seems to us to be best for Ireland quite regardless of the opinion and so-called dignity of British Members and absolutely careless of the penalties you may devise for our punishment.

Lord Hugh Cecil, the brilliant youngest son of the Marquis of Salisbury who sat for Greenwich, with what proved to be prophetic vision, reminded the Liberal party that the time might come when they would be in a majority and might be anxious to rally their supporters in a contest or dispute with the House of Lords. If the House of Commons did not make a stand against disorder now where would their material authority be?

Before the session ended the House asserted its power to "deal with" outside offenders against its dignity.

It was almost forgotten save by the historians that in olden times the Serjeant-at-Arms on the warrant of Mr. Speaker had upon divers occasions arrested and brought before the House persons charged with "Contempt of Parliament" and drastic penalties had been imposed upon the delinquents. In the Clock Tower underneath the world-famed "Big Ben" there is a chamber which does duty as the gaol of the House of Commons. In the early days of the Parliament elected in 1880 Charles Bradlaugh, the Member for Northampton, was imprisoned here for defying the Chair. The right to punish Members of the House—or members of the public—had not been exercised since that day, though persons had been brought before the House and had "purged their contempt" by apologies.

These memories were recalled by an article which appeared in the "Globe", a London paper conducted on vigorous, full-flavoured, fighting Conservative lines, containing suggestions against the integrity of certain Members. The attack in the article was upon Irish Nationalists. The House in its corporate capacity knew nothing of political differences. The words were regarded as a breach of privilege, and the Serjeant-at-Arms was asked to bring the Editor and the publisher of the paper "to the Bar".

A few feet inside the door of the Chamber there is a brown line across the floor. This represents the "Bar", beyond which none but Members and duly accredited officials may pass when the House is in session. The Bar itself is a dividing Brass Rod telescoped into wooden pillars on either side.

On this afternoon in August 1901 the Brass Rod was drawn out and joined at the middle, thus forming an imposing barrier to "strangers". The Serjeant-at-Arms, bearing on his shoulder the huge gilded Mace, which ordinarily rests on the table when the House is in full session as the emblem of parliamentary authority, brought in the two offenders.

Standing at the historic dividing rail between Parliament

and public outside, the Editor and the Publisher apologised for the appearance of the article. The House insisted upon withdrawal of the suggestions in the article as well as an apology. The Editor, when asked categorically whether he withdrew the imputation, said "I do, Sir". The Publisher, when the question was put to him, replied "I must, Sir".

"There must be no quibbling over words", said the Speaker sternly.

The Publisher then substituted "I will" and hurriedly corrected it to "I do".

After being admonished by the Speaker, both Editor and Publisher walked backwards under the constructive authority of the Mace, which the Serjeant-at-Arms held over them till they disappeared through the folding doors.

When Members of Parliament had dispersed to their country homes for the Autumn, Great Britain and the civilised world were shocked at the news that came from America. While President McKinley was attending a Pan American exhibition at Buffalo a revolutionary assassin fired two shots at him. At first it was thought that the President would recover, but he suffered a serious relapse and died on the 14th September. A fine type of the American with great traditions—simple-living, earnest and God-fearing, William McKinley was admired as a Statesman and held in high esteem by all men. Horror at the outrage which deprived his country of his services, and sympathy with his family, mingled with universal tributes to his memory. His life was quoted for the benefit of younger members of the Anglo-Saxon race as a noble example.

Chapter 4

TURMOIL. SCIENCE. ART

ANY person who paid particular attention to a squad of Police marching casually from one of the doors of the Birmingham Town Hall on the 18th December 1901 might have noticed that the Sergeant was somewhat smaller in

stature than an ordinary policeman. As a seething mob
were besieging the Hall such a minor detail escaped observation. The rioters were waiting for Mr. Lloyd George and
they waited on oblivious of the fact that the dapper little
Sergeant was in fact their man.

Mr. Lloyd George and his friends had transferred their
attacks upon the policy of the Government from the floor of
the House of Commons to the platform. The "Welsh pro-
Boer" had invaded Birmingham and literally "bearded the
Douglas in his Hall". His attempt to address a meeting in
the stronghold of Mr. Chamberlain was met with furious
opposition which developed into so serious a disturbance of
public peace that baton charges were made by the police in
course of which several people were injured—one fatally.

The resource of the police in marching off the object of the
riotous attack in the Sergeant's uniform provided cartoonists
with pictures, music hall artists with popular tags, and the
public generally with the most exciting topic of the hour.

The incident occurred just two days after a less turbulent,
but more important, gathering. Lord Rosebery—the nation's
orator—had previously declared that he could not voluntarily
return to the Liberal Party. "I must plough my furrow
alone," he said, which declaration of independence provoked
Mr. Thomas Gibson Bowles, an Independent Conservative,
to compare him with Alexander Selkirk (the original of
Robinson Crusoe), who cried in his loneliness:

> I am out of humanity's reach,
> I must finish my journey alone :
> Never hear the sweet music of speech,
> I start at the sound of my own.

In response to requests from people of various shades of
thought Lord Rosebery heard the sound of his own voice in
an address known to history as the "Chesterfield speech"
in the course of which he remarked significantly:

> Some of the greatest peaces and greatest settlements in the
> world's history have begun with an apparently casual meet-
> ing of two travellers in a neutral inn.

That useful hint was left to mature in public and political thought, while the war pursued its sporadic course. Mr. Joseph Chamberlain, in the course of a speech in the country, observed that it might become necessary to take measures of greater severity in order to bring the campaign to a close. Precedents for anything we might do, he said, could be found in the action of German troops in the Franco-Prussian war who had adopted methods of severity which we had never yet approached.

Count von Bülow, the German Chancellor, resented this reference in a speech to the German Reichstag, and Mr. Joseph Chamberlain promptly retorted at the Silversmiths' Dinner at Birmingham with a speech which has become a classic. Quoting the observations of Count von Bülow, the Colonial Secretary went on to say:

> What I have said I have said. I withdraw nothing, I qualify nothing, I defend nothing. As I read history no British Minister has ever served his country faithfully and enjoyed popularity abroad. I do not want to give lessons to a foreign Minister and I will not accept any at his hands. I am responsible only to my own Sovereign and my own country.

A notable event marking a new era in the treatment of disease was the announcement in January of 1902 that an anonymous philanthropist—afterwards revealed as Sir Ernest Cassel—had placed two hundred thousand pounds at the disposal of the King who had decided that the sum should be applied to the erection of a sanatorium for the open-air treatment of tuberculous patients in England.

Strange as it may seem in these days, fresh air was the "enemy" up to the later years of the nineteenth century. Medical men and scientists of the modern school preached in vain against the evils of ill-ventilated rooms. A gentleman of substantial position in the country told the present writer that a near relative of his had died of consumption in a room where the windows and door were kept firmly shut and a screen perpetually placed round the bed. With grim and sad satire it was remarked in enlightened circles that a very big proportion of sick people really died of suffocation by bad air.

It is said that in this respect civilisation acquired wisdom from savagery. In the wars with the native tribes of South Africa it was noticed that the primitive warriors carried their wounded to the tops of the hills and left them with their wounds exposed to the pure air, the healing effects of which were practically infallible. The natural inference was that if fresh air could cure an open wound, its effect must be equally good upon the whole system.

Public opinion, however, was only just coming round to this view and, as events proved, science still had a long journey in its task of convincing all classes of the community that the artificial warmth of a sealed room is more prejudicial to health than the winds of Heaven. The generous benefaction of Sir Ernest Cassel and the wise choice of an object by the King provided a propitious starting point.

Turning to recreation the opening years of the century began with a revival of Shakespearean productions. During the nineteenth century the drama had passed through many vicissitudes. In the earlier years it had for some reason fallen into disrepute, and notwithstanding the fact that there were individual instances of genius the "play-actor" was not popular. For many years into the Victorian period respectable middle class society looked upon the theatre as a "gay place". Where religious teachers were not actually hostile they did not encourage their congregations and young people to visit places where plays were performed. That attitude still had its adherents. In the profession itself the old stock company attached to a particular theatre had been superseded by the provincial touring company though there was a feeling that this was not altogether a good change.

The principal theatres were now in the hands of men of high repute. The first actor knighthood was conferred on Henry Irving in 1895. Younger than Irving but contemporary with him at the beginning of the century were Mr. Tree, Mr. Alexander, Mr. Forbes-Robertson, Mr. Martin

Harvey, Mr. Lewis Waller, and Mr. Benson, all of whom were subsequently knighted. Mr. and Mrs. Kendal were playing with charming grace and skill their delightful comedies; Mr. Cyril Maude and Miss Winifred Emery were accomplished exponents of a newer and equally cultured school.

Sir Henry Irving opened his 1901 season with "Coriolanus". Mr. (afterwards Sir Frank) Benson had a Shakespearean Season. Mr. (afterwards Sir Beerbohm) Tree produced "Twelfth Night" at His Majesty's Theatre with the perfect setting of which he was master. His Majesty's was leading the way in a period of ornate production, but the dramatic world was not quite sure whether the splendid presentation or the simple rendering was the correct thing—for Shakespeare at all events. People were pining for something new. Melodrama was struggling to maintain its own. Irving occasionally revived it in its most impressive form in "The Lyons Mail" and "The Bells". Provincial towns and some parts of London still supported at least one theatre each where "the legitimate" attracted its regular patrons. The orthodox hero, heavy villain, heroine, and bad woman were respectively cheered and hissed night after night, while the knock-about comedian created roars of laughter as a relief to the strain of continuous pathos till virtue triumphed and villainy was vanquished.

The London theatres and the more important playhouses in the big provincial cities were producing problem plays. The riddles of social and domestic life were being solved by playwrights according to their respective views of society. The stage was inaugurating a rivalry with the pulpit. On the other hand the light side of the drama was growing lighter. No attempt was made to emulate the comic opera of Gilbert and Sullivan; that was impossible. The musical comedy or musical play, with its songs, dances, and chorus, all independent of each other and innocent of arbitrary plot had now thoroughly established itself at several London theatres and was drawing big audiences on tour. At Drury Lane, with its huge stage accommodating racehorses, yachts, and flocks and herds, the drama of life was presented with all the probabilities and possibilities of topical incidents.

In music there was a British revival—more especially in the effort to produce English opera.

Literature was depending very largely upon the later Victorian writers—or rather their works were gaining their just appreciation. There was a tendency in many quarters to misunderstand Thomas Hardy. His wonderful word paintings of Wessex life were temporarily obscured by a restricted controversy as to the wisdom of portraying such crude pictures as the tragic failure of "Jude the Obscure" and the pitiful story of "Tess of the D'Urbervilles". Strange to say the same people were able to appreciate the works of Rudyard Kipling despite the barrack-room ballads. J. M. Barrie from a fascinating Scottish story teller was at the beginning of his career as a writer of plays. Hall Caine's moving romances were read by many thousands. The popular sixpenny magazine was finding short story writers and watching expectantly for more detective romances from Conan Doyle whose Sherlock Holmes was the unchallenged king of criminologists.

When Parliament met in 1902, Mr. Balfour endeavoured to expedite business. The parliamentary device of discussing unimportant details at inordinate length for the purpose of impeding the progress of legislation and harassing the Government of the day had been invented by the Nationalists and often used by the two great Parties in the State. The Closure—the power to move that "the question be now put" —had been created by a Liberal Government to defeat the obstructive tactics of the Nationalists before Home Rule for Ireland became part of the Liberal policy. The innovation was then strongly resented by many Conservatives. The time had now arrived when a Conservative Leader of the House thought it necessary to obtain further powers.

In the process of framing the new Rules all kinds of changes were proposed, including a fixed hour-and-a-half adjourn-

ment instead of half an hour for dinner. Old parliamentary
hands on either side resisted this. They saw in imagination
the social life of Westminster broken up. Members they
said would go out to dinner and the little impromptu parties
of friends and opponents dining together in the precincts of the
House would no longer soften the acerbities of Party warfare.

Another innovation called special attention to changing
society habits.

Hitherto Parliament had met at noon on Wednesdays and
adjourned at five o'clock. This gave a mid-week rest from
late hours to Members and Officials. These new Rules
altered the short day to Friday. Sir Henry Campbell-
Bannerman with pawky humour thus put his finger on the
underlying reason:

> There has grown up of late years a practice in what I believe
> calls itself smart society of having what is called a ' week-
> end '. It is an expression which is novel and I believe that
> this week-end in the country has become almost indispens-
> able not so much to smart society as to that larger number
> in the community who wish to be thought to belong to
> smart society.

The observant Scot further went on to say he had been
given to understand that where members of the household
were still at home the blinds of the front rooms were drawn
down from the Saturday morning till the Monday in order to
give the outside world the impression that the occupants
had gone out of town for the fashionable week-end.

There was little doubt that these changes in hours had been
forced upon the Government by those younger men who insisted
upon dining with their fashionable friends and commencing
their week-ends in the early hours of Friday evening.

The proposals were carried, as were various minor provisions against obstruction of a semi-technical character, and
then came the question of suspension of unruly Members.
The periods for the suspension in the old Rules were cut out.
The Government suggested longer periods and proposed also
to insert an additional proviso to the effect that the suspen-

sion of the Member should continue until he had written a letter to the Speaker expressing "his sincere regret to the House for the offence for which he had been suspended".

This was stoutly resisted in various quarters of the House. Some Conservatives of the older school who had seen fiery youths mature into sedate parliamentarians—as rowdy students acquire the best "bedside manner"—thought there might be punishment or apology but not both. Their advice prevailed. The apology clause was dropped. So much time had been taken over the discussion that it became imperative to proceed with other necessary business, and the House never got back to the discussion of the new Rules. As a consequence the manual was printed with a blank where the former period of suspension had been omitted, and for a quarter-of-a-century Parliament went on working with the empty space as the period fixed for the exile of an unruly Member.

Chapter 5

EASTERN CIVILISATION.   WESTERN EDUCATION

THOUGHTS were diverted from West to East by the announcement that a formal Treaty had been entered into between Great Britain and the Government of Japan. The average person in Great Britain, and in other Western European countries, pictured in his mind's eye dancing girls and quaintly dressed men when Japan was mentioned. The popular mind obtained its information concerning this Asiatic Power from Gilbert and Sullivan's superb creation "The Mikado".

There had been a war with China, followed by certain diplomatic negotiations, and men whose fate it was to study international politics realised that this island people in the Far East had emerged from Oriental exclusiveness to enterprising Western civilisation. The conclusion of the Treaty with Great Britain was a conspicuous landmark. Japan was not inaptly designated the "child of the world's old age", and she attracted all the enthusiastic interest which the description suggested. "Japs" coming to this country were no longer regarded as romantic visitors. They were received as serious guests who might be useful friends and good customers, although it must be recorded that there were people who still admired the adherence of the Chinese to their old-world civilisation. The Treaty moreover marked the end of the policy of "Splendid isolation" which had been the pride of Victorian Statesmen all of whom kept out of alliances with other Powers.

In British home politics the train of events brought about a temporary alliance between the Irish Nationalists and the Conservatives. This was not a new experience. Apart from their demand for Home Rule there were many points upon which a number of the Irish Members, with their ancient Catholic religion and rural instincts, were Conservative at heart. This was especially so in the matter of education, and a Bill brought in by Mr. Balfour in the early part of 1902 dealing with Elementary Education became the Aaron's Rod of political argument. It revived old-time discussions and historic events stretching back over several generations.

In order to appreciate the new controversy it became necessary to recall the work of Andrew Bell and Joseph Lancaster—the one a Church of England Clergyman (Rector of Swanage) and the other a member of the Society of Friends. In the days of George the Third the English man or woman of the wage-earning classes who could read or write was the exception. The King spent much of his time at Weymouth, and as related in "The Marches of Wessex" (Darton) wished that every child should be taught to read the Bible. The Grand Jury of the County of Dorset assembled at the Lent Assizes, passed a Resolution, and a meeting was arranged of the "Nobility, gentry, clergy and inhabitants" in accordance with the King's wish. A Committee was formed to educate the poor, who were to be taught useful arts "but not educated so as to render them discontented with their station".

No girl was "to be permitted to write or cypher till she has completed her ninth year nor then unless she can read the Bible fluently, repeat the catechism, prayers, &c., knit stockings and do all sorts of common plain work".

The Reverend Andrew Bell from such beginnings became the protagonist and organiser of the "National Society for promoting the education of the children of the poor in the principles of the Established Church". At about the same time Joseph Lancaster, encouraged and supported by his brethren of the Society of Friends (Quakers), whose zeal for education is second only to their religious devotion, began his crusade for the spread of knowledge. Both men in the need for economy adopted the system of inducing the advanced pupils in the capacity of "Monitors" or "Pupil Teachers" to educate the younger children. It is still a matter of controversy as to whether Bell or Lancaster should receive the greater credit for the method which is historically known as the Madras system—the claim being that it was first used there by Bell. Between them the two men founded Elementary Education. The work progressed slowly. The modesty of the first Church of England Committee was really expressive of the attitude of the English rural districts towards education. In her engrossing novel "The Mill on the Floss" George Eliot no doubt faithfully depicts the prevailing sentiment of the period in the sincere belief of the Miller's head man that knowing too much was what brought folks to the gallows.

Midway in the nineteenth century William Edward Forster, a young Quaker born at Bradpole in the county where Bell first applied himself to the subject, became "profoundly depressed by the terrible ignorance that characterised the great mass of the nation". Comparatively early in life Forster had gone to Bradford. He received encouragement in his efforts to promote popular education from Canon Jackson of Leeds and Dr. Hook, a Unitarian Minister of Leeds. By the year 1870 Forster had become a Member of Parliament and a prominent statesman. The great work of his life was the Education Act of 1870, under which the State, through the Local Authorities, undertook the responsibility of providing Elementary Schools. Following upon Bell's work, National (Church) Schools had been founded throughout England. The question arose as to what should be done with those Institutions. Forster decided that they must be brought into the State Scheme and that for this purpose they should be assisted by grants from public funds. On this point he was opposed by people who contended that the Schools should either be transferred to complete representative control or be carried on without any assistance whatever from the State. Forster, although personally belonging to a Faith which does not recognise ritual or ecclesiastical orders, stubbornly insisted on what came to be known as "the Dual System", combining Board and Voluntary Schools.

The Board Schools were provided and maintained by the ratepayers and controlled by School Boards directly elected for that purpose. The Church of England, Wesleyans, Jews, Roman Catholics, Baptists and some other denominations, as well as undenominational local Committees, possessed the Voluntary Schools, which were controlled and maintained by the particular bodies with which they were associated, aided by the Government grant. There were other Voluntary Schools maintained it was said to "keep out the Board Schools" and save the rates. Attendance at School had also been made compulsory upon every child in the land.

It was now urged—more especially by the Church of England—that the task of maintaining these Voluntary Schools was "an intolerable strain". A new Education Act had become necessary because of certain difficulties in the way of defining what should constitute Elementary Education and to what extent local Educational Authorities were entitled to give advanced teaching. Mr. Balfour introduced a comprehensive system which abolished the School Boards and, while placing upon the ordinary Local Authorities (Town and County Councils) the responsibility for financing all Elementary Schools, conferred upon the denominations the power to retain their own religious "atmosphere" and staff direction in the "Voluntary" or "non-provided" Schools.

The Bill revived the old controversy in a very acute form. The objection to grants from the central fund of Forster's day was a minor matter compared with the indignant protests against the proposal that denominational teaching should be provided out of the rates. The supporters of the Denominational Schools urged that they were compelled to pay rates for the maintenance of the publicly controlled or "provided" Schools which neglected what they considered the essentials of religious education. And so the discussion went on—"Clericalism is the enemy" declared Mr. Lloyd George, speaking as a Welsh Nonconformist. "There can be no real religion without specific declarations of Faith", retorted the supporters of the Anglican and Catholic Schools. The Irish Nationalists, on behalf of the Roman Catholic Schools in England, welcomed the Bill, and for the time being were staunch supporters of the Government.

Parliamentary reputations were built up in the struggle. The most striking figure in the Church party was Lord Hugh Cecil. Up to this time he had been regarded as an *enfant terrible* making a playground of the popular representative assembly. Once when a Member of his father's Cabinet was in the middle of a rather lengthy speech he startled old Members by ejaculating "Vide! Vide!!"—the abbreviation of "Divide! Divide!!", a parliamentary method of orderly disorder ostensibly signifying a desire to proceed at once to a division but really a blunt expression of boredom.

The little band of young seigneurs whom this unconventional new statesman had gathered around him were called the "Hughligans"—a nickname rightly or wrongly attributed to the grim humour of his father.

As the Education Debates proceeded men saw a new Lord Hugh Cecil emerge. His genius as a debater and his passionate devotion to his Church revealed him as a force in political life. The days of the inspired peroration had gone and the House as a rule resented appeals to sentiment. Hardly any other man would have risked the intense feeling which this youth threw into his speeches. He had none of the conventional attributes of an orator. His voice lacked the bell-like note; his gestures would shock the eye of any trained elocutionist. Yet he possessed the native eloquence of brain and soul.

Throughout the country the Debates were followed with intense interest and the arguments were repeated on innumerable platforms. The Bill passed through its various stages and went to the House of Lords, where it was stoutly defended by the Bishops.

As an Act of Parliament it was destined to provide substance for many a stirring political situation.

Chapter 6

PEACE AND ITS LESSONS

THE South African War definitely came to an end and Peace was formally declared on terms made between the British Government and the Boers at Pretoria on the 31st May 1902. The two Dutch Republics as separate Governments disappeared and the burghers agreed to "desist from any further resistance to the authority of His Majesty King Edward VII, whom they recognise as their lawful Sovereign". It was further agreed that " Military administration of the Transvaal and Orange River Colony will at the earliest possible date be succeeded by civil government, and, as soon as circumstances permit, representative institutions leading up to self-government will be introduced".

The Declaration was in time to ensure that the King should be crowned in peace. The day fixed for this event was the 26th June, but two days before this date came the startling news that King Edward was seriously ill. An operation for appendicitis performed by the famous Surgeon, Sir Frederick Treves, restored his Majesty to his normal health, and the 9th August was decided as the postponed date.

c

Early in July the Prime Minister, having seen the new reign inaugurated, quietly withdrew to his books and country life in the historic home of the Cecils at Hatfield. Lord Salisbury's resignation had been expected and occasioned no surprise. For a few days the political Clubs were in a state of animated speculation as to the choice of a successor. The King sent for Mr. Arthur Balfour and asked him to form a Government. It has happened in history that the statesman sent for by the Sovereign has found it impracticable to form an Administration. The co-operation of his colleagues is, of course, essential. There were some murmurs that the Liberal Unionists—still nominally a distinct body—and some Members of the Conservative Party might have desired Mr. Joseph Chamberlain as the man of the hour to lead them. Mr. Chamberlain was at the time suffering from the effects of a cab accident. He sent a message to a Party Meeting through his son, Mr. Austen Chamberlain, that he was prepared to serve under Mr. Arthur Balfour.

The new Prime Minister thus entered upon his task with the Empire at peace and the unanimous support of a strong Party.

There were personal breaks between the old century and the new in the religious world. The Wesleyans lost one of their greatest men—the Rev. Hugh Price Hughes. Dr. Parker, the eminent Nonconformist preacher of the emotional Victorian School, passed away. John Kensit, a Protestant Churchman who took a leading part in denouncing certain Church of England clergymen for bringing into their services ceremonials similar to those practised in the Roman Catholic Churches, died at Liverpool subsequently to injuries received after a Protest Meeting at Birkenhead.

Intense feeling had arisen between the "High Church" and the "Low Church". The Low Church, or Evangelical Party, who during the Victorian era wore black or Geneva gowns in the pulpit and restricted ceremonial to severe simplicity, had gradually been replaced by what were known as "Broad Church" clergy, who introduced surpliced choirs and used such terms as "Altar" instead of "Communion Table".

Another body in the Church that had been growing in numbers comprised those clergy and laity who contended in effect that at the Reformation the Church of England, while denying the authority of the Pope, still retained pre-Reformation observances and vestments. These Anglo-Catholics, or "Ritualists" as they were generally known, exercised a strong influence in the thickly populated areas of the big towns and the industrial districts. They were known to be tireless workers who did an immense amount of good amongst the poor. Their practices were nevertheless denounced as unlawful by Broad Churchmen, as well as by the remaining members of the old Low Church.

The Archbishop of Canterbury, Dr. Temple, a former Headmaster of Rugby and a man of robust but kindly old-world West Country sincerity and piety, endeavoured to hold a just balance in the heated controversy. With his brother Bishops he called upon the clergy to act in conformity with the law, and certain practices held to be outside the Rubric of the Church of England were officially condemned.

Dr. Temple, like other leaders of the Victorian era, was destined to see very little of the new reign. While he was delivering a conciliatory speech in the House of Lords on the Education Bill he fell back in his seat. After a temporary recovery he was assisted from the House but he died very shortly afterwards.

Dr. Randall Davidson, a Churchman of moderate views and friendly disposition towards all religious denominations, was appointed to succeed Dr. Temple as Archbishop of Canterbury—and Head of the Church—at a time when many old-world institutions were called upon to face new problems. The Education Act apart from its political aspect opened up new channels for educational effort. Secondary education was co-ordinated with the other branches of the educational system. It was now recognised as part of the legitimate activities of the Public Education Authorities. A link was thus established between Elementary and Higher Education. A step was taken towards building up what enthusiasts described as "the inclined plane" from Elementary to Higher Education. Educationists predicted that this would have a beneficial effect on social life. Some of them who were dubious of the rate aid for denominational schools were reconciled by the thought that certain parts of the Act supplied a public need. It was, moreover, predicted that since the rates were to become responsible for the schools a very large proportion of the voluntary schools would gradually come under complete public control on the initiative of their existing governing bodies.

The year 1902 saw the establishment of a most important system for dealing with the perplexing problem of youthful offences against the law. No branch of modern social science had caused greater anxiety to public spirited men and women than the treatment of child criminals. In the old days under English law only one penal method for persons of all ages was recognised. Children were sent to ordinary prisons where they acquired the criminal atmosphere. They herded with hardened offenders and were virtually nurtured in crime. It was asserted that more than half of the criminals had made their first lapse in their teens. Society naturally wondered whether something should not have been done to prevent that first lapse being followed by a career of crime.

Charles Dickens, Charles Reade and other publicists by pen and voice roused public opinion in the mid-Victorian era to the necessity for providing a remedy. A beginning was made by the first Reformatory School Act under which children up to sixteen years of age might be sent to these disciplinary institutions instead of to prison. There still remained a gap between sixteen and twenty-one. During this critical period when character might still be formed or reclaimed some thousands of offenders were sent to penal servitude. The desirability of still further measures of reform was strongly felt by those whose duty it was to administer the law. In common with other public men and with society generally they desired to mould legal methods to the growing opinion that regeneration was more important than punishment. This was the object in view when in 1902 the Borstal scheme was inaugurated. Under this system a special class of establishment for youths over sixteen was created—a half-way house between school and punitive institution in which healthy physical exercises and education were blended with field work, gardening and handicrafts.

A Borstal association supported by Judges, Statesmen, and distinguished leaders of religious thought was founded for the purpose of helping the youths thus released on the verge of manhood to obtain regular employment.

This was probably the vital breaking point between ancient and modern penal history. Its development and results will be discussed in a subsequent chapter.

While Society was developing its newer ideals for the solution of social problems, travel was proceeding towards a revolutionary stage. In 1902 came the projection of the vast system of underground tubes in London. There had been underground railways and a short electric line from the southern suburbs to the city; then followed the "two-penny tube"—all to be embraced in a network of lines destined to connect up London with the surrounding counties and bring into being an enormous moving underground population day by day.

Chapter 7

THE NATIONAL GAME
AND THE NATION'S WORKERS

NINETEEN hundred and two was a cricket year. The game unfortunately was played under unfavourable conditions. The weather was bad and the actual play was in consequence not at its best. The importance of the season rested on the fact that the Australians came over for the first visit of the new century. Since the 'seventies Australian and English teams had played test matches alternately in England and Australia. A feature of this year's tests which recorded the relentless march of time was the absence from the English Team of Dr. W. G. Grace. This marvellous cricketer was the idol of the later nineteenth century schoolboy. His massive figure and flowing beard were portrayed in countless pictures and prints upon the walls of mansions and cottages. He played in the Test Match against Australia at the Oval in 1880, and from then up to 1899 when he played in a Match at Nottingham he was an essential member of the All England Team whenever the Australians came to this country. Dr. Grace was still in the front rank of good cricketers, but by general consent the day had come for younger men in the Test.

The 1902 Team included C. B. Fry—probably the finest athlete of his day. Prince Ranjitsinhji (afterwards the Maharaja Jam Saheb of Nawanagar) who first played in Test Matches in 1896, was also in the Team. A picturesque figure in the field, lithe, swift and enterprising, he was a tremendous favourite with the public. The Hon. F. S. Jackson in his prime as a great cricketer maintained the triumphs he scored at Cambridge and for Yorkshire. Rhodes the all-round Yorkshire bat and bowler was also in the Eleven; and A. C. MacLaren; with G. L. Jessop the mighty hitter, and others whose names are easily remembered in the world of cricket. The first of the Test Matches at Birmingham was stopped by the rain, as was the second at Lords. Australia won the third at Sheffield by a hundred and forty-three runs; and scored a sensational win at Manchester by three runs. This gave them the rubber, but England won the last Match at the Oval after a struggle that lives still in the annals of cricket. G. L. Jessop who was in splendid form scored a hundred and four in an hour and a quarter. This exciting game revived the spirits of cricket enthusiasts. The bad weather had produced a depression in spectators and players and there was a disposition to talk of cricket as a lost cause. The Letter Writer to the papers was ready with his lamentations about the decadence of English cricket, but in spite of the unpropitious season cricketers cheerfully faced the future.

The infant growth of a new political Party was one of the early events of the new century and the new reign. On the King's Birthday, at the New Year and at such rare events as a Coronation, distinguished men are promoted to the Peerage. In the List of Honours on the Coronation of King Edward VII appeared the name of Sir Ughtred Kay-Shuttleworth, the head of an influential Lancastrian family and an ex-Liberal Minister. Sir Ughtred had represented the Clitheroe Division of Lancashire since 1885, and on his elevation to the House of Lords the seat became vacant. Mr. David Shackleton, a Lancashire man and one of the most substantial Trade Unionists in the country, was adopted as a Candidate. Hitherto Mr. Shackleton had been known as a Liberal. It was at first suggested that he would be called —like several other Trade Unionists—a "Liberal Labour" or "Labour and Liberal" Candidate; but neither designation was adopted. He was nominated as a "Labour" Candidate and as such was elected without opposition. Comparatively little comment was aroused by this change in nomenclature. The average person knew very little about any Labour political Party as such.

As far back as 1869 a "Labour Representation League" had been formed under the Presidency of Mr. R. M. Lathom, a Chancery barrister, with Mr. Henry Broadhurst, a working stone-mason, as Secretary, for the purpose of providing opportunities for the return of working-class Members. The miners of Northumberland in 1874 sent their Secretary, Mr. Thomas Burt, to Parliament. Mr. Alexander Macdonald, a man with some private means who had been a miner, was also returned for Stafford. Neither of these was opposed by the Liberals, and Mr. Henry Broadhurst joined them in 1880 with Liberal support. Mr. Joseph Arch, the Norfolk agricultural labourer M.P., was also regarded as a Liberal. In 1885 the Northumberland miners sent Mr. Charles Fenwick "direct from the coal face" to join Mr. Burt; the Yorkshire miners sent Mr. Ben Pickard, their Secretary, and the Durham miners Mr. John Wilson. Other men with a

direct claim to have worked with their hands were returned
from other parts of the country, including "Mabon", the
miner bard of Wales, but they were for all practical purposes
Liberal Members.

In Scotland unsuccessful attempts to establish independent
labour representation had been made from time to time by
Mr. J. Keir Hardie, who had been a messenger boy at nine,
and at the age of ten went down the mine.   Mr. Keir Hardie
inherited the Scottish passion for education; became in turn
a Trade Union official and the local Representative and
Sub-Editor of the "Cumnock News", published in conjunction
with the "Ardrossan and Saltcoats Herald", a Scottish weekly
newspaper of remarkably high standing and literary merit.

Self-taught and brimful of rugged vigour, he spoke with
an unrestrained Scottish accent, but, grammatically, his
English was perfect.   At the General Election of 1892 he
was elected for West Ham, avowedly and ostentatiously as
a Labour Member.   There was no Liberal Candidate against
him.   He made a dramatic appearance at Westminster
escorted by an East London crowd with cornet accompani-
ment, but his presence did not affect the orientation of
Parties.   Mr. John Burns, who was undoubtedly the most
striking personality in the Labour movement at that time, was
returned for Battersea, but with the goodwill of the Liberals.

In 1893 a few men who agreed with Mr. Keir Hardie met
at Bradford and formed the "Independent Labour Party".
The movement gathered adherents from semi-middle class
young men who believed that the regeneration of Society
depended upon the nationalisation of all the means of production, distribution and exchange—a proposal which a few
years previously had been worked out with fascinating ability
by Edward Bellamy, an American writer, in a popular book
entitled "Looking Backward".   This work was the most
successful of the many treatises issued during the last
quarter of the nineteenth century on nationalisation or
collectivism, or, to use the most generally accepted term,
Socialism.   The Independent Labour men, known as "I.L.P."

Candidates, became the apostles of the Socialistic theory. They were put up in constituencies here and there, but they only attracted stray votes.

The Trade Union movement, which had its beginnings much further back, was essentially a combination among workers in each particular trade or industry, with the direct object of making the best bargain possible on wages and working conditions for their members. Officials of Trade Unions as such had no position in politics, though they took sides individually, many as Liberals and some—especially in Lancashire—as Conservatives. A Resolution was passed at the Trade Union Congress in 1893 which included the nationalisation of the land and the "means of production, distribution and exchange". It came up annually and was regarded by Trade Unionists proper as a pious opinion, concerning some state of affairs in the dim future, which pleased the young folk and did no particular harm. The subsequent developments belong to another chapter.

Chapter 8

THE RISE OF THE LABOUR PARTY

MR. J. RAMSAY MACDONALD, an advanced young Radical, arrived from the Highlands just about the time that Mr. Keir Hardie came to London from the Scottish Lowlands. With the fire and fervour of youth and the eloquence of a born orator, the black-haired, handsome "unknown" was an object of curiosity at elections where an "extreme" Candidate was in the field. He stood as an advanced Candidate for Southampton, but found himself entirely out of touch with the orthodox Liberals.

After taking part in a bye-election in the Attercliffe Division of Sheffield in 1894, where Mr. Frank Smith, a former worker in the Salvation Army, was an Independent Labour Candidate, Mr. Macdonald wrote to Mr. Keir Hardie announcing his willingness to join the Independent Labour

Party. He became an indefatigable worker with the little group of men and women who went out into the highways and byways preaching the elementary doctrine of State Socialism to sparse audiences, mostly sceptical and oft-times hostile.

In the latter years of the old century these persistent apostles began to approach other organisations. An effort was made to bring in the Co-operative Societies with the object of securing the help of a movement which had become a powerful institution in the daily lives of people in the industrial districts.

The history of co-operation, immensely important to twentieth century development, has its roots in the early part of the nineteenth century, when various efforts were made by certain altruists to establish a system under which workmen might found self-supporting communities, first purchasing collectively and ultimately producing directly for each other. Most of these attempts failed, but in 1844 twenty-eight weavers and workers in Rochdale got together a capital of twenty-eight pounds, formed a Co-operative Society, and opened a small shop in Toad Lane. The members took turns to serve in the shop and gradually built up an organisation which spread throughout Lancashire and the north of England, and from thence to Scotland. The older Utopian idea of self-contained communities was dropped, and the shrewd Lancashire artisans, whose example was copied by other small Societies, applied business methods to their ventures while retaining as an ideal the principle of mutual help and social improvement.

The movement which the new Labour Party now endeavoured to link up with its political fortune had become a federation of many limited liability co-operative societies. Any person might become a member by payment of a nominal entrance fee on taking up a share which might be purchased on easy conditions. The Society as such bought goods in the usual wholesale market and resold them to members at ordinary prices. The difference between the "Co-op" and the ordinary shop was that after paying a

small interest on the shares the "Co-op" profit was paid out
to the members according to the amount of their purchases.
A Co-operative Wholesale Society had also been established.
The Societies were non-political and it seemed very unlikely
that there would be any enthusiasm here for a proposal
to join the new political Labour movement.

The miners and the textile workers also at first kept
stubbornly out of the proposed combination. Mr. James
Mawdesley, the well-known official of the Lancashire cotton
workers, had in fact been put forward as a Conservative
Candidate, though he was not elected.

The effort to amalgamate the various industrial Organisa-
tions into one group, however, continued. A Conference
was held at which Mr. Keir Hardie and Mr. Ramsay
Macdonald represented the Independent Labour Party;
Mr. H. Quelch and Mr. H. R. Taylor, the Social Democratic
Federation, an old-established Socialist body. Mr. G.
Bernard Shaw, best known then as a dramatic critic, and
Mr. E. P. Pease were appointed to represent the Fabian
Society. The "Fabians" were nearly all literary and
professional people. They accepted the Socialistic theory but
had hitherto proceeded on the belief that it would ultimately
succeed by gradually, or imperceptibly, permeating other
Parties with Socialism, on the tactics of Fabius, the Roman
General who avoided frontal attacks and captured points of
vantage by drawing his opponents away from their base.

A constitution was drawn up for a "Labour Representation Committee", comprising those of the Trade Unions who
could be induced to come in, the Independent Labour
Party and the other Socialist Societies. Under the constitution the affiliated Unions and Societies nominated
their own Candidates, who, on receiving the approval of the
Central Committee and signing a general undertaking not
to appear on the platforms of either of the existing political
Parties, were supported by the Central Organisation.

Mr. Ramsay Macdonald, who was appointed Secretary to
the new movement, approached his task with the zeal of a

crusader. His wife, a lady of deep sympathies and high intellectual gifts, whose tender thoughts for the poor and distressed are commemorated by a statue to her memory in Lincolns Inn Fields, also devoted herself to the work. The seed fell on stony ground. Only a small percentage of the Trade Unions were enrolled; the Co-operative Societies steadily refused to join. The Social Democratic Federation withdrew. The general public knew little or nothing of these early pioneers on the apparently unconquerable prairie.

The turning point came as a consequence of what is known to history as "The Taff Vale Case".

The Trade Union Acts passed in the 1870's after a searching enquiry into the whole subject of workmen's organisations had enacted that Trade Unions might conduct disputes without incurring criminal proceedings. Before that an individual could leave his employer if dissatisfied, but it was a crime for men to combine if their purpose were held to be "in restraint of trade".

The Trade Union Acts, however, did not specifically deal with the possibility of civil proceedings, and after many years that aspect was tested in an action brought by the Taff Vale Railway Company against the Amalgamated Society of Railway Servants.

A strike having arisen, the Company sought an injunction restraining Mr. Richard Bell, the General Secretary of the Society, Mr. Holmes, the Organising Secretary for the district, as officials of the Union, and the Society itself from "watching or besetting or causing to be watched or beset" the railway station or works for the purpose of "persuading or otherwise preventing persons from working for the plaintiffs". The injunction was granted in a carefully considered Judgment as a matter of law, and ultimately confirmed on appeal by the highest legal Tribunal in the land.

Two points of vital interest with respect to Industrial disputes arose on this. It was now settled that as the Law then stood a Trade Union as such could be sued and its funds made liable. Furthermore, picketing during a dispute

for the purpose of persuading persons to join in the strike
might be an actionable proceeding.

The Trade Unions gradually concentrated their thoughts
upon an endeavour to secure the election to Parliament
of Members directly concerned with industrial questions
who would endeavour to secure a change in the law.

Such was the history in brief of the developments leading
up to the return of Mr. David Shackleton (afterwards Sir
David Shackleton, Principal Adviser to the Ministry of
Labour) as a Labour Member elected under the auspices
of the Labour Representation Committee.

By that glorious uncertainty of political life which is its
greatest fascination, all forecasts of a peaceful and prolonged
period of Office for Mr. Balfour were disappointed.

The Prime Minister's majority was apparently overwhelming, but complicated problems followed in the aftermath
of the war. Dr. Macnamara—one of the new men on the
Liberal side, a former President of the National Union of
Teachers and a forceful speaker—received strong support from
Members in different parts of the House when he urged upon
the Government that the deplorable shortage of decent housing
accommodation should be taken in hand without delay.

In the course of a Debate Mr. Keir Hardie estimated the
number of unemployed "at not less than four hundred
thousand". Mr. Walter Long (afterwards Lord Long) on
behalf of the Government said he had reason to believe
this estimate was exaggerated but there was no doubt a
very serious want of employment.

The Low Churchmen demanded very severe discipline
for ritualism, and called upon the Government to apply it.
Others agitated for Army Reform. The reaction after what
was colloquially known as "the Khaki Election"—held, as
it was, while the war enthusiasm was strongest—had set in.

Bye-elections were going against the Government. One
was doubly significant. A vacancy occurred at Woolwich,
where the Conservative Candidate at the previous election
had been returned with a majority of two thousand, eight

hundred and five. Mr. Will Crooks—a prominent London Trade Unionist who had been born in a workhouse—was put forward as a Labour Candidate under the auspices of the Labour Representation Committee. The Liberals stood aside and Mr. Crooks defeated the Government Candidate by a majority of three thousand, two hundred and twenty-nine.

Mr. Chamberlain, who had been on a long tour to South Africa, landed at Southampton in the Spring of 1903 to find the popularity of his colleagues chilled and drooping in the keen March winds.

Chapter 9

HISTORIC EVENTS ABROAD
NEW LEAD AT HOME

A VISIT to King Victor Emmanuel of Italy from King Edward VII was welcomed with inspiring enthusiasm by the people at Rome. During his stay King Edward visited Pope Leo XIII at the Vatican. This act of courtesy, conceived and conducted with tact and grace, excited no feelings of displeasure among the vast Protestant majority of the British Empire and was greatly appreciated by Catholics in Great Britain and the Dominions.

From Rome King Edward went to Paris, and, on a sunny May day destined to be memorable in history, was received with passionate cordiality by huge cheering crowds as he passed through the streets gaily decorated in his honour.

During the South African war the feeling towards the English in many parts of France had been very unfavourable and at times distinctly hostile. Bitter cartoons had appeared in the popular French papers, and some influential journalists had written fierce attacks upon British policy. The phrase "perfidious Albion" summed up the attitude of many French writers. An amusing example of this was provided in the experience of a distinguished English "pro-Boer" journalist who had resigned a coveted editorial position rather than support the war policy of the Government. Travelling on a holiday through France, he was assailed with cries of "Vive les Boers" from small boys in the village street.

The King's visit to Paris was the beginning of the new era in Anglo-French relations—and thus in the history of the world.

When attention was again directed to domestic affairs Mr. Joseph Chamberlain's friends wistfully looked to him for a lead out of their difficulties. The lead came with startling effect. It carried men's minds back into the pages of what was virtually regarded as a closed book in English history.

The controversy between the two economic policies popularly known as Free Trade and Protection might be traced from the seventeenth century and thence to the year 1815, when, at the end of the Napoleonic Wars, a Corn Law was passed closing British ports against the importation of foreign grain until the price had reached eighty shillings a quarter. This was followed by Acts establishing a sliding scale under which when the price of home-grown wheat rose to a certain height the duty on imported wheat sank in proportion.

Rioting, incendiarism and other forms of violent protest were associated with the early opposition to these Acts, but the most historic agitation, in which men who were still in politics had taken their part, was identified with the names of Charles Villiers, a man of aristocratic family, Richard Cobden, a manufacturer, of yeoman farmer ancestry, and John Bright, a member of a Quaker family engaged in the manufacture of carpets in Rochdale. Bright, relating one of those poetic incidents that occur sometimes in political life, thus describes the circumstances in which he was recruited by Cobden :—

I was then in the depths of grief—I might almost say of despair—for the light and sunshine of my house had been extinguished. All that was left on earth of my young wife, except the memory of a sainted life and an all too brief happiness, was lying still and cold in the chamber above us. Mr. Cobden called on me as a friend and addressed me, as you may suppose, with words of condolence. After a time he looked up and said ' There are thousands and thousands of homes in England at this moment where wives and mothers and children are dying of hunger. Now when the paroxysm of your grief is passed I would advise you to come with me and we will never rest until the Corn Laws are repealed '.

This was the beginning of a comradeship which has no parallel in the records of politics. Mr. Cobden, as his contemporaries testified, was convincing and persuasive. Mr. Bright had all the natural gifts of the orator. His language was the pure, simple English of everyday life. Mr. Justin McCarthy, the historian, wrote of him :

> The fire of his eloquence was a white heat—intense, consuming, but never sparkling or spluttering.

When the Bright and Cobden agitation began it was a settled belief amongst men on both sides and in both Houses of Parliament—the House of Lords almost unanimously, the House of Commons by an overwhelming majority—that the tax was necessary for the encouragement of the growth of corn at home and as a safeguard for the supply of food in time of war. The annual Motion for its repeal which Mr. Villiers brought forward was received with the same amused tolerance as was accorded in subsequent years to Resolutions in favour of Woman Suffrage or Bills for legalising marriage with the Deceased Wife's Sister.

The intervention of an unhappy stroke of fate changed the whole aspect. Mr. Bright many years after summarised the crisis in a sentence—"Famine itself, against which we had warred, joined us ". In 1845 the Irish potato crop was ruined and the mainstay of the food of the people in the South and West was practically destroyed. People clamoured for the opening of the ports. Lord John Russell, the Whig Leader, announced his conversion to the principles of the Anti-Corn Law League. Some of the Tories were inclined to open the ports. Sir Robert Peel, the Tory Prime Minister, went further. Not only did he agree with the policy of opening the ports, but he boldly declared himself in favour of the repeal of the Corn Laws.

The fight did not end there, but after a vigorous and severe struggle protective duties on grain were abandoned. The principle of untaxed imports was extended to manufactures and every description of produce except for revenue purposes. Lord Beaconsfield frankly told his Conservative followers that Protection was "dead and damned".

Now after a long lapse of years rumours and murmurings floated through places where politicians most do congregate that as a solution for unemployment Mr. Joseph Chamberlain —who during the later period of John Bright's career had been the friend and colleague of the great Free Trader—was a convert to Protective import duties on foreign corn and goods.

Mr. Chamberlain did not keep his friends in suspense very long. On the 15th May 1903—just two months after his return from South Africa—he addressed his Birmingham constitutents. He repudiated "the Manchester School"— so named—partly—because Manchester was the centre of the Bright and Cobden movement—and raised the standard of Imperial Preference or "Free Trade within the Empire". Briefly his proposal was that we should be prepared to put duties on goods coming to this country from abroad, and, by remitting the tax on goods from our Dominions and Colonies, build up through this preference a system of free interchange within the Empire.

An opportunity for further debate arose in the House of Commons by the procedure under which a Motion to adjourn for a specified period at Easter or Whitsuntide is necessary. It is customary on this Motion to initiate a general discussion of current topics, and attention was called to speeches made by Mr. Chamberlain and other Members of the Government on Tariffs.

In the course of this Debate Mr. Chamberlain outlined the principles on which Preference should be given to the Colonies, and pointed out that the main product of the Colonies is food. Then followed a passage which was seized upon as the keynote of the new movement:

Therefore we come to this. If you are to give a Preference to the Colonies—I do not say you are—you must put a tax on food.

D

The point of the qualifying phrase "I do not say you are" was that Mr. Chamberlain at this stage urged that all he demanded for the present was an enquiry into the whole fiscal question with a view to considering the advisability of Imperial Preference.

Mr. Winston Churchill promptly declared himself an opponent of the new proposals. It would be impossible, he said, to stop at a simple system of Preferential Tariffs. The manufacturers would insist upon some tangible return, and the only one possible would be an elaborate system of bounties and duties. Developing this aspect he went on to say:—

> This move means a change not only in historic English Parties but in conditions of our public life. The old Conservative Party with its religious convictions and constitutional principles will disappear and a new Party will arise . . . rigid, materialistic and secular—whose opinions will turn on Tariffs and who will cause the Lobbies to be crowded with the touts of protected industries.

Attention was directed for a while to other interesting incidents. A further step was taken towards Anglo-French friendship by the return visit of the President of the French Republic, who was met by the King at Victoria Station and received with popular enthusiasm. After enjoying Royal and Civic hospitality the President despatched a telegram on his way home thanking the King and the people of Great Britain for the hearty welcome given to the representative of "France, the friend of England". King Edward, in reply, expressed his earnest desire that the friendship between the two nations might be lasting.

Just about this time public opinion realised that a new mode of traction had come to stay. Motor cars, since their introduction towards the end of the nineteenth century, had been regarded as noisy playthings with an unpleasant smell, owned and used by eccentric people. The "eccentrics" grew in number, and it dawned upon the public that they were going far beyond the generally accepted speed of twelve miles an hour above which in the case of the horse "furious driving" would be presumed.

Accordingly Parliament came to the conclusion that the new pastime should be officially recognised and regulated. In July, 1903, a Bill was introduced compelling the registration of all motor cars by County and County Borough Councils and calling upon each owner to affix a number to his car, which number should be always visible. A good deal of discussion took place in both Houses as to the speed limit. There was a proposal to give discretion to Local Authorities to fix their own limit without establishing a general figure, but eventually twenty miles an hour was adopted as the maximum speed.

The assumption still was that this "hobby" would be indulged in by men of leisure upon the high roads between the small towns and outlying villages.

The month of July brought with it a solemn event of sentimental interest for all civilisation and intense importance to a big proportion of the religious world. Pope Leo XIII had been head of the Church of his faith since 1878. During his Pontificate problems of the gravest religious and international importance had been discussed. Leo XIII had dealt with them according to his beliefs. Towards his character and person there was the deepest respect in Great Britain as elsewhere, which naturally increased as he grew more venerable with the weight of years. On the 20th of July, 1903, he passed away at the age of ninety-three amid manifestations of world wide sympathy.

Chapter 10

THE TARIFF REFORM CRUSADE

"TARIFF REFORM" as a subject for conversation and argument gripped the popular imagination. It was debated on every village green; discussed in every morning train.

While the controversy was still at the "Inquiry" stage, nominally, an active campaign for and against tariffs began. Free Traders attacked Mr. Chamberlain's proposals as old-time "Protection". Mr. Chamberlain and his friends contended that the reform of the tariff was a subject of its own with no reference to ancient "Shibboleths". They urged that, just as in the days of Cobden and Bright, Protection had become an obsolete method of encouraging trade, so the Free Trade system initiated after that campaign was now unsuited to modern conditions. Half-a-century, they contended, had made vast differences, and the growth of trade between the various parts of the Empire rendered the Empire as a whole comparatively independent of foreign goods.

Some Members of Mr. Chamberlain's own Party, however, declined to accept these arguments. One section who were opposed to a tax on corn founded a "Unionist Free Food League". The uncompromising opponents of all kinds of protective tariffs inaugurated a "Free Trade League"; supporters of Mr. Chamberlain formed a "Tariff Reform League".

The "Cobden Club" which had remained in existence for many years, pressing for more and more freedom from taxation on imports, became very active. At every Debating Society and every political meeting Tariff Reform monopolised all the time and energy. The country was flooded with statistics by able economists. Patients argued Tariff Reform with their doctors and even with their dentists.

It is contended to this day by many shrewd judges that if Mr. Chamberlain had been Prime Minister and thus in a position to obtain an Election on his proposal for an Inquiry, he might have carried the country with him on the wave of popular interest. He had yet to convince his Leader that an appeal to the electors on the subject was desirable, and so the controversy went on, mainly outside Parliament.

The Liberal Party forgot all domestic differences and sprang into line against Protective duties in any shape or form.

It is fairly safe to say that Mr. Chamberlain expected support from the skilled artisans and the factory workers

who were members of the more substantial Trade Unions.
His services to such causes as Workmen's Compensation
were remembered with gratitude in the country.   Personally
he was popular with the wage-earners, and it was urged
that, in principle, Trade Union provisions for regulating
conditions of labour were similar to proposals for safeguarding the market for British-made goods.

An opportunity for testing the feeling of Trade Unions
arose in the North-Eastern area. The Iron Founders'
Society had accepted the formula of the Labour Representation Committee and had chosen Mr. Arthur Henderson
as a prospective Candidate when occasion should arise.
It arose immediately after Mr. Henderson's adoption by
reason of a bye-election in the Barnard Castle Division
of the County of Durham rendered necessary by the death
of the Liberal Member, Sir Joseph Pease.

Many Liberals were disposed to give the Labour Candidate,
who had been a Liberal Organiser, a clear run against the
Conservative, but a Liberal Candidate was put forward and
strongly supported by Mr. Samuel Storey, then a powerful
leader in local Liberalism, who subsequently became a convert
to Tariff Reform and joined the Conservative Party.

Mr. Henderson and his supporters throughout the election
emphatically championed Free Trade and declared themselves opposed to Mr. Chamberlain's proposals. Speakers
in favour of the Conservative Candidate strongly advocated
Tariff Reform. The Liberal Candidate inserted in his
Address a paragraph favouring an Inquiry, though he
mentioned in his speeches that he believed the Inquiry
would show the advantages of Free Trade.

Mr. Henderson's victory at the poll was therefore a definite
pronouncement against Mr. Chamberlain by the constituency
and by the Trade Union movement officially, although
the supporters of Tariff Reform no doubt attracted to their
ranks many individual Trade Unionists.

It was at first thought that the Irish Nationalist Members
as representing agricultural interests would be in favour

of Protection against imported foreign foodstuffs, but they were now working whole-heartedly with their old allies, the Liberals, and Mr. Chamberlain got no support there.

The Barnard Castle election was perhaps even more significant as a landmark in the Labour Movement than as a stage in the Fiscal controversy. There had been in the old days occasional three-cornered contests, but the Labour Candidate was invariably at the bottom—generally with a very small percentage of votes. Mr. Shackleton and Mr. Crooks, as has already been pointed out, were returned with the support or assent of the Liberals. Barnard Castle was the first direct victory of the new Labour electoral organisation.

When in response to the customary invitation from the Speaker, "Members desiring to take their seats will advance to the Table", Mr. Henderson—introduced, according to the traditions of the House, by his two sponsors Mr. Shackleton and Mr. Crooks—walked up the floor, fortune was kind to the Labour Representation Committee.

Will Crooks, the good-hearted, ready-witted Cockney, David Shackleton, the embodiment of Lancashire stability, Arthur Henderson, a blend of Scottish caution and Tyneside fervour, were all tried and tested public workers. They were men of unimpeachable personal character and responsibility. Nobody looking down upon the House could conjure up thoughts of a "Red Terror" from these pioneers of a new parliamentary force.

The importance of the incident was not fully realised by the general body of Members of Parliament or of the public outside until a later period in political history. There was still a general belief that the new Labour Members were advanced Radicals and unattached allies of the Liberal Party, especially in view of the fact that a little while afterwards Mr. Johnson, an official of the Durham Miners' Union, was returned as a Liberal.

During another brief interval in domestic argument, a further stage in Anglo-French relations was reached when some eighty Members of the French Legislature were

JOSEPH CHAMBERLAIN AND BALFOUR

By permission of the "Westminster Gazette"

invited to confer with Members of the House of Commons respecting International Arbitration. Their reception was thoroughly representative. Mr. Balfour, Sir Henry Campbell-Bannerman, and Mr. Chamberlain all addressed the visitors at a Dinner given in their honour and spoke of the friendship between the two countries.

Although the Tariff controversy absorbed the platform and the Press, Mr. Balfour contended that as the subject was still in the Inquiry stage no direct Debate on its merits or demerits was necessary so far as the House of Commons was concerned. On this hypothesis he skilfully parried all attempts to draw a definite declaration of faith from him. Many cautious Members of the Conservative Party also held aloof and suggested that Mr. Chamberlain's policy should be modified so that the taxation of foodstuffs—if any—would be insignificant.

These timid approaches and retreats were ridiculed in scathing terms by Lord Hugh Cecil, who took a similar view to that expressed by Mr. Churchill and was now devoting his gifts to the cause of Conservative Free Trade. He summed up the attitude of Mr. Balfour and his "Free Food Friends" on the one hand and the ardent Tariff Reformers on the other in the lines:

> But those behind cried "Forward",
> And those before cried "Back";
> And backwards now and forward
>   Wavers the deep array;
> And on the tossing sea of steel
> To and fro the standards reel
> And the victorious trumpet's peal
>   Dies fitfully away.

While the new controversy was developing the last of the Conservative Prime Ministers in the Victorian era passed peacefully to his long rest. Lord Salisbury, who had remained in retirement since his resignation, died at Hatfield on Saturday, the 22nd August, 1903. The final break with the past called attention to the fact that a new generation was asserting itself. The Conservative Party included amongst its influential personages a far greater proportion of men connected with trade and commerce than had participated in the guidance of its destinies during Lord Salisbury's earlier days. The great governing families merged with the captains of industry. The landed gentry were no longer the dominating guardians of the young heir to the venerable Tory Party.

A public sensation which for a while obscured even Tariff Reform was created by the publication of the Report of the Royal Commission on the South African War. Firm supporters of the Government argued that the weaknesses revealed were such as could not have been avoided and the mistakes such as could not have been foreseen. A very large body of critics drawn from all Parties, however, interpreted the Evidence and the Report as showing an unpreparedness in general plans and an appalling lack of proper equipment and stores.

Still the country at this period drifted from every other subject back to Tariff Reform. The Trade Union Congress discussed Mr. Chamberlain's proposals in the autumn. Two delegates from small Unions were in favour of an Inquiry, the rest voted solidly for a motion to the effect that the change proposed by Mr. Chamberlain was "most mischievous and dangerous".

Another significant Debate arose at the same Congress on the subject of Parliamentary Representation. A number of the older Trade Unionists had urged the new movement to keep in touch with the older Parties and had warned them against the "Ishmaelite" policy. Mr. Thomas Burt at a Liberal Federation meeting good-humouredly reminded them of the fate of Ishmael: "He shall be as a wild ass among men".

Mr. Richard Bell, who was the Chairman of the Labour Representation Committee—but still retained Liberal sympathies and had been returned for Derby at the General

Election with the approval of the Liberals—urged that it would be unwise to push independence to the point of isolation. A proposal to give Candidates under the Labour Representation Committee a wider latitude and to withdraw the clause prohibiting them from appearing on other Party platforms was, however, defeated by five hundred and six thousand to two hundred and eighty-five thousand on a card vote—each delegate having the voting powers of the full number of members he represented.

The Autumn Recess had still more sensational developments for the political world. The Duke of Devonshire, who, as Lord Hartington, for a short time held the position of Leader of the Liberal Party during Mr. Gladstone's temporary retirement, and whose profound influence as a Liberal Unionist had been the most potent personal force in the defeat of Mr. Gladstone's Home Rule Bill of 1886, was still a staunch Free Trader, as were Mr. Ritchie (afterwards Lord Ritchie), the Chancellor of the Exchequer, and Lord George Hamilton, the Secretary of State for India.

Mr. Ritchie and Lord George Hamilton resigned and close upon that—in fact contemporaneously with it—came the further news that Mr. Chamberlain had resigned. Apparently Mr. Balfour had such an open mind that neither side was satisfied. The master stroke of diplomacy was that he had contrived to keep the Duke of Devonshire in the Cabinet, but Lord Balfour of Burleigh, Secretary of State for Scotland, who held a position in Scottish politics somewhat analagous to that of the Duke of Devonshire in England, resigned.

The Conservative boat was obviously rocking on a troubled sea, with its principal oarsmen out of stroke. At the Annual Conservative Conference held in Sheffield supporters of Mr. Chamberlain were present in force. During the day meetings they gave Mr. Winston Churchill and Lord Hugh Cecil a noisy reception when these two sons of past chieftains endeavoured to lead them back along the paths of Free Trade. A Motion was tabled pledging the Party to Mr. Chamberlain's full scheme. At this point the Conference adjourned till the following day.

Meantime, Mr. Balfour addressed a Mass Meeting in the evening and devoted his masterly methods as a tactician to the task of steadying the boat. His speech was a general disquisition on Economics, but it mystified the majority of his huge audience. He declared against the doctrine that protective taxation was necessarily wrong but on one point he was clear. "I believe", he said, "this country will not tolerate a tax on food."

How then did the Tariff Reform Motion stand? When the Conference reassembled the following morning Mr. Chaplin (afterwards Viscount Chaplin), the typical old-world squire whose faith in Protection had never wavered, felt compelled to call off the hunt. The full-blooded Tariff Reform Motion, if carried after Mr. Balfour's speech, would be in effect a vote of no confidence in their Leader. Mr. Chaplin was not prepared to go so far as that.

It was thus open to any section to carry on its propaganda without committing the Leader of the Party. This did not satisfy the Duke of Devonshire. He was a man who acted slowly and with deliberation. There is a legend concerning him that he dreamed one night he was addressing the House of Lords. Then he woke and found he was. His mind once made up, however, he was a man of unswerving consistency and iron determination. When he realised that Mr. Balfour was not prepared to adhere to the established principle that Free Trade was the fundamental rule of our Fiscal and Commercial system, he decided finally to leave the Cabinet.

On the same day that this decision was announced Mr. Chamberlain commenced his independent campaign by addressing a meeting at Glasgow at which he outlined a tariff that included a duty of two shillings a quarter on foreign corn and flour—maize to come in free—also a duty of five per cent. on foreign meat and dairy produce, excepting bacon; and a tax average not more than ten per cent. on foreign manufactured goods.

Mr. Chamberlain declared one industry after another to be either "gone" or "going". A conflict raged around pearl buttons. One set of disputants contended they had "gone" because of foreign competition. Another body of controversialists ascribed the lack of trade in this dainty article of clothing to the invention of the wringing machine and the consequent substitution by the thrifty housewife of linen buttons, which were not so prone to be crushed.

At a crowded meeting Mr. Chamberlain held up two loaves. One was reduced by a quantity of flour representing the amount of the whole tax that he proposed, and he challenged anybody to answer at sight the sporting question which loaf was the bigger.

"Your food will cost you more", was the battle-cry of the Free Traders. "Tariff Reform means work for all", was the slogan of Mr. Chamberlain's followers.

Chapter 11

PROBLEMS
DIPLOMATIC, SOCIAL AND POLITICAL

THE completion and signature on the fourteenth of October 1903 of an arbitration agreement between Great Britain and France with respect to questions that might arise between the two countries was the first definite outcome of the new Anglo-French relations.

At home the ever-recurring autumnal influenza claimed its victims. Among them was Lord Rowton, the friend and secretary of Lord Beaconsfield. Before he became associated with the political career of the great Statesman, Mr. Montagu William Lowry-Corry, as he then was, practised at the Bar on the Oxford Circuit. His name, however, is known to fame, neither as a lawyer nor as a politician but as the social reformer who instituted "the Poor Man's hotels" which in London bear his name. In conjunction with Sir Edward Guinness (afterwards Lord Iveagh) he investigated personally the conditions under which the poor lived in London and Dublin. As a consequence he advanced a

large sum of money to build a "Rowton House"; furnished
it himself and opened on a scale of charges fixed at sixpence
a night for bed and use of living rooms, with board prices
which enabled a single man to be comfortably lodged at an
inclusive charge of some ten to thirteen shillings a week.
A Company was formed with a wider range of activities and
at Lord Rowton's death in 1903 the capital had reached a
very large figure and the operations covered a very wide
area. The houses which now extend to all parts of London
were so conducted that the boarders were "paying guests"
on an economic basis and had no occasion to feel any charit-
able restraints on their independence. The idea has also
been taken up in other parts of the country and the principle
of the scheme applied to the provincial towns. It has also
extended to Europe and America. By initiating and
developing this system Lord Rowton undoubtedly established
for the respectable poor a blessed alternative to the grimy
lodging house and back street inn which till the Rowton
plans spread were their only places of refuge.

The growing problem of new occupations for women
became the subject of a leading legal decision. Miss Bertha
Cave applied for admission to Grays Inn. The four Inns
of Court—the Middle Temple, the Inner Temple, Lincoln's
Inn, and Grays Inn—are the historic institutions possessing
the exclusive right to confer upon candidates the privilege
of pleading as Barristers-at-law in the higher English Courts.
An applicant is first admitted a Member of the Inn as a
student. After having "kept Terms" or "eaten dinners"
by attending a specified number of times in the Dining
Hall attached to his Inn, and after passing certain examin-
ations, the aspiring advocate is "Called" by name in the
presence of the senior member of the Inn on "Call Night".
This ceremony of being "Called to the Bar" establishes the
right of audience in the Courts of England and Crown
Colonies. Scotland has its own Bar, as have Ireland and
the self-governing Dominions beyond the seas. Each of
the English Inns of Court is controlled by its Benchers—

chosen from senior members—who may admit or call whom they please, subject to a general "overlordship" by the Judges of the High Court.

Miss Bertha Cave wished to become a student at Grays Inn. From time immemorial only male students had been accepted and men only called to the Bar. The Benchers declined to vary this practice. Miss Cave appealed to the High Court. A special tribunal, presided over by the Lord Chancellor, held there was no precedent for ladies being admitted to the English Bar and the tribunal were unwilling to create one—There the matter ended for the time being.

An Act of Parliament passed in 1903 was welcomed by everybody associated with the work of the Criminal Courts and by the general public. In the English Courts a prisoner at Assizes or Quarter Sessions may call upon any junior barrister present in Court and not appearing for the prosecution to defend him at a fee of one guinea. This is known as a "Dock brief" or a "Docker". Prisoners without any means hitherto defended themselves. The Court always exercised a keen supervision in such cases in order that the accused might have the full benefit of any points in his or her favour. But it was felt that direct legal assistance would be a more satisfactory system. Accordingly by the Poor Prisoners Defence Act, 1903, in cases where the defence set up by a poor prisoner in the evidence or the statement made by him or her before the committing Justices is such that legal aid seems desirable, either the committing Justices or the presiding Judge at the trial can assign counsel and solicitor at the public expense. This is a very long way from the seventeenth century, when counsel were not allowed to appear for defendants on a charge of felony except to argue points of law for them.

*   *   *   *   *

When Parliament met in 1904 Mr. Joseph Chamberlain took his seat below the gangway.

The scene recalled memories of those times when every sound Conservative squire linked the name of Joseph

Chamberlain with that of such persons in history as "Jack Cade". Lord Salisbury the Conservative Leader had indeed likened the then Birmingham Radical to that early English rebel. Now he sat beside that typical squire Mr. Henry Chaplin fighting for the cause which Squirearchical Conservation had never surrendered.

Although the distinguished convert had gone below the gangway in order that he might have a free hand, it was assumed that Mr. Chamberlain had not such a very wide difference of view from that of Mr. Balfour, especially in view of the fact that his devoted son, Mr. Austen Chamberlain, of whom he was justly proud, had found it possible to accept the post of Chancellor of the Exchequer in Mr. Balfour's Government.

Public attention was once more turned from West to East for a while when news came that Japan had declared war on Russia. The immediate problem upon which the Japanese Minister in St. Petersburg had been instructed to sever diplomatic relations was a demand from Japan that Russia should recognise the territorial integrity and independence of China and Korea, and that there should be equal opportunities for Russia and Japan in both these two countries. The main interest to this country was that the Power which had emerged from the mists of antiquity was now adopting the orthodox method of asserting her position in modern civilisation. Our Treaty with Japan did not involve us in this particular dispute. The usual proclamation of neutrality was read in the City of London from the steps of the Mansion House and warnings were issued to ship-owners and shipbuilders against actively taking sides. The general tendency after the first interest had subsided was to "wish the little 'un good luck" and turn again to our own affairs.

A new problem had arisen in South Africa. Until such time as the clause in the Treaty of Peace with respect to representative institutions came into force the two new Colonies were under direct control from the Colonial Office. The mineowners there asked for an Ordnance permitting them to import Chinese labourers, who were to be indentured for three years and live in compounds.

Mr. Alfred Lyttelton had succeeded Mr. Joseph Chamberlain as Colonial Secretary. He was an International cricketer, a member of the famous indomitable Cambridge team of his day, a thorough sportsman and a perfect English gentleman. The irony of fate ordained that he should be the object of fierce attacks from press, platform and Parliament.

The Colonial Office agreed to grant the Ordnance for the introduction of the Chinese labourers. Their action was strongly resented, and it came at a time when the Government were subjected to acute and alert opposition in the House of Commons.

One afternoon early in March, 1904, the Irish Nationalist Party moved a reduction of One hundred pounds in the estimates for Irish Education. A long Debate was expected. Secure in the thought that many Irishmen would have grievances to discuss the Government supporters took things calmly.

Suddenly the Debate collapsed. No more Irish Members rose and the Conservatives had nothing to say on this matter. The division bells rang throughout the building. Members filed into the Lobbies and came leisurely from the "Aye" and the "No" Lobby respectively, past the enumerators, or "Tellers"—one from each side at either entrance—who check the counting.

At the end of the division the "Tellers" communicated their figures to the officials and lined up at the Table facing the Speaker. When the Clerk handed the slip of paper containing the numbers to the Irish Teller a mighty shout went up from the Opposition benches. As it is the duty of the senior Teller of the side that has won to read out the figures, it was evident that the Government were defeated.

Shouts of "Resign! Resign!" greeted Mr. Balfour.

The refusal of supply is one of the most emphatic forms of humiliation that the House of Commons can inflict upon the Government. If done deliberately it is usually followed by resignation and a General Election. Mr. Balfour, however, treated this as a chance vote and decided to go on.

Chapter 12

OLD PARLIAMENTARY JOKES AND NEW MEN

WOMAN'S Franchise had long been a favourite topic for political pleasantries. Sir Charles McLaren (afterwards Lord McLaren) secured an opportunity one evening for moving a Resolution to the effect that the restrictions which then prevented women from voting at parliamentary elections ought to be removed by legislation.

The Motion was carried by One hundred and eighty-two to Sixty-eight. In the course of the Debate, Mr. Labouchere, the Liberal Member for Northampton, then nearing the end of his career as a famous parliamentary wit, called attention to the fact that an iron grille was placed in front of the Ladies' Gallery behind the Speaker's Chair. "Why was it there?" They were told that the sight of so much beauty would so disturb the minds of honourable Members that if it were moved they would not be able to continue their deliberations quietly. But, he asked, with what was then regarded as crushing finality, what would prevent ladies being admitted as Members of the House if they were given the vote? What, he persisted, would happen if ladies were transferred from the Gallery to the Treasury Bench and mixed hugger mugger with honourable Members? Personally, he was an old man and the transference would not affect him very much. He was speaking more out of sympathy with the younger Members of the House, and he would not consciously submit them to temptation—such at that period was the accepted note of discussions on this topic.

Feeling on more immediately controversial topics grew very acute. Processions accompanied by bands and banners marched in protest to Hyde Park and to other popular

meeting places in the great towns throughout the country
to protest against indentured Chinese labour in South
Africa.   In the House of Commons Sir Henry Campbell-
Bannerman, as the official Leader of the Opposition, proposed
a Vote of Censure on the Government.   In the course of
the Debate Major (afterwards General) Seely, the handsome
young Unionist Member for the Isle of Wight, with the
deep smooth voice and urbane manner, condemned the
Ordnance from the Government side.   He spoke in the
capacity of a candid friend, and he toiled on amid what is
described in the verbatim Reports as "Ministerial interruptions".   His assailants next adopted an old device of
talking to each other in audible tones, drowning his voice
in a monotonous murmur.   Still he strove to get in a few
words here and there.   The murmurs next developed into
deafening shouts and jeers.

Mr. Winston Churchill, who was sitting near the object
of this fraternal demonstration, jumped up and, addressing
the Speaker, said:

Owing to the vulgar clamour among the Conservative Party
I am unable to hear what my honourable Friend is saying.

Whereupon an old-fashioned Conservative, pointing
dramatically at Mr. Churchill, retorted:

Allow me to say, Mr. Speaker, that the vulgarest expressions came from the honourable Gentleman.

The intervention did not pour oil upon the troubled
waters, and later on when Mr. Balfour rose to speak reprisals
from the other side came with a chorus of "Vide! Vide!!".
The "head boy" suffered for the riotous conduct of his
turbulent juniors.   "No Seely, no Balfour" was in effect
the cry.   Mr. Balfour urged that he had taken no part in
the demonstration against the Member for the Isle of Wight.
He assured the House that he had made an appeal to his
friends to give the honourable Member a hearing.   On this
he was allowed to proceed.

The Vote of Censure was defeated, but the agitation

E

against the Ordnance went on in and out of Parliament. The conditions under which the coolies were confined to their compounds for the period of their indentured service was roundly described as "Chinese slavery"—a description responsible for the enrichment of the vocabulary by Mr. Winston Churchill, who, whilst strongly opposing the Government policy, admitted at a later stage that the use of the word "slavery" in this connection was a "terminological inexactitude".

The Conservative party was growing very angry with its troublesome young men. One afternoon when Mr. Winston Churchill was criticising his Leaders a number of his fellow Conservatives and Unionists began to walk out of the House. As he proceeded with his speech more of them departed in twos and threes. Some were to be seen watching through the glass panels at the side of the doors the gradual dwindling of the audience and motioning to their friends. Ultimately Mr. Churchill found himself talking to upholstery so far as the back benches on his own side of the House were concerned.

In a very few weeks an incident occurred in which the comradeship of parliamentary life rose superior to Party differences.

A Member on the Liberal side asked the House to amend the law—in the light of the Taff Vale decision—by removing the possibility of civil actions against Trade Unions and their leaders in the event of a strike. Mr. Churchill rose to speak in favour of this appeal. He called attention to the strong representation in the House of the landed interest, gentlemen of the Law, and the Commercial classes, and asserted that by comparison in view of its numbers in the country the representation of Labour was ludicrously small. He was proceeding to draw the moral that the House thus had a special responsibility for safeguarding the interests of labour when he paused in the middle of a sentence as though seeking the right word.

He began the sentence again; stopped; and looked nervously around. Members realised that memory was playing a trick with him. He was struggling hard to collect his thoughts. Political hostility vanished in an instant. A sympathetic cheer went up from all parts of the House. The object, obviously, was to afford the bewildered speaker time to unravel the tangled skein of his argument. But the skein was broken. After another effort Mr. Churchill, in a faltering voice, apologised to the House and sat down.

Consoling cheers, deep and sincere, greeted him. Sir James Ferguson, one of the oldest Members of the House— an uncompromising Conservative—left his place and, sitting beside Mr. Churchill, chatted encouragingly to him.

The Lobbies buzzed with comments on this strange lapse on the part of a Debater who had exhibited such confidence and promise. Events proved that it was only a temporary check arising out of an attempt to deal with a new subject upon the spur of the moment instead of marshalling facts in advance.

Mr. Churchill took this useful lesson to heart and commended its teaching to his friends. Ever since that day, by example and precept, he has advocated thoughtful preparation of speeches—particularly on new or unfamiliar subjects.

The Anglo-French friendship went steadily on from stage to stage. Easter of 1904 saw the publication of three documents simultaneously in Paris and London, settling some highly delicate international points. The public looked on with feelings of general approval and regarded it as another result of the interchange of courtesies which the King had initiated.

In personalities, as in problems, the new was displacing the old. Fresh names appeared in the headlines of the newspapers; voices hitherto unfamiliar claimed the ear of Parliament and country. One evening shortly after the 1900 Election, while a tall man with a bushy black moustache, high cheek bones and spare figure, was addressing the House, Mr. Balfour was seen turning over the pages of "Dodd's Parliamentary Companion"—the authority on biographical particulars of Members. It was presumed that he was looking up Mr. Bonar Law. Within a very short time after that the new Member was Parliamentary Secretary to the Board of Trade. As a junior Minister he applied himself to administration rather than to discussion. When Leaders of his Party went out to Mass Meetings he was in demand for the overflow gathering. He spoke with the sharp decisive tongue of the educated and travelled Scot. His gift for ready, close reasoning was almost unique. His speeches had all the atmosphere of thoughtful preparation, yet he never used notes.

Born in Canada, Mr. Bonar Law returned to the land of his forefathers for the completion of his education, and until he gave his energies to politics had been actively associated with a firm of Glasgow Iron Merchants. The Fiscal controversy was his real political baptism. He was a Tariff Reformer and very quickly became one of the strongest forces on that side. He ceased to be an "overflow". He was a principal speaker.

Another man came quickly into prominence on the other side. Mr. Reginald McKenna, a junior barrister (afterwards the great banking expert), relinquished law and was throwing himself wholeheartedly into politics as an ardent young Liberal. He became famous in a day. Mr. Austen Chamberlain, as Chancellor of the Exchequer, had made an excellent impression on introducing his review of the Nation's finance known in parliamentary phraseology as "the Budget". Among his proposals for providing the money required to meet expenditure in the coming year was a provision for putting an additional tax on tobacco leaf that came into this country "stripped", or, in other words, with the part of the stalk that runs through the leaf already extracted by labour employed at the place of shipment. Free Traders observed in this "a whiff of Protection". Experts urged that there were other objections. Mr. McKenna, quoting these views, made an onslaught upon the possible consequences of the duty and had an exciting encounter with the Chancellor of the Exchequer. The following morning Mr. McKenna's name was displayed throughout the country in big type. His position as a public man was established, and his abilities enabled him to maintain it. The stripped tobacco tax subsequently disappeared from the Budget.

Chapter 13

LICENSING. ARBITRATION. SALVATIONISTS

PUBLIC excitement centred for some weeks on Licensing Law. Legal tribunals had decided some years before that a licence for the sale of alcoholic liquors was for one year only and the licensee had no inherent right to a renewal. The Government now introduced a Bill the effect of which was to grant compensation to the owner of licensed premises when the licence was taken away on any other ground than that of misconduct.   The fund out of which the compensation was to be taken was to be provided by an annual levy upon existing licensees in proportion to the volume of their trade.

It was contended by the Opposition that the measure, by recognising a property in license where no such property existed, was setting up a new vested interest.   The supporters of the Bill argued that since the licensees themselves were providing the fund, it was an equitable method of reducing redundant licences.

Temperance Societies throughout the country led a vehement and vigorous campaign against the proposal and there were heated Debates in the House upon it.   The rejection of the Bill was moved by Mr. Thomas Burt, the leader of the Northumberland miners, once described by Earl Grey—a member of the old Border aristocracy—as "the finest gentleman I ever knew".

Mr. Burt dissociated himself from any "fanatical and exaggerated" utterances that might have been made by over-zealous people. He remarked that he was not going to attack the publicans. "I have it from the Archbishop of Canterbury," he said, "that there is apparently a great rivalry between the Church and the trade as to which of them rear the most virtuous families." He went on to say that the Archbishop, quoting from the Licensed Victuallers' Annual, had stated that this organ of the trade actually declared and deliberately affirmed as a matter of statistical proof that the publicans' families turned out much better than the clergymen's.

When the laughter subsided Mr. Burt continued:

> Now I would just warn my publican friends that it does not necessarily follow that the public house is a better school of morals than the Church—look at the pains that we take in selecting the publican.

Then he paused, and everybody rocked with laughter. None laughed more heartily than the Bishops who were sitting in the special gallery reserved for visiting Members of the House of Lords.

"I hope", added Mr. Burt, after giving some examples of rigorous character tests imposed by magistrates before granting a licence, "that this wholesome rivalry in the rearing of virtuous families will go on with moderation and without acrimony."

On the merits of the Bill he contended that it was a step in the backward direction—that it did nothing for John Bull's family, "many of whom", he pleaded, "are in rags, living on the verge of starvation, and their poverty, their misery and their crime is largely caused by traffic in intoxicating liquors".

Heated discussions verging on turbulent scenes arose upon the Bill night after night. The opposition strenuously held to their contention that this was in principle a recognition of a legal right to the renewal of a licence where no such right existed. In the course of one of the many Debates an incident occurred which marked the beginning of another kind of parliamentary revolution.

Up to this time it was, and continued to be, an unwritten code of etiquette that only Members of the front Benches, or Party Leaders, should appear in the precincts without their hats. The exceptions were made to distinguish these quasi-official Members from their colleagues. Any ordinary Member of Parliament would no more dream of sitting in the House bareheaded than a lady would think of going into a Church hatless. Even Mr. Keir Hardie, who was always unconventional, never departed from this rule. He declined to don a tall hat, but on the day of his arrival he wore a cloth cap which was afterwards replaced by a soft felt. Mr. Burns clung to his bowler, as did Mr. Richard Bell. Sir William Allen, a picturesque Viking, appeared in a poetic wideawake; every other Member wore the regulation silk hat.

The hat indeed played, and is still assumed to play, a most important part in parliamentary life. A Member is expected to lift it when addressed by the Chair or referred to by another Member in debate; also when he speaks to another Member personally; interjects a remark in debate, or passes the Teller at the Lobby door. Of course he keeps his hat off when he addresses the House or remains standing anywhere within the Chamber.

One night during the Debates on the Licensing Bill Mr. Will Crooks desired to put a point of order after the division had been called.

"If the honourable Member wishes to address me on a point of order he can do so during the division if he will sit covered", came the warning instruction from the Chair.

This pronouncement alluded to the rule that a Member submitting a point of order to the Chair while other Members are walking towards the Division Lobbies with their hats off remains in his place with his hat on and is thus as conspicuous to the Chair as he would be rising with his hat off when other Members are seated.

Mr. Crooks looked about him in bewilderment. Points of order are very seldom put at this stage, and the need for a hat had not yet been brought home to this comparatively young Member.

It now dawned upon the House that a terrible innovation was being perpetrated. A "back-Bencher" was in the sanctuary hatless!

A Member sitting near by happened to be wearing an opera hat. He passed it to Mr. Crooks, who put it on and tried to press it over his forehead from the top. As a consequence it "concertinaed". Roars of laughter greeted the puzzled man's efforts to balance the flattened "crush". At last somebody took it off for him, touched it inside and sent the crown up with a bang. Perceiving now the style of the borrowed hat Mr. Crooks succeeded in pulling the brim over his right eye.

The point of order was eventually put and dealt with. The incident, however, was more serious. It called attention to the fact that Mr. Crooks' colleagues—Mr. Shackleton and Mr. Arthur Henderson—were also invading the Chamber without their hats. To these three well-thatched men belongs the terrible responsibility for initiating a custom which spread insidiously till years later a disgruntled cynic of the old school, gazing down from the Gallery, declared one might be looking at a bird's nest!

While internal Party politics were exciting keen controversy our relations with other Powers once more became interesting by reason of the King's visit to the German Emperor at Kiel, where a gala dinner was given on the "Hohenzollern" with the customary exchange of cordial speeches and toasts. British and German sailors on the war-ships also had supper together.

King Edward travelled on to Hamburg and was present at various other functions. This visit was not of a diplomatic character but an Anglo-German Arbitration Treaty was shortly afterwards concluded on somewhat similar lines to that between Great Britain and France.

A gracious act of the King at home was appreciated as recognising the remarkable growth of a vast religious movement within a single lifetime.

William Booth, born in Nottingham in 1829, became a Minister of the Methodist New Connection Church. Coming to London he was struck with the destitute condition of the people in the East End. As early as 1865 he made special efforts through the Christian Mission to do something for their spiritual and temporal welfare. In 1878 his zeal for his Mission promoted the foundation of the Salvation Army—officered by deeply religious men and women, with William Booth as its General. The new movement, organised on military lines,

GENERAL BOOTH

Standing with his hands on his hips and his head thrust forward Mr. Churchill flung back stinging retorts. Scraps of sentences heard above the din suggested that his infuriated colleagues would be outmatched in any contest of barbed wit. They replied with shouts in varying tones and keys which effectually drowned the offending voice.

Mr. Shackleton, one of the new Labour Members, rising to a point of order, said:

> Mr. Speaker, for the last ten minutes I have been endeavouring to listen to the speech of the honourable Member and I have been unable to follow him. I think it is one of the privileges every honourable Member is entitled to that he should be heard.

Here Mr. Shackleton was assailed with cries of "Order! Order!!". Again addressing the Chair, he said:

> I do ask you as Speaker of this House to try to keep order for us.

The Speaker replied that it was impossible for him to compel every Member to keep silence, but he trusted every honourable Member would observe the Rules of the House.

Mr. Churchill made another attempt and spoke, as the official records say, "amid continued interruptions". He remarked that he saw the Prime Minister in his place. Was it to be supposed that he was a consenting party to this uproar?

More angry shouts followed upon this. The Speaker rose and, addressing the House in tones of some emotion, said:

> I cannot of course compel the silence of every honourable Member of this House, but I would remind them that the Rules of this House as they existed more than two hundred and fifty years ago make it the duty of every Member to maintain silence whilst a Member is addressing the House. No Speaker can enforce that regulation, but I appeal to the House whether it is not more conducive to the dignity of the House when a Member is speaking—whether his opinions be popular or not—that he should be allowed to proceed.

Concluding his speech shortly afterwards amidst a renewed chorus of "Vide! Vide!!" Mr. Churchill appealed to the good sense of the House of Commons to say whether he had received fair treatment—whether the carefully organised attack upon the liberties of debate in which he declared the right honourable Member for West Birmingham (Mr. Joseph Chamberlain) was an accomplice and a consenting party——

Here there were roars of "Order!" and "Withdraw!" from the Conservatives and cheers from the Liberals in the midst of which Mr. Chamberlain, springing to his feet, said: "Mr. Speaker, I rise to a point of order". He was met with shouts of "No, no," and for a moment or two was unable to proceed. "I merely wish to know," he said, "whether it is in order"—more cross fire and shouts of "Order! Order!!" held him up again. Then he went on—"for the junior Member for Oldham to say that there is a conspiracy against him of which I am an accomplice—a statement which is absolutely untrue". Derisive cries of "Oh! Oh!!" from the one side and "Order! Order!!" from the other, with cheers and counter-cheers greeted this disclaimer.

"The honourable Member should not make charges of that kind", said the Speaker.

At this there were cheers and shouts of "Withdraw!" from the Conservatives, when Mr. Churchill, in carefully chosen words, said:

> Mr. Speaker, if I have said anything which passes in any degree the limitation of the order of debate I completely withdraw it. I have made my protest which I venture to commit to the good sense and calmer consideration of the House.

To veterans like Mr. H. W. Lucy (afterwards Sir Henry Lucy), famous as "Toby" of Punch, this scene was a weird reproduction of an incident that occurred twenty years before, in October, 1894—when from that same corner seat Lord Randolph Churchill moved an amendment to the Address and in the course of his remarks charged Mr. Joseph Chamberlain with making speeches which were "an incitement to interference with the freedom of political discussion and a justification of riot and disorder".

That incident arose out of a Conservative meeting at Aston Park, Birmingham, which was to have been addressed by Sir Stafford Northcote and Lord Randolph Churchill but was broken up amid riotous scenes. Mr. Chamberlain then, as now, strongly repudiated the charge that he had incited the disturbance. Mr. Balfour, sitting now on the same side as Mr. Chamberlain watching this contest between his former opponent and the son of his old colleague, must have been moved to reminiscent and philosophic thoughts on the changes and chances of time.

Mr. Winston Churchill very soon improved on the "fourth Party" methods. According to the testimony of all the veterans, the little band which he joined were the authors of the most virile Opposition that the House of Commons had witnessed in the time of any living man. Mr. Lloyd George was recognised tacitly as the unofficial leader of the group. He still sat in the corner of the second Bench below the gangway. Behind him on the third and fourth Benches were the Irish Nationalists, ever ready to lend a hand. Mr. McKenna and Mr. Churchill sat near each other on the front bench. Close by, and working with them, were such rising politicians as Mr. Walter Runciman, Mr. Trevelyan and Major Seely, who had also crossed the Floor. Mr. Herbert (afterwards Sir Herbert) Samuel was less insistent but very sure and effective. Mr. J. H. Dalziel (afterwards Lord Dalziel), still young in years but with a long parliamentary career, took a somewhat independent line but was always to the fore.

Mr. J. A. Pease (afterwards Lord Gainford), then a Junior Leader of the Liberal Party, was ever on the alert from the front Bench and took care that the advance guard below the gangway received fair recognition.

All-night sittings were special opportunities for the new combination. The House normally adjourned at midnight. Certain business, such as that arising out of Committee of Ways and Means, i.e., the provision of money, might be taken after twelve. The Government, by Motion at the commencement of the day's proceedings, might also by a majority of the House suspend the Twelve o'clock Rule for other business. It invariably happens in the case of every Government that some business must be taken after twelve in order that they may complete their arranged programme. The presence of an active Opposition debating every possible point therefore means that the supporters of the Government are kept within the precincts during long weary hours, patiently waiting for the sound of the division bell. The contention of the Opposition—every Opposition— has always been that in the absence of such disciplinary watchfulness a Government might rush through legislation upon inadequate discussion, or obtain sanction for the expenditure of huge sums of public money without criticism.

Some of the more brilliant young men in the Conservative Party who acted with Lord Hugh Cecil were out of sympathy with the Government and gave them no assistance against the corresponding talent in the Liberal camp. Mr. Churchill and his versatile comrades had no serious competition in the rapier play of debate. The middle-aged Conservatives and Unionists in their wisdom silently and steadily voted. When some of the younger Conservatives protested vocally they merely provided openings for the expert fencers opposite.

"If honourable Members insist upon going on they will spend their time walking through the Lobbies—an exercise more in keeping with their political attainments than taking part in serious debate", observed Mr. Churchill one evening when a proposal to postpone certain business till another day was under discussion.

Chapter 15

HOUSING. "STONEWALLING". OUTRAGE

THE Garden City and the Garden Suburb were practically unknown till the eve of the present century. Towards the end of the old century Mr. George Cadbury and Mr.

W. H. Lever (afterwards Lord Leverhulme) founded at
Bournville and Port Sunlight respectively model villages
for workmen. They were the pioneers of a movement
for transferring the family of the wage-earner from the
house opening on the street to a cottage and a garden in
some spot with preserved free spaces. From this idea
of model villages for workmen the Garden City evolved :
first at Letchworth, then at Hampstead, and in other
directions. From about 1903 onwards through 1904 was
a critical period of public education on the subject. To
this date can be traced the beginnings of that country life
enjoyed by comparatively well-to-do families, owning dwellings on co-partnership lines, in picturesque settlements at a
convenient distance from the big towns. These communities
were able at their foundation to set a high example, and their
development proceeded side by side with the movement—in
which most of their members took part—for improving the
housing conditions of people in less prosperous circumstances.

It may fairly be said that during these years the country
witnessed an awakening to the importance of healthy
houses for all classes. Other captains of industry directed
their attention to similar schemes on the lines of the Port
Sunlight and Bournville undertakings for brightening the
lives and improving the stamina of the future generation.
Mr. Joseph Rowntree established the Earswick Garden
Village with quiet pastoral roads and cottages deeply set
back in gardens just outside the city of York. A passage
in the Trust Deed gives an interesting and comprehensive
summary of the objects which the founders of these early
garden suburbs had in view:

> The object of the said Trust shall be the improvement of
> the conditions of the working classes (which expression shall
> in these presents include not only artisans and mechanics,
> but also shop assistants and clerks, and all persons who earn
> their living wholly or partially, or earn a small income by the
> work of their hands or their minds, and further include
> persons having small incomes derived from invested capital,

pensions, or other sources) in and around the City of York, and elsewhere in Great Britain and Ireland, by the provision of improved dwellings with open spaces and, where possible, gardens to be enjoyed therewith, and the organisation of village communities, with such facilities for the enjoyment of full and healthy lives as the Trustees shall consider desirable, and by such other means as the trustees shall, in their un-controlled discretion, think fit.

A Garden Village was also established at Hull by Sir James Reckitt. In the mining areas the model village at Bolsover in Derbyshire had already led the way under the direction of Mr. J. P. Houfton, an enterprising mining engineer and coalowner. It was followed some years later at Woodlands, near the Brodsworth Colliery in Yorkshire established by Sir Arthur Markham. Other similar villages sprang up in different parts of the country, though there was in many quarters a hesitating tolerance of the new idea. Some people argued that individual effort and privacy were threatened by it.

At about the time when the Garden Village was struggling for recognition the National Housing and Town Planning Council came into existence. The movement began among a number of public spirited people led by the then Bishop of Durham who were deeply concerned with the housing conditions among the mining villages of the North of England. The Association broadened its membership and established friendly relations with housing reformers in other countries. It should be added that a certain contro-versial difference of view existed in these early, as in subse-quent, years between the claims of the villa or cottage as against the well-appointed flat or the efficiently equipped tenement. Far seeing men predicted that it would become a question of convenience in transit.

*   *   *   *   *

The hardest-worked man in Great Britain in the years 1904 and 1905 was Sir Alexander Acland Hood, affectionately known as the "Pink 'Un"—a hunting Squire from the

West of England, who, as Chief Government Whip, now directed the pace for Members of Parliament.

A French journalist is said to have informed the continental public that British Members of Parliament were being "lashed" into the Division Lobbies. The confusion over the same word with a different meaning would very naturally occur in translating the descriptive account of an important division. By long custom certain alert looking men representing the respective Parties stand at the two Lobby doors and "whip" their own Members— some of whom may not have heard the Debate—by nodding towards the side on which they expect their men to go.

As Chief Government Whip, Sir Alexander Acland Hood occupied the official position of Parliamentary Secretary to the Treasury. His juniors were Lords of the Treasury or held other minor Government appointments. In the discharge of their main duty of keeping a majority for the Government within hail they had a strenuous task. After the Government defeat, when the Irish Members ceased talking suddenly, special precautions were taken against a similar collapse of discussion at an inconvenient juncture. Hour by hour almost minute by minute—the lists of Members kept by the checking clerks at the door of the Whips' Office adjoining the circular "Inner Lobby" between the main entrance and the Debating Chamber were examined. The names of the incomers —as ticked off on these lists when they arrived—often showed that there were not enough Government men within the precincts. This meant that a "snap" division might be taken if the debate collapsed; and the Government would be defeated.

One afternoon towards the end of the Session, when it was absolutely necessary to get the Finance Bill through one of its stages, the Opposition were waiting to pounce. Their Whips' lists showed that their men were present in force and the Government men were not. They wanted to divide. The Government Whips could only avert defeat by inducing their men to go on talking for a full hour while urgent messages were 'phoned to the absentees.

F

Incited by this prospect of catching the slackers out, the George-Churchillian combination prepared to make a night of it for the Government. It was a favourable opportunity for continuous attempts at "snapping". The Budget proposals for the taxation of the coming year had been duly embodied in the Finance Bill which had been debated in general principle on the Motion "that this Bill be now read a second time", and was passing through the usual examination in detail by a Committee of the whole House. Amendments to every line might be moved and discussed.

The Government were determined to get the Bill through its Committee stage before the House adjourned. Hour by hour that hot summer night they wrestled with amendment after amendment. The small hours lengthened to the dawn. The young Liberals, backed by the Irish Nationalists, were taking turns at oration and recuperation. Ever and anon during these alternating spells of rest and argument the division bell would summon the jaded supporters of the Government from their efforts to sleep away dull care in the reading room or the library.

Daylight succeeded dawn and still found Mr. Churchill and his friends in full cry. Between six and seven Mr. Claude Lowther, a young Cumberland Conservative, recalled the attention of the House to a sensational report discussed a few days earlier that a tropical disease known as "beri-beri" had broken out among the Chinese labourers in South Africa. He suggested that Mr. Churchill had taken such a great interest in Chinese labour that he was suffering from this malady. Reminded from the Chair that this had no bearing on the Motion immediately before the House, Mr. Lowther replied:

> I bow entirely to your ruling, Sir, but I made that remark because I have heard that the most marked and character-istic symptom of the disease is a terrific swelling of the head !

The Kitchen Department produced breakfast shortly after this, for which men went out in relays. With the energy of nourished morn the combatants continued the contest of endurance. Lunch found them still smiting hard. The afternoon dragged on. The business ultimately went through and at twenty minutes to four—after having sat over twenty-five hours—the House adjourned.

The honours of the combat were carried off by Mr. Spencer Charrington, the Conservative Member for Mile End. He was one of the partners in the old-established London brewery, said to have been the model for the philanthropic firm in Walter Besant's "All Sorts and Conditions of Men". Though eighty-six years of age, he went through the whole of the sitting and voted for the Government in every division. His example to the younger men was recognised in the presentation of a silver bowl by Mr. Balfour at a meeting of the Party a few days later, much to the delight of the Chief Whip, who naturally welcomed the encouraging effect of this tribute to loyalty and zeal.

Trouble arising out of the Education Act was haunting the Government. In various towns and districts "passive resisters" refused to pay that portion of their rates which represented the amount required for the upkeep of the denominational schools. Money in some cases had been recovered by distraining on household goods. In other cases the resister had gone to gaol. The protest movement included eminent Nonconformist Ministers, manufacturers, professional men, shopkeepers and others usually accounted the most law-abiding classes of the community.

Certain Welsh Authorities were adopting inter alia the plan of applying only as much public money towards the upkeep of some Non-provided Schools as had previously been available for them before they came upon the rates. The Government brought in a Bill entitling them to deduct from any sums payable to the Authorities on account of Parliamentary grants sums thought necessary for the effective maintenance of the schools. This measure was denounced by the Liberal Opposition as "the Welsh Coercion Bill".

One afternoon the Closure was moved on some three pages of amendments. A group of Welshmen led by Mr. Lloyd

George protested vehemently, and when the division was called they declined to go into the Lobby—a gesture in which they were joined by several English Liberals invariably decorous in their parliamentary demeanour, some of whom afterwards held high Office.

The difficulty was solved by the resourceful cool-headedness of Mr. Asquith and the calm dignity of Mr. Lowther. Amid the general excitement the Deputy Speaker suggested that the question should be put again, in which case honourable Members having made their protest might proceed to the Division Lobbies in the usual way. Mr. Lloyd George said he would in that case walk out and take no further part in the business.

Mr. Asquith promptly intervened and recommended that the Deputy Speaker should carry out his suggestion and that Welsh Members should formally register their protest by leaving the House. He added that if they did so he would support them.

The doors were then thrown open and Mr. Asquith, followed by the rest of the Liberal Members led the Welshmen out.

The Bill passed and the House shortly afterwards went off for a needed holiday.

The autumn brought some interesting events. At a Trade Union Congress at Leeds a significant sign of the popular appreciation of the Sovereign's personal influence was provided in the enthusiasm which greeted a reference by Mr. John Ward (afterwards Colonel Ward) of the Navvies' Union, to King Edward as "almost our only statesman".

A startling piece of news from the mists of the ocean which at first sight had in it the possibilities of war aroused intense public excitement. Just after midnight of Friday, the 21st October, 1904, a fleet of some thirty steam trawlers belonging to Hull were peacefully fishing on the Dogger Bank in the North Sea when shot and shell suddenly began ploughing the waters around them. One trawler was sunk; her skipper and third hand killed, and members of the crew wounded. Other trawlers were struck and the "Hospital Mission to Deep Sea Fishermen" damaged.

It was ascertained that five Russian warships had opened fire upon these inoffensive and unarmed toilers of the sea.

The surviving fishermen got back to Hull and reported their experience to the proper Authorities. Lord Lansdowne, the Foreign Minister, immediately hurried to London and saw the King. The crowds in the London streets hooted the Russian Ambassador. As events afterwards disclosed themselves such steps were taken by the Navy as would have given prompt and effectual meaning, if necessary, to the demands made upon the Russian Government for explanations, apologies and compensation.

The incident recalled attention to the Russo-Japanese War, which had been watched with the languid interest naturally devoted to events occurring a long way off. The man in the street gathered from what he read in the papers that the "Japs" were getting the best of it. He had no animosity towards Russia, but in accordance with his indulgent nature he expressed passing satisfaction at the fact that the "bantam" was putting up a good fight.

Now the Russians had chosen to interfere with British subjects who were carrying on their lawful occupation. Various suggestions were made as to the cause of this astounding occurrence—described by Lord Rosebery with general concurrence as "an unspeakable outrage". The broad belief was that the Russian officers were either drunk or had lost their nerve. It was discovered that they had fired at other vessels and other trawlers. It was also stated that one of their own ships had fired upon another Russian vessel and mortally wounded a Chaplain.

The Russian Government expressed profound regret to the British Government. The Tsar also telegraphed his personal regrets to the King and promised the most liberal compensation. It was further announced that an Inquiry would be instituted into the facts by an International Commission.

When public interest swung back to Home affairs the Fiscal question was still predominant. The Liberals, now thoroughly united, were carrying on a concentrated campaign.

Lord Selborne, speaking at the Liberal Union Club—one of
the recognised centres of the Liberal Unionists—said the
policy of the Opposition was merely to disunite the Unionists.
He declared the real Opposition Leader was Mr. F. C. Gould—
thus recording a recognition of one of the most successful
careers in the history of pictorial argument.

Mr. (afterwards Sir) Francis Carruthers Gould was the son
of a Barnstaple architect.   In his early days he was a member
of the London Stock Exchange.   He made no claim to
perfection or even efficiency in the technique of drawing,
but he had an extraordinary faculty for hitting off a situation
as it presented itself to the popular mind, and a remarkable
aptitude for reproducing the features of public men with
their outstanding characteristics strikingly emphasised.   He
studied his subjects from life, spending hour upon hour in
the Inner Lobby and the Press Gallery of the Houses of
Parliament.   Each picture caught the central figure in a
certain familiar mood.   In addition to this, he also took a
keen personal interest in politics.   The cartoons initialled
"F.C.G." which appeared in the "Westminster Gazette"
(then an evening paper) overnight and were produced in
several provincial papers next morning provided a daily
stream of argument more deadly to the Government than
the thunders from the platform.

Chapter 16

SCOTTISH THEOLOGY.   RUSSIAN TRAGEDY
WESTMINSTER TUMULT

SCOTLAND was thrilled with an acute religious problem
arising out of a decision of the House of Lords sitting in
its capacity as the highest Legal Tribunal.   Every educated
Britisher knew of course that in Scotland Presbyterianism
was the State religion.   If he lived or travelled in the North
he might have heard the Church of England, or Episcopalian,

services put into the category of an eccentric form of devotion by the couplet:

> Pisky Pisky, Amen!
> Doon on your knees and up agin.

Outside Scotland it was necessary to explain in some detail the developments which at this time of day divided Presbyterians into three main bodies. The Established Church—colloquially known as the "Auld Kirk"—adhered to State connection and State control. The Free Church, under certain conditions, were willing to recognise a State connection but repudiated Civil control. The United Presbyterian Church declared for absolute freedom from either State connection or State control. Another body, known as the "Original Secession Church", consisted of highly esteemed and deeply religious people who were a free and independent body also but did not appear in the controversy which had been sprung upon a wondering British public.

The immediate trouble arose out of a decision to unite the Free and the United Presbyterian Churches under the designation of the "United Free Church". A small minority of the Free Church who became known as the "Wee Frees" refused to assent to the union and brought actions with the object of restraining the transference of the funds to the new body. They claimed that the fusion was an abandonment of the Free Church doctrine on the political side, and also contended in arguments that went beyond the Southern comprehension that there was a fundamental spiritual difference between the Free Church and the United Presbyterians upon the doctrine of "Predestination".

The Scottish Court in Edinburgh decided against the protesting parties, but the House of Lords by a majority found in their favour—following broadly the rule of law that a Church might change its doctrines but not the application of the property left to it in Trust; and if the Trust did not provide for the event of a schism the right to control the property claimed by those who adhered to the original opinions of the body held good.

The whole of the funds, buildings and general possessions of the Free Church thus became the property of the "Wee

Frees". They numbered about thirty Ministers, most of whom were in charge of congregations in the Highlands and Islands. They were obviously too small a body to cope with the responsibilities of so extensive a trust.

The Archbishop of Canterbury, as the head of a friendly Church, offered his services as mediator in a voluntary settlement. Other public men of various denominations suggested a friendly arrangement. Ultimately it was decided that the legal position should be respected and the property divided according to the ability of the recipients to administer it. Thus the "Wee Frees" retained their independence, with a considerable proportion of the buildings and possessions.

An event of historic importance heralded the close of the Russo-Japanese war. The Chinese strategic sea front of Port Arthur was captured by the Japanese in their war with China in 1894, but, largely through Russian diplomacy, the victors were prevented from retaining their prize, and subsequent arrangements gave Port Arthur to Russia.

A stronghold with such memories naturally became the central object of hostilities. The Japanese forces assailed it by land and sea and the dramatic surrender by a Russian General on the 1st January was the turning point in the war. The news was received with broad satisfaction in this country and it had a tragic sequel in Russia. The autocratic system had no Parliament to be agitated, and no representative Government to be turned out; no safety valve was provided for public feeling. The Tsar surrounded by—and it was gener-ally assumed dominated by—the Grand Dukes nominally controlled every soldier, every police officer and every subject in his dominions, in his capacity as an absolute Monarch.

Prince Troubetskoi, Marshal of the Moscow nobility, warned his Royal Master that Russia was on the eve of "not a simple disturbance but a revolution". Strikes of workmen were organised not merely for an increase of wages or for better working conditions but for the institution of reforms leading up to representative government. A communication was sent to the Tsar to the effect that the strikers intended to march in a body to the Winter Palace for a conference with the Monarch personally, as they had no faith in the bureaucracy or in his Ministers. A petition was at the same time sent for presentation to the Tsar urging that he should throw down the wall that separated him from the people and order at once a Convocation of representatives of all classes including the working classes.

On a day which came to be known in history as "Red Sunday" adults and children singing hymns paraded the streets carrying the religious emblems of the Russian Church. The Cossacks—rough-riding cavalry recruited from the Eastern part of the Russian Empire—first rode at the procession, striking the people with heavy whips. As this did not disperse the crowd, the troops attacked with swords and rifle shots. Thousands were wounded and hundreds killed. Some of the men in the procession rushed to the workers' quarters for knives and sharp tools. The conflict was renewed sporadically day by day and soldiers were killed by the crowd. The strike spread to Barristers and Solicitors who, as a protest against the action of the Authorities, declined to plead in the Courts. Maxim Gorki, a renowned writer, with other literary and learned men, also protested, and they were arrested for expressing sympathy for the new movement. In this country it was difficult to follow the trend of events or to appreciate the exact condition of public and social life in Russia. Some people asserted that the Tsar personally yearned after a sound and safe way of introducing constitutional government on the lines of Western civilisation, but was induced to believe that the autocratic power inherited by him was a sacred trust which he had no right to surrender.

Another incident on the Continent of some special interest at about this time was an extensive strike of German miners on the Ruhr, and, as an indication of the growth of international relations between Trade Unions, the Executive of the British Miners' Federation decided to grant the German miners two thousand pounds a week during the dispute.

When the two Houses assembled men were prophesying freely that this would be the last session of the Balfour Parliament. Under the Constitution there must be a General Election not later than seven years after the last General Election, but all Parties were clamouring for an early dissolution. Throughout the country the election had, in argument, already commenced. The Tariff Reform League, the Free Trade Union and various other Organisations were increasingly active.

Mr. Chamberlain, fighting valiantly and attracting the personal admiration of all his fellow-countrymen, was conducting a tireless campaign. Mr. Asquith, the most effective speaker on the other side, was also addressing crowded meetings.

Wherever men walked or talked together it was safe to assume that at some period of every conversation they were discussing Free Trade and Tariff Reform. The House of Commons, as Mr. Thomas Gibson Bowles, a Conservative Free Trader, one night observed, was the "only place on God's earth" where the subject was not debated.

Various attempts to raise the subject here were skilfully evaded. Mr. Balfour was still trying to steady the boat by preventing his crew from quarrelling with each other. He took up the simple position that nothing could be done until after the General Election and therefore why discuss in the present House a subject which had no relation to this Parliament?

For a while Ireland diverted attention. Mr. George Wyndham, who had been Chief Secretary since 1900,—one of the most attractive men in public life—pleasant, eloquent and chivalrous—handed in his resignation. He had piloted through Parliament a scheme of immense importance to Ireland under which, by Government aid, landlords were bought out and Irish tenants became the owners of their farms. Although his colleagues had supported him, the older Tories declared that his policy would result in the disappearance of the Irish gentry. The Irish Unionists now accused him of flirting with Home Rule because of feelers in the direction of devolution which had been thrown out from certain quarters.

That sound Territorial Conservative, Mr. Walter Long, was moved from the Presidency of the Local Government Board to succeed Mr. Wyndham in the Irish Secretaryship.

While the incident helped to keep the Fiscal question at arm's length for a little while, Mr. Balfour could ill afford to lose so brilliant a colleague as Mr. Wyndham in these difficult times. The seeds of trouble in the House of Commons were growing and blossoming rapidly.

Every opportunity provided by the Rules however failed to draw the Prime Minister. Mr. Churchill, who happened to be speaking one evening when Mr. Balfour rose from his place and passed along the front Bench towards the door behind the Speaker's Chair, remarked:

> The right honourable Gentleman need not go out. I am not going to talk about Free Trade.

The Conservatives resented "Winston's cheek". Some of the Liberals laughed. The rest of the Liberals had ceased to find any humour in the situation.

On another occasion after one of the fiscal Debates when Mr. Balfour stayed away Mr. Churchill said:

> To keep in Office for a few more weeks and months there is no principle which the Government are not prepared to abandon; no friend or colleague that they are not prepared to betray and no quantity of dirt and filth that they are not prepared to eat.

The protest was voiced with equal fervour, though in less picturesque terms, by staid and solemn gentlemen to whom the serious business of the House of Commons was almost a religion. Mr. John Ellis, a strict Quaker, whose appearance, speech and actions were one continuous, consistent assertion that "Life is real, life is earnest" declared: "Mr. Speaker, this thing cannot go on".

On the 22nd of May Mr. Balfour was asked if Fiscal Reform would be considered at the Colonial Conference which in the ordinary course would be held in 1906. If so, would the Government feel free to commit the country to the elementary stages of discussing Preference with the

Colonies, or was Mr. Balfour pledged to a declaration made by him in a speech at Edinburgh that there should be two elections—first to obtain a general mandate to ask the Colonies to come into a Fiscal Conference, then another as to the question of approving or disapproving the results of the Conference?

Mr. Balfour repeated his assertion that the Government did not mean to deal with the Fiscal question in the present Parliament. As to the Colonial Conference, he had not in his mind when he made his Edinburgh speech that the Colonial Conference would meet in the course of the present Parliament. "Perhaps it will not", he added cryptically.

Sir Henry Campbell-Bannerman took advantage of the Rule under which he might move the adjournment of the House, with the assent of not less than forty Members, in order to call attention to a matter of urgent and definite public importance; the matter in this case being, as he ultimately phrased it, "the statement made by the Prime Minister that the question of Colonial Preference may be submitted to the Colonial Conference in 1906 before the country has had an opportunity of expressing its opinion thereon".

According to the Rules, the Debate on the Motion came on at nine o'clock at the evening sitting, which automatically concluded at midnight. Sir Henry Campbell-Bannerman spoke for about twenty-five minutes. He quoted from the Edinburgh speech of Mr. Balfour in support of his contention that Mr. Balfour had definitely stated that if his Party came into power "after the next General Election" they would ask the Colonies to join a Conference whose discussions should be free but whose conclusions would be subject to the approval of "the various electorates". Sir Henry asked if Mr. Balfour had now departed from that? The Leader of the Opposition concluded by saying: "What we have to consider is the effectual means for preserving the dignity and character of pledges given by the Prime Minister, and the honourable traditions of our public life".

When Sir Henry Campbell-Bannerman sat down the Colonial Secretary (Mr. Alfred Lyttelton) advanced to the Table.

"Balfour! Balfour!!", the Opposition cried in unison. "Let him defend his own honour", shouted one. "An insult to the House", yelled another. "He wants to speak when he cannot be replied to," suggested somebody with a voice that rang out above the din. The Speaker was absent, and it was the task of Mr. Lowther, the Deputy Speaker, to quell the storm. His soothing powers availed not. "The question of the Colonial Conference surely comes within the province of the Colonial Secretary", he suggested.

"No—the Prime Minister's personal honour", protested the Opposition.

Mr. John Ellis, the man of peace and stern justice, rising to a point of order, demanded a precedent of a Prime Minister's personal honour being challenged when he had not at once risen to reply.

The Deputy Speaker held that this was not a point of order, and Mr. Lyttelton again came up to the Table. The united call for "Balfour! Balfour!!" drowned every syllable he attempted to utter.

Mr. Winston Churchill endeavoured to offer a few words of advice, but protesting supporters of the Government promptly drowned his voice.

Mr. Churchill left his place below the gangway, and, marching up the floor to the music of angry voices, shouted his message at the ear of the Deputy Speaker. He was understood to be asking for some sort of undertaking that the Prime Minister would speak next.

Mr. Lloyd George also had a point to make while both sides were resting their lungs. The Leader of the Opposition, he said, had put a question to the Prime Minister and asked for an explanation. Was not the House entitled to that explanation from the Prime Minister?

The Deputy Speaker said he had not the least doubt in the world that the Prime Minister would give an explanation, but he pointed out that other honourable Members might desire to ask questions and if the Prime Minister spoke at once he would be debarred from making any further answer.

The Deputy Speaker added that he would himself give an assurance that other honourable Members should have an opportunity of replying to the Prime Minister.

Mr. Lloyd George urged that the Prime Minister could speak now and when other questions were asked he could answer them by leave of the House.

After this temporary lull, Mr. Lyttelton came up again and stood grimly asserting his position at the Box. Words were uttered by him but nobody heard them. From the Irish Benches, where Members had been looking on with the critical eye of experts at this Saxon contest, Mr. Michael Flavin offered a solution.

"I have had the pleasure of being removed by the Police", he shouted. "Is it not now the turn of some of the gentlemen of England to be removed?"

The Deputy Speaker reminded honourable Members on the Opposition side that they were employing a dangerous weapon. "If used on one side to-night", he said, "it may be used by the other side another night."

"It has been used already", retorted several Members, recalling the experiences of Mr. Churchill and Major Seely.

Sir Henry Campbell-Bannerman's rising gave his own followers a brief period for recuperation and the Conservatives an opportunity for reprisals.

"Vide! Vide!!", shouted honourable Members on the Government side. During a pause Sir Henry said the Leader of the House must see that it would be impossible for this Debate to proceed unless he, in the first place, made a statement.

"Keep your own side in order!", sharply ejaculated Mr. Austen Chamberlain from the Treasury bench.

The Irish Members reiterated Mr. Flavin's remedy "Send for the Police!"

The Deputy Speaker obtained a hearing for Sir Henry Campbell-Bannerman, who appealed to the Prime Minister on the ground that the question for the House was one to which no one could reply except himself.

Mr. Balfour placidly remarked that he could not understand all this trouble and turbulence. He would endeavour to rise at a time which would give honourable Gentlemen opposite the right to reply to any observations he might make.

Mr. Lyttelton, the international wicket-keeper, once more stood up to the bowling and was heard to say he intended to stand there. Others stood also and points of order chased each other in rapid confusion. Beyond the tumult resounded a consistent Irish demand for the Police. Nationalist eyes hungered after the sight of the Saxon constabulary at work upon the Saxon gentry. Lest this should be considered an insufficient compliment to the "quality" one Nationalist Member proposed as an amendment "Send for the Horse Guards"!

Stolidly standing up to the wicket, Mr. Lyttelton held his ground for just a minute or two under the hour. At length the Deputy Speaker decided it was perfectly obvious the scene could go on no longer.

By virtue of the power invested in him under the Rules he adjourned the House on the ground that a state of grave disorder had arisen, and, as the official record states, it was "adjourned accordingly at half after ten of the clock".

Chapter 17

"MR. SPEAKER"
SENSATIONS IN POLITICS AND PASTIME

MR. WILLIAM COURT GULLY, who had been Speaker of the House for ten years, took his place in the historic Chair for the last time on the 7th June, 1905. His farewell was the dignified speech of a man conscious that he held an Office of the highest responsibility. Tributes to his services came from all parts of the House, including a short speech from Mr. Richard Bell, the Chairman of the Labour Representation Committee. This was the first ceremonial occasion on which Labour had claimed to speak as a separate and distinct entity.

There was no question as to Mr. Gully's successor. Mr. James William Lowther, the Deputy Speaker and Chairman of Committees, allied to his thorough experience, possessed a happy gift of sweet reasonableness and strength in reserve. He was duly proposed, seconded, and, with the approval of the House, "Led to the Chair", a legend dating from the days when the Speaker, as the head spokesman of the Assembly, was responsible to the Crown for its deeds or misdeeds. In troublous times when Parliament sometimes evoked the displeasure of the Sovereign, suitable men very reluctantly accepted the task and it is said the person called upon by his fellow-Members was literally dragged to the Chair. Centuries alter circumstances but stabilise customs at Westminster. Thus, the proposer of the Speaker takes him by the right arm, the seconder takes him by the left arm, and he is technically forced into the Chair as an assertion of the traditional right of Parliament to demand the performance of any necessary duty by any one of its Members.

The ancient and impressive ceremony happened to fall at Whitsuntide. Before the House separated for a short holiday the eternal topic was once more ventilated. Lord Hugh Cecil found an opportunity of resenting Mr. Chamberlain's influence on the Conservative Party and of repudiating the suggestion frequently made that Unionist Free Traders should follow Mr. Churchill to the other side. In the course of a stinging speech Lord Hugh recalled the year (1885) when Mr. Chamberlain was a Member of the Radical Party. "At that date," said Lord Hugh, "I undertook my first active political work by acting as the Editor of a political poster." This poster, he went on to explain, was issued as a vehement protest against the falsehood— or, as Lord Iddesleigh (formerly Sir Stafford Northcote), a distinguished Leader of the Conservative Party, described it —the "downright thumping lie"—that the Conservative Party proposed to tax the food of the people. Lord Hugh continued:

> My right honourable friend [Mr. Joseph Chamberlain] has succeeded in making that poster out of date to some extent but although we can no longer say it is a falsehood we still earnestly wish we could, and I hope Unionist Free Traders

will continue their Membership of the Unionist Party until they bring that poster back into fashion again. At any rate, we will not consent to leave the Party at the bidding of one who however distinguished a Member of it now is after all in his origin only an alien immigrant.

Just at this period there was a strong agitation for more stringent regulations as to the admission of alien immigrants into this country.

*　　　*　　　*　　　*　　　*

In the Whitsun recess Lord Roberts, the great General and popular soldier of his day, appealed to the country to make rifle-shooting "a national pursuit". He recalled the days when archery was a national accomplishment, and urged that if rifle-shooting had been as skilfully taken up most of the unfortunate incidents of the South African War would never have occurred. Lord Roberts casually mentioned conscription, and added that, failing this, the security of the State depended in the last resort not only on the willingness—which might be assumed—but on the ability of the nation to take up arms in self-defence.

A movement for encouraging rifle-shooting was commenced and took a modest place with golf and other hobbies which had been added to cricket and football.

A domestic topic of interest was provided by the Whitsuntide Congress of the Co-operative Societies. It was pointed out that they numbered two million, two hundred thousand members, having a Loan and Share Capital of thirty-six million, five hundred thousand pounds and an annual trade of ninety-two million pounds. A Resolution was passed to the effect that so important an Organisation should exercise some direct influence on the legislation and administration of the country, but a proposal to join forces with the Labour Representation Committee was defeated by eight hundred and one votes to one hundred and thirty-five after a heated discussion in the course of which one Member declared that such a step involved handing over the Co-operative movement bag and baggage to a body financed by Trade Unions and controlled by Socialists.

G

When the House met again the lengthening summer evenings did not bring greater peace for Sir Alexander Acland Hood. The adjournment for an hour-and-a-half for dinner was playing havoc with Party discipline. London is a glorious place at this time of year and nine o'clock is an early hour for a young man to desert cheerful society. The junior Members of the Party went out to dinner early and came back very late.

Sir Alexander Acland Hood fought like a sportsman. He stood at the Bar of the House and by a twirl of his long red moustache or a nod of his head gave one of his trusted men the signal to continue the Debate. His best "stonewallers" were Sir Frederick Banbury (afterwards Lord Banbury) and Mr. James Fitzalan Hope. Others might also be relied on for a useful speech while the wanderers were sauntering down to the House.

In spite of these strenuous tactics the Chief Whip could only command small majorities. The burden fell most heavily on the silent, patient men of the Party. One instance was quoted of a loyal Member who rushed to Westminster from the country immediately after his wedding in order to vote for the Government the same evening.

At times these plodding toilers lost their patience. In the early hours of one morning, when Mr. Winston Churchill was at somewhere about his thirteenth—or thirtieth—speech a middle-aged, country Conservative Member accustomed from his youth up to roost and rise with the lark, suddenly ran down the gangway and, pausing opposite Mr. Churchill on his way out, shouted "I cannot stand this any longer".

Mr. Balfour made a special appeal to his followers. Sir Alexander Acland Hood continuously emphasised the supreme importance of regular attendance. He referred to it almost daily in the message sent out according to custom from the Whip's Office overnight informing each Member of the Party as to the business of the day. On every Conservative breakfast table lay the Injunction underlined three times, thus constituting what is known as a "three-line Whip"; but the young bloods wanted a vigorous lead. The older men were tired and did not intend to seek re-election.

The climax came on the night of the 20th of July. Mr. John Redmond moved an amendment to reduce the vote of the Irish Land Commission. The Debate dragged on slowly. It got an enlivening few minutes from Mr. T. P. O'Connor and came to a full stop at about quarter-to-twelve.

As the Members filed out of the lobbies it was seen that the Tellers at the doorway of the Lobby for the supporters of the Government had finished their counting first. The others completed their task a little later. Obviously it was a narrow division. Instead of strolling out after they had voted Members crowded the Benches and stood at the Bar in animated conversation.

A triumphant roar went up from the Opposition when the Clerk handed the paper to Sir Thomas Esmonde, the Irish Teller.

The Government were beaten by two hundred to one hundred and ninety-six. Mr. Balfour took time to consider the position, and ultimately decided that he would still remain in Office.

Meanwhile popular public attention centred on cricket. The Surrey County had discovered a young man whose name was ultimately known throughout the world. John Berry Hobbs appeared in the Surrey Team this year with scores in his first two matches of eighteen and eighty-eight against the Gentlemen of England, and twenty-eight and one hundred and fifty-five against Essex. Cricketers realised that a man of first-class batting capacity had entered the field. The general public heard this with interest, though they were thinking mainly of the visit of the Australians. The Team against the visitors won two matches, and the other three tests were drawn. F. S. Jackson was Captain; A. C. MacLaren, Hayward, and Rhodes were in the Team. C. B. Fry made 144 against the Australian Team at the Oval. The three draws incited the controversy carried on for so many years as to whether three days was long enough to finish a Test Match.

Before Parliament was prorogued Lord Stanley (after-wards the Earl of Derby) explained the conditions under which the State became the owner of the telephones, to which people in Great Britain were slowly growing accustomed. Many business and professional men in London up to the end of the old century regarded it as a nuisance to answer the telephone and in some London establishments the impression still remains that the person at the other end of the telephone is a hostile intruder who should be warded off if possible by the office boy. The telephone, however, was appreciated much more in the industrial districts and became a necessary part of every enterprising business concern. The early system was a private undertaking. Speaking on behalf of the Government, the Postmaster-General said he had become convinced that the telephones must in the future be in the hands of the State for purposes of inter-communication throughout the Kingdom.

During the autumn another stage was reached in the friendship between Great Britain and Japan by the Treaty for "the consolidation and maintenance of peace in the regions of Eastern Asia and India". In the Treaty it was agreed that if by reason of unprovoked attack either country should be involved in war in defence of its territorial rights the other country would go to the assistance of its ally. Peace had been concluded between Russia and Japan, and Russian diplomatists began to speak of the prospect of an agreement with Great Britain.

At about the same time an agreement was arrived at between France and Germany as to a conference on affairs between the two countries in Morocco. This was followed by a sensational statement in the Paris "*Matin*" that the French Government had been verbally informed that if France were attacked by Germany, Great Britain was ready to back up France to the very end.

Details as to the possible action to be taken were given which made the statement sound unlikely, but feeling was generally gaining ground that Great Britain would not remain an onlooker if and when a struggle arose out of an unprovoked attack on France. The incident was sufficient to arouse bitter attacks on this country by the German

Press. British statesmen on both sides of politics repudiated the suggestion that because there had been an approximation between Britain and two great and friendly Powers there must necessarily be an estrangement between ourselves and any other Power or Powers.

In November a new German Navy Bill was accepted by the German Federal Council providing for an increase in construction. In the presentation of the Bill it was urged that the experience of the Russo-Japanese War and the action of other nations compelled Germany still further to increase the tonnage of her vessels so that German warships and torpedo boats might not fall behind the warships and torpedo boats of other countries in respect of fighting power.

Affairs at home were saddened by the spectre of unemployment. The Prime Minister received a deputation of wives and relatives of men out of work, who presented a petition stating that many thousands of women and children in the East End of London were suffering misery and degradation through their menfolk being unable to obtain employment. A touching appeal for money to alleviate the suffering of the poor and starving during the winter was made by the Queen, who headed the list with two thousand pounds.

Chapter 18

ACTORS AND STATESMEN

THE death of Sir Henry Irving in the Autumn of 1905 concluded a distinguished career; and called attention to the changes in the drama as well as among its patrons.

The new generation of playwrights was coming into its own. J. M. Barrie's charming humour and pathos in "Quality Street", were followed by such clever studies as "The Admirable Crichton" and "Little Mary". Perhaps his most important work in that it influenced the passing of old customs was "Peter Pan" (The Boy who would not grow up), played with such skill by gifted actors and actresses

—including Gerald (afterwards Sir Gerald) Du Maurier.
Hitherto the old-fashioned pantomime was as regular an
occurrence as Christmas itself. The harlequinade, however,
was almost a tradition. The Harlequin and Columbine;
the Pantaloon; the Clown; and the Comic Policemen were,
alas, forgotten or left out by Producers of the gorgeous
transformation scene that closed the story of Cinderella—
or whatever happened to be the fairy tale of that particular
year. Adults, so consistently "just took the children"
that the theatre managers with a shrewd idea of the real
position were actually catering for grown-ups. As a consequence the pantomime was losing its character as a children's
show. "Peter Pan", a real children's play which adults
also could enjoy, was hailed with delight. It was destined
to become a greater Christmas feature than the pantomime,
and it set the fashion of light plays in substitution for the
once orthodox Christmas fare.

Playgoers were beginning to appreciate the humour of
George Bernard Shaw. Born in Dublin in 1856 "G.B.S."
came to London twenty years later and soon began to write
and talk Fabian Socialism. As a dramatic Critic and as a
public speaker he was a little too subtle for that time of
day. His plays, with their interwoven admixture of wit,
irony, and caustic comment on the ways of Society were for
a long time produced at private subscription performances
or read by unconventional young people. They were now
attracting big houses at the London theatres.

The sons and daughters of the old-fashioned well-to-do
families, forming what are known as the "comfortable
middle classes", who represent such a big proportion of
the remunerative support of all undertakings had been
educated on modern lines. The Classics and business
were not assumed to be necessarily dissociated. The
descendants of the stern, inflexible Victorian parents—to
whose sturdy, genuine character the British race owes so
much—were seeking to alternate work with play. The
increasingly strenuous competitive element in the former

was rendering the latter more necessary. The newer recreations took various forms. There were more tennis clubs, and a greater number of social gatherings of all kinds. The movement extended with beneficial results to young men and women employed in shops and sedentary occupations. The Heads of big business establishments realised the desirability of encouraging athletics among their staffs.

Towards the theatre an entirely different tone had been created before Henry Irving passed away. This eminent man's original name was John Henry Brodribb. He was born at Keinton near Glastonbury in 1838; educated in London; and for some few years was in the counting-house of a London firm of East India merchants. During his spare time he studied elocution, and in 1856 he joined one of the old-fashioned Stock companies at the Theatre Royal, Sunderland. Playing all sorts of parts, comedy, tragedy, and pantomime, he worked hard at his profession, and in 1871 first became famous as a tragedian. He had secured a place at the Lyceum Theatre, London, and there played "The Bells", his weirdly fascinating study of a mind obsessed with remorse. Other parts followed which gripped public interest, and for thirty years Irving made the Lyceum Theatre the home of the grand emotional style of acting.

He raised the prestige of the stage to a higher standard than it had ever before reached. He saw the old gulf between theatrical Bohemianism and normal educated society bridged. Many men and women of culture and talent were attracted to the stage by this great actor who was a personal friend of Statesmen like Lord Beaconsfield and Mr. Gladstone.

Irving's greatest triumphs were shared by that gifted lady Ellen Terry (afterwards Dame Ellen Terry).

When as already mentioned the honour of a knighthood was conferred upon Mr. Irving in 1895, a precedent was established. The first actor knight also held the degrees of D.Litt. Dublin, Litt.D. Cambridge, and LL.D. Glasgow.

His last and in some respects his biggest effort was "Becket", which he produced in London and took on tour in the principal

Provincial cities, where adoring crowds had always flocked to see him. On the night of 13th October he appeared at the Bradford Theatre, and shortly after playing the historic scene in which the martyred Prelate is murdered at the altar he was seized with a fatal illness, and thus died amid the full glory of success in the profession he loved and adorned.

Irving's old friend J. L. Toole who for many years held in comedy almost the corresponding position to that which Irving occupied in serious drama died in 1906.

When the public mind reverted to politics the state of trade intensified discussion on the Fiscal question. Tariff Reformers asserted again that "Tariff Reform means work for all". The Free Traders still retorted "Your food will cost you more". Differences between Ministers were illustrated by speeches in divergent tones from different Members of the Cabinet. Mr. Winston Churchill declared:

> Cabinet Ministers abuse, contradict and disavow each other. Members of the Government and of the Conservative Party fight over the Prime Minister as dogs worry a bone.

Mr. Joseph Chamberlain while declaring the current talk about divisions in the Unionist Party to be "grotesque exaggeration", insisted that the majority in the Party could not sacrifice their convictions to the prejudices of the minority. He went on to say:

> No army was ever led successfully to battle on the principle that the lamest man should govern the march of the army.

Thus matters stood on Monday the 4th December 1905 when Mr. Balfour in the calm atmosphere of the recess asked to be relieved of his responsibilities as Prime Minister; and the King sent for Sir Henry Campbell-Bannerman.

Innumerable rumours and counter-rumours kept political circles busily engaged with Cabinet-making gossip. Instances were recalled from history in which the Party Leader sent for by the Sovereign on the resignation of a Government had been unable to obtain the services of the men whom he desired as his colleagues. Some people doubted whether Sir Henry Campbell-Bannerman would be able to blend the "Liberal Imperialists" with the Radical Members of his Party into one harmonious Administration. The Cabinet—necessarily comprising the effective and responsible heads of the great Departments of State—must be chosen from men of proved capacity.

It was indeed suggested in some quarters that Mr. Balfour's resignation was a clever piece of strategy in that it presented Sir Henry Campbell-Bannerman with the difficulty of trying to form a Government, and possibly failing, before the now inevitable General Election. Mr. Balfour, with his experience, was, however, very unlikely to forget that the occasion invariably produces the man.

The Government was formed practically without delay. Of the "Imperialists", Sir Edward Grey had made a special study of Foreign affairs, and addressed himself to topics associated therewith. It was possibly natural that, in London, he should have been regarded as a diplomat only with little interest in domestic affairs, but his own friends and neighbours knew him as a man with strong progressive views on social problems. He accepted the post of Minister for Foreign Affairs.

It was noted with interest that Sir Henry Campbell-Bannerman obtained the collaboration of Mr. Asquith as Chancellor of the Exchequer. Mr. Asquith had been Mr. Chamberlain's most formidable antagonist in the country. He had Mr. McKenna, one of the swift forwards from below the gangway, as his Secretary to the Treasury. Mr. Lloyd George became President of the Board of Trade, and Mr. Winston Churchill Under-Secretary to the Colonies. Thus the Free Trade front line of defence against Tariff Reform and Preference was skilfully drawn.

The surprise of the Cabinet was Mr. Haldane (afterwards Lord Haldane), an eminent Chancery lawyer, who was appointed Secretary of State for War. Mr. Haldane had been foremost in the Imperialist activities of the "Liberal League". He was generally credited with having led a determined movement organised to supersede Sir Henry Campbell-Bannerman and induce Lord Rosebery to resume the leadership. Because of his Imperialism Lord Haldane was assumed to be a "Whig". It would have been more correct to have described him as a "Collectivist" with Imperialistic tendencies. Members of the Fabian Society regarded him as a non-official sympathiser and, as subsequent events proved, he had little or nothing in common with the old-fashioned Liberals on social matters.

Lord Rosebery, the polished orator whose literary pursuits were interwoven with his political activities, clearly intimated that he preferred to remain an interested onlooker and could not serve under any banner on which Home Rule for Ireland was inscribed. Politics aside, many people in all Parties wanted to hear his charming speeches for their own sake, and preferred him as a brilliant free lance.

Mr. John Burns took Office and rank as President of the Local Government Board. Thus there was a direct connecting line between the Cabinet Council and the experiences of wage-earning labour. No man was more thoroughly a representative of labour, though there was only one " John Burns". His personality dominated every circle he entered. In the course of a Debate one evening he mentioned that he had worked in parts of Africa and had organised cricket matches in which the natives played. Mr. Lyttelton, speaking later, remarked "I am sure my honourable Friend was the Captain of the Eleven".

Mr. Burns had many interests outside politics. He knew XXth century London in all aspects of its life better than Charles Dickens knew mid-Victorian London. He possessed an excellent library, founded in his youth out of hard-earned savings. He could recall the day when it was a choice between a book and a new pair of boots—and the book won. A man of strong individuality had thus been secured as the first person chosen from the wage-earners to take Cabinet rank.

Chapter 19
THE NEW GOVERNMENT

AT a huge meeting in the Albert Hall Sir Henry Campbell-Bannerman acknowledged the tributes of friends and opponents alike to his success in the task of forming his Government.

At this gathering there was an early indication of one of the troubles which awaited the Liberal Party. During the Prime Minister's speech a well-dressed young woman in one of the galleries unfurled a banner and demanded a pledge that the Liberal Government would give "Votes for Women". Her banner was confiscated and she was ejected. A girl scarce out of her teens attempted another demonstration in one of the boxes and was led out. As usual, there was more disturbance by people in the audience who protested against the interruptions than by the interrupters. This died down in a few minutes and the meeting continued in blissful innocence of the hurricane these storm petrels portended.

By the statutory limit, then seven—now five—years the House of Commons elected in 1900 had another two years of legalised existence, but, as was anticipated, Sir Henry Campbell-Bannerman advised the King to exercise his constitutional authority and dissolve Parliament at once. Thus writs were sent throughout the country calling upon the constituencies to elect new Members.

In the election campaign Chinese labour in South Africa again became an exciting topic. The Education Act and the Licensing Act stimulated the enthusiasm of Non-Conformists and Temperance people, who threw themselves energetically into the campaign against the Conservative Party. The Trade Unions directed active efforts to the return of Candidates who were in favour of Labour Legislation with special regard to the alteration of the law as laid down by the Taff Vale decision. A very large number of people with no strong political partisanship discerned a lack of foresight and an absence of sound administration in the conduct of the South African War. The general tendency of the floating mass of unattached opinion was to vote against the supporters of the late Government.

Over and above all these considerations the speeches, arguments and literature in the constituencies were overwhelmingly devoted to the conflict between Free Trade and Tariff Reform. Mr. Chamberlain fought strenuously but the Conservative Party were handicapped by the feeling openly expressed that they were going to lose. With West country bluntness they were warned by Lord Halsbury and Sir Alexander Acland Hood that no fight was ever won by the combatant that went in "tail down," but they failed to get their "tails up".

The advocates of Tariff Reform urged that the unrestricted importation of goods from foreign countries competed unfairly with British labour in the towns and that agriculture would become a more prosperous industry for the farmers and the labourers under Mr. Chamberlain's proposals for regulating the importation of agricultural produce. Free Trade speakers contended that exports upon which British labour was employed went abroad to pay for the imports and that taxes would mean high prices for consumers and less interchange of trade. The economic discussions on either side were conducted with zeal and skill, but the most potent argument came from a more homely source.

In every little community there was still sitting at the fireside or eking out a pathetic old age in the workhouse at least one man or woman who as a child lived through the later days of the Corn Tax. These old folk probably knew little about the complications of XIXth century politics. They remembered acutely that they were hungry in the days when there was a tax on corn. Their tales of old times overshadowed all the efforts of the platform and the press. Mr. Chamberlain had frankly declared that if you had Imperial Preference you must have a tax on corn. That was sufficient for the families and the neighbours of these survivors of what were popularly called "the hungry 'forties".

The day of each election under the procedure at that time was fixed locally. The contests were on different days for different constituencies. East Manchester was among the early declarations. Mr. Balfour had represented this constituency for many years. At the 1900 Election his majority was well over two thousand. When the news came that Mr. Horridge, K.C., (afterwards Sir Thomas Horridge, a Judge of the King's Bench) had defeated him by just under two thousand the Clubs went wild with excitement.

Old electioneers predicted that the defeat of the ex-Prime Minister was the keynote of the Election. Their forecast was amply justified. Members of his Government fell one after another and prominent Conservative back-Benchers were beaten North, East, South and West. Liberal Candidates did not "get in". They "tumbled in".

The result of the polls showed that Liberals had three hundred and seventy-seven Members with twenty-four "Liberal Labour" men who were included in the Liberal Whip's lists as adherents of the Party. The Conservatives had one hundred and thirty-two and the Liberal Unionists twenty-five; the Nationalists eighty-three. There were twenty-nine Members elected under the auspices of the Labour Representation Committee. In effect, therefore, the position was:—Government supporters four hundred and one: Opposition one hundred and fifty-seven with eighty-three Irish Nationalists and twenty-nine Labour Members who were declared opponents of the Conservative policy. Reviewing these figures, Mr. Joseph Chamberlain, on the day of the first meeting of Parliament, frankly declared

"There is no possible combination we can form by which we can turn the Government out of Office".

It was a physical impossibility for six hundred and seventy men—the number of Members of the House of Commons in that day—to find seats within the Chamber. On ordinary days in the past, when many Members were absent and others wandering about the precincts, the accommodation sufficed. When the new Parliament assembled brimful of enthusiasm the numerous followers of the Liberal Ministry crowded the seats behind the Treasury Bench and packed themselves as closely as possible into the Benches below the gangway. Some of them found places in the balconies on either side of the House which are available for "listening" Members. Still the Government side was a congested area.

From the point of view of comfort it was a happy arrangement for the Liberals when Members of the newly-established Labour Party sat in front of the Irish Nationalists upon the Opposition Benches below the gangway. There was a further significance in the choice of places. At the Election in several constituencies returning two Members one Liberal Candidate and one Labour Candidate had been put forward against two Conservative Candidates. In many instances local Liberals had kept an open field for the Labour Candidate and in such cases had supported him. It was indeed understood that Sir Henry Campbell-Bannerman would have liked Mr. Shackleton to join his Cabinet.

The new political force, however, now, by their choice of seats, emphasised that they were a separate and distinct Party. They appointed Whips of their own and chose a Leader on the lines of the Irish Party by electing Mr. Keir Hardie as their Chairman for the Session.

Mr. Keir Hardie was a Socialist open and avowed. In this respect he differed from many Members of the new Party. Representatives of influential and old-established Trade Unions, like Mr. John Hodge of the Steel Workers, asserted that they were in the Labour Party as Trade Unionists, not Socialists. The miners still refused to go into the new Labour group. Their representatives—men of the old guard who exercised a strong moral influence over their supporters —were Liberals and sat on the Liberal side of the House.

The most comfortable place in the House was the front Opposition Bench. So many Ministers had suffered bad fortune at the polls that it was difficult to give this part of the House the appearance of a tenanted habitation. When ex-Ministers and Whips had taken their seats there according to parliamentary custom, a long stretch of green leather remained visible. It was remembered that a Member of Parliament who is also a Privy Councillor is by courtesy entitled to a seat on this Bench "if there be room".

In the far off days subjects of the King summoned to his Privy Council were his advisers upon matters of State, but although the Cabinet first was, and nominally remains, a Committee of the Privy Council it is a Committee with full powers. Members of the Privy Council are entitled to the prefix of "Right Honourable" and they wear a special uniform on State occasions. They are summoned for formal business, and membership of the Privy Council is a high honour. The privilege of a seat on the front Opposition Bench is the one remaining parliamentary distinction. When those Members of the Opposition who happened to be Privy Councillors exercised their right in the new Parliament the Bench still had a desolate appearance.

Older parliamentarians of all Parties looked with a longing eye for one absent face. Mr. Arthur Balfour had been defeated because of his policy—or absence of policy. On every personal consideration his absence was a sad blank. The place was not the same. Debate lacked an essential something.

Soon after the House met there were rumours that the Chiltern Hundreds would be invoked. The uninitiated were informed that certain lands belonging to the Crown have Stewards, or Bailiffs. Their duties are nominal but technically they hold places of profit under the Crown. A Member of Parliament who at that time of day accepted any place of profit under the Crown thereby vacated his seat in the House of Commons but might seek re-election if he so desired. No Member may resign his seat. His service as a Member of the House of Commons is a public duty which he has been called upon to perform. A simple solution of the difficulty is an application to the Chancellor of the Exchequer for a Stewardship of one of the Crown estates collectively known as "the Chiltern Hundreds", which application is granted as a matter of course.

The City of London, as a two-Member constituency, was represented by Sir Edward Clarke and Mr. Alban Gibbs (afterwards Lord Aldenham). Mr. Gibbs made an application for the Chiltern Hundreds and at the bye-election Mr. Balfour was returned without opposition. A cordial welcome awaited him in all quarters of the House, and Mr. Horridge, his opponent at Manchester, was among the first to congratulate him.

Chapter 20

SOCIAL LEGISLATION AND COMING MEN

FOR a long time the children coming to school ill-fed and physically unable to apply themselves to their lessons had been the despair of humane and conscientious teachers. Sir John Gorst, a former Conservative Education Minister, in the course of many speeches upon the subject, pointed out that under compulsory education the children were brought into the schools and kept there by the authority of the law. They were thus prevented from earning or foraging food for themselves. The State thereby accepted a moral responsibility for the consequences to the stamina of the growing generation. Efforts had been made from time to time by humanitarians to cope with the problem by private charity.

Mr. Tyson Wilson, a Lancashire Labour Member, had the fortune to draw a place in the ballot which decides the precedence in which upon the earlier Fridays of each session Bills other than those introduced by the Government may be brought in by ordinary, or "Private", Members. He seized the opportunity of bringing in a Bill empowering the local Education Authority to provide meals at the schools for necessitous children and charge the parents if they were in a position to pay. There was no question as to the general and genuine sympathy with the children, but some rigid economists pointed out the danger of lessening parental responsibility. The case for the Bill was summed up by Dr. Macnamara, speaking from the experience of his younger days as a schoolmaster: Make the parent pay if he can. "If he is a drunken worthless person who starves his child to indulge his own vices whip him at the cart-tail", but feed the child.

In the course of the discussion Mr. Jowett, the Labour Member for Bradford, speaking from the front Bench below the gangway, described the scenes he had witnessed at some schools where meals were provided by private subscription. He paid a warm tribute to the voluntary and kindly supervision given by the teachers. In addition to their physical improvement, it was, he said, noticeable that the children benefited in their general behaviour. The teachers were able during the meals to give them friendly hints on good manners.

A Member making his way to the Opposition Benches above the gangway passed in front of Mr. Jowett and thus came between the Speaker and the Member addressing the House—a flagrant breach of parliamentary etiquette. The offender was assailed with angry cries of "Order! Order!".

Mr. Will Crooks, in an indulgently explanatory tone, observed "He's been absent at meal time".

The erring Member having thus innocently driven home one of Mr. Jowett's best points, made his apologies and Mr. Tyson Wilson's measure went smoothly on its way. As a Private Member's Bill to which there was some opposition it had very little chance of passing through all its stages, in the limited number of Fridays available, but it was adopted by the Government and eventually became law.

This was the first step towards a more general application of the principle of State responsibility. It revived memories of Victorian struggles. The orthodox "Manchester School" held a rigid faith in the combined advantages of free trade plus individual freedom from State interference. Another Victorian school led by that great Conservative philanthropist, the Earl of Shaftesbury, the tireless advocate of such Acts as those regulating the conditions of employment of women and children in factories and mines, had the sympathy and support of advanced Liberals and Radicals of those days.

The Whigs and Liberals of the Manchester School had now either modified their views or been superseded by the newer type in the Councils of Liberalism. Mr. Harold Cox, the Member for Preston and Secretary of the Cobden Club,

H

was almost the only representative of the old order in the House of Commons. In speeches of conspicuous ability and close reasoning power he preached the orthodox gospel of individualism in opposition to Mr. Tyson Wilson's Bill and all subsequent legislation of a similar nature. He found a few supporters, such as Sir Frederick Banbury and occasionally—in some of the other discussions—Lord Robert Cecil, on the opposite side, but no appreciable help on the Liberal side. The Conservative Party—especially the Tariff Reform section of it—moreover contained a large proportion of Members, imbued with the spirit of Lord Shaftesbury, who, while disavowing and opposing Socialism, had inherited the feudal instinct that the State, as the modern overlord, exercised a parental guardianship over all within its domains.

Amid all social problems the Fiscal question still lingered as a leading political topic despite its defeat at the polls. In order to "draw" Mr. Balfour as to the future place of Tariff Reform in the programme of the Party, a Motion was put down by Sir James Kitson (afterwards Lord Airedale), an influential Yorkshire leader of Commerce, recording the determination of Parliament to resist any proposal—whether by way of taxation upon foreign corn or a general tariff upon foreign goods—to create in this country a system of Protection.

Mr. Balfour, with all his pre-election skill, played with the Resolution. He described it as ambiguous and, instead of making a declaration of policy which his opponents demanded, put a series of questions to the other side.

Sir Henry Campbell-Bannerman retorted that the right honourable Gentleman seemed to be like the old Bourbons, who forgot nothing and learnt nothing. He little understood the tone of the new House. "Enough of this foolery", cried the stern Caledonian. "Move your amendment and let us get to business."

There was no "business" in the sense that the Prime Minister intended the word. Sir James Kitson's Motion was carried, but no declaration was made by Mr. Balfour on the main question.

The most striking parliamentary interest of the Debate was the discovery of new men destined to exercise magnetic influence in political life.

An impassioned and impressive speech on the Labour attitude was contributed by Mr. Philip Snowden, who had just been returned for Blackburn. Several Members rose to continue the Debate and the choice fell upon the man who "caught the Speaker's eye". It was not altogether a surprising coincidence that two men bearing the name of Smith should be in the House of Commons. They happened to be near each other on the Conservative side, and each assumed he had caught the Speaker's eye. For a few minutes both men addressed the House in an entertaining duet. Mr. Speaker indicated that the Member upon whom his eye had alighted was "Mr. Smith of Liverpool".

Members who had left their places with the intention of strolling into the Lobby after Mr. Snowden sat down paused a moment at the sound of two voices in unison. They halted a while for the opening sentences of the subsequent solo and then returned to their seats to hear more from this tall, dark, clean-shaven young man.

The maiden speech of "F.E.", as Mr. F. E. Smith was invariably described (even after he became Lord Birkenhead) is one of the classics of parliamentary eloquence. He spoke as an unrepentant Tariff Reformer and attacked the other side with such biting satire and brilliant epigram that his Party might have been the victors completing the rout of the vanquished. The only criticism by those who heard him was that in the enthusiasm of youth he had used up too many good things in one speech.

In the Lobbies afterwards people were told the new Member was a Cheshire man born at Birkenhead. After a distinguished career at Oxford, where he was President of the Union, he now practised as a Barrister on the Northern Circuit and represented the Walton Division of Liverpool.

In Conservative quarters many people wished the Leaders had been as emphatic in their adherence to Tariff Reform

as this outspoken recruit. But Free Trade and Protection
were having the last match of a long season, to be followed
by a longer interval. The King's Speech had indicated
a list of social changes some of which involved acute controversy. The Debate on Sir James Kitson's Motion was
in a double sense a breaking-off point. It signalled the
arrival of new men with new ideas. It marked the parliamentary conclusion of a distinguished career.

Sir Edward Clarke, K.C., the senior Member for the City
of London, was the forensic orator of his day and a powerful
force in public life. He had appeared in almost every *cause
célèbre* of his time. Some of his speeches at the Bar and in
Parliament were printed and preserved as models of finished
eloquence. Politically he disdained modern designations
and always called himself a Tory. He stood by the "creed
of the Tory Party". In the Kitson Debate he asserted
boldly that the Tory Party should refuse to accept the corn
and meat tax policy of Mr. Chamberlain. He took his
stand upon the declared Tory policy of Mr. Disraeli (Lord
Beaconsfield) and of a former Tory Leader, Lord Derby,
who in 1852, after an election in which a corn tax was defeated, declared that the Tory Party would accept and adopt
without any reserve whatever the verdict of the country.

The speech made from the Front Opposition Bench,
where Sir Edward Clarke had a seat as a Member of a former
Administration, was by no means the first sensational incident in Sir Edward's experience. As a young Tory he won
a bye-election in Southwark. The victory following upon
other signs of confidence convinced Lord Beaconsfield that
Public Opinion was with his party, and on the strength of this
belief the Conservative leader decided to advise the election of
1880, which led to the triumphant return of Mr. Gladstone.

Some few years after that Sir Edward Clarke was chosen
by the Leaders of his Party to move the rejection of Mr.
Gladstone's Home Rule Bill in the House of Commons.
At a still later date he was one of the very few Conservatives
who opposed Mr. Chamberlain's South African policy and

made a memorable speech in the House against it on the
eve of the Boer War. He now sought to shield his Leader
and colleague from the Chamberlain section of his Party,
but in so doing brought upon his own head the bitter resentment of the Tariff Reformers. A few months later Sir
Edward Clarke applied for the Chiltern Hundreds and passed
out of parliamentary life, but he continued to take a keen
interest in the work of the House. On the occasion of any
important Debate his alert, taut figure, set off to advantage
in the well-fitting early-Century grey frock coat, is still a
welcome sight, as he steps nimbly across the Inner Lobby
and up the stairs leading to the Distinguished Strangers'
Gallery.

Chapter 21

JUBILEES IN ART. "TAFF VALE"
SUFFRAGE SLOGAN

A celebrated actress and a distinguished singer were
specially honoured by a grateful public in the year
1906. Ellen Terry reached her stage jubilee. She made
her first appearance in 1856 as one of the Company of which
Charles Kean the popular nineteenth century actor was the
chief. As already mentioned, she shared the greatest
triumphs of Irving. After playing every important part
in the whole repertory of classic drama for fifty years she
was still appearing in revivals and also in modern drama.
A remarkable performance was given by the theatrical profession at Drury Lane in recognition of her jubilee. Crowds
thronged the theatre and many of the audience had taken
places in the queue in the early hours of the previous day.

At a later period of the year Adelina Patti, amid general
manifestations of affection, formally bade farewell to the
British public. So far back as 1861 this famous vocalist
sang at Covent Garden and from that time her career was
one continuous triumph in London, Paris, and the other
big cities. Although she left the operatic stage in the

eighties, she continued to sing at concerts; and audiences throughout the country were delighted by her beautiful voice, which she preserved with wonderful freshness. For some years previous to her farewell Madame Patti had practically retired to her Castle at Craig-y-nos, where she had a private theatre. The public eagerly welcomed her occasional returns to the concert platforms, and after her final retirement many thousands still remembered her inspiring rendering of "Home Sweet Home".

These poetic aspects of life provided soothing interludes for people engaged in serious public and private business.

Since the Taff Vale decision three Bills dealing with Trades disputes had been introduced by Private Members. The first of these was lost; the other two were read a second time and thus approved in principle.

Sir John Lawson Walton, the Attorney-General, introduced a measure in the new Parliament on behalf of the Government, and a further Bill was brought in by Mr. Walter Hudson, one of the representatives of the Railwaymen's Union. The principle of Mr. Walter Hudson's Bill was ultimately adopted, and for all practical purposes this became the Bill of the Government.

The crucial point was a clause which provided that an action should not be brought against an Association for recovery of damage sustained by any person or persons by reason of the action of a member or members of such Association.

The House was reminded in the course of the debates that as there are strikes in which the workmen as a body refuse to continue their employment unless certain terms are granted, so there is the "lock-out" by which employers dismiss all the men in a body in order to enforce certain conditions. The principal movers in a dispute on either side might endeavour to persuade their fellow employers or fellow workmen to act with them, and out of this arose the clauses legalising persuasion, or as colloquially expressed "peaceful picketing". In that respect the Taff Vale decision as it stood might—so it was contended—apply to strikes and also to lock-outs, but although the clauses of the Bill were so modelled that they protected employers' associations as well as workmen's organisations the opponents of the Bill retorted that employers desired no such privlege.

Mr. F. E. Smith moved the rejection of Mr. Hudson's Bill in one of his clever speeches. Fresh talent sprang up in the new House as one Debate succeeded another. During the discussion on the later stages of the Trades Disputes Bills a young man from the Liberal Benches rose to support the measure. His smooth, musical voice, soft yet penetrating, and his quiet, confident manner inspired the inevitable "Who's this?"

Dodd's Parliamentary Companion disclosed the information that John Allsebrook Simon had been returned for the Walthamstow Division of Essex. Further investigation showed that he was the son of a Congregational Minister; had been President of the Union at Oxford, and, like Mr. F. E. Smith, his contemporary at College and the Bar, was a promising Junior Counsel.

Mr. (afterwards Sir) John Simon's speech revealed the precision of thought and grasp of facts which make the successful debater. He pointed out that since 1870 it had been assumed that Trade Unions and other Associations were in the position which the Bill now before the House placed them. No one would have thought of bringing an action against the Tariff Reform League for a libel on the Cobden Club, whatever might have been the assumption of their rights against any individual official. This, as the decision of the highest tribunal showed, had been a misinterpretation of the law, but lawyers had hitherto accepted it as correct.

The most interesting feature of Mr. Simon's intervention in Debate was the fact that the Liberals had discovered a rising man to counter the new man discovered by the Conservatives. There was a sharp contrast between him and Mr. F. E. Smith in method and in style. Mr. Simon was seldom epigrammatic. He had no biting cynicisms but there was a gentle effective irony the more damaging because of its delicacy of touch.

His arguments on the Bill, and those of other supporters, apparently expressed the will of the majority on both sides of the House. The Second Reading was carried by four hundred and sixteen votes to sixty-six, and the Bill as ultimately constructed in Committee was read a third time without a division. Later on, when the measure reached the House of Lords, the Leaders of the Opposition advised its acceptance. Lord Halsbury, who had been Conservative Lord Chancellor for many years—a sturdy, unflinching, outspoken, old-world Tory—stoutly protested that they were doing a great wrong, but the House of Lords nevertheless followed the advice of the Opposition Leaders and the Bill duly became law.

Another pre-election controversy now began to monopolise parliamentary interest. Mr. Augustine Birrell had been appointed Minister of Education. His cheery good nature, his sense of humour and his general popularity induced his Leader to entrust him with delicate work.

His new task was to establish public and popular control over all the Elementary Schools. The first step must necessarily be a settlement of the apparently interminable religious difficulty. The Minister for Education was not prepared to leave religious instruction out of the school curriculum. "Where no vision is the people perish", was his emphatic declaration, and it was evident that any Bill which might have a chance of passing would have to abide by that guiding thought.

Mr. Birrell's proposal was a non-denominational or "simple Bible" teaching in all schools, with the proviso that in the schools which hitherto had been under denominational control it might be part of the arrangement of the transfer to the public Authority that the denominations should give denominational teaching to those children whose parents so desired, provided that the cost was not paid by the public Authority.

Instead of providing a solution the proposed plan only succeeded in expanding the political vocabulary. "Birrelligion"—as the scheme was sarcastically described—was denounced as heresy in countless drawing-rooms. Strong Churchmen asserted that it was a mockery of what they considered essential religion in the schools.

Once again the Irish Nationalists made common cause with the Anglican Conservatives. They severed themselves on this question from the Liberals and stubbornly resisted the application of Mr. Birrell's proposals to the English and Welsh Catholic Schools.

The Education Bill of 1902 had discovered Lord Hugh Cecil. The Bill of 1906 found another gifted son of the great Lord Salisbury. Lord Robert Cecil had given up a lucrative practice at the Parliamentary Bar on his election to the House. He threw himself into the conflict against the Government Bill with all the fervour of his younger brother and with a wider knowledge of the world.

Another social problem now came within the range of political activity. The feminine warning sounded at the Albert Hall Meeting was emphatically re-echoed in the House of Commons. Ardent supporters of Woman suffrage contended that by tradition, and by reason of the fact that the National Liberal Federation—the representative body of Liberal delegates from the constituencies—had passed resolutions in favour of it, the Liberal Party was morally committed to a policy of votes for women. This the leaders declined to admit. The resolutions were pious opinions and, so it was contended, not formal declarations of policy.

Shortly after the new House assembled a Private Member's Motion was put down to the effect that sex should cease to be a bar to the exercise of the parliamentary franchise. On the evening of its discussion an eager crowd of young women secured seats in the Ladies' Gallery. At that time of day ladies were permitted to occupy only the enclosed balcony behind the Speaker's Chair, high above and farther back than the gallery reserved for representatives of the Press. Technically they were not within the House. The massive iron grille (referred to by Mr. Labouchere, as recorded in a previous chapter), through the bars of which they gazed at the men below, typified this assumption.

As the Debate on the Suffrage Motion proceeded, a restless movement behind the grille indicated an unusual interest in the proceedings. Mr. Herbert Gladstone (afterwards Lord Gladstone) rose to speak for the Government in his capacity of Secretary of State for Home Affairs. The son of the great Liberal Leader, was naturally regarded as the special custodian of Liberal principles. He said the Government intended to leave the Motion an "open question".

Loud murmurs of "Shame" from behind the iron grille greeted this pronouncement. The meaning was clear. Leaving the proposal as an "open question" signified that Members of the Government attached no significance to the result of the division. It was generally known that some Members of the Ministry were strongly opposed to Woman Suffrage. The Home Secretary now in parliamentary terms ruled it out of the Government programme.

Just before midnight Mr. Samuel Evans (afterwards Sir Samual Evans, President of the Probate, Divorce and Admiralty Court) rose. It became obvious that he intended to continue the discussion until the clock struck twelve. This meant that the Debate would automatically come to an end without a division and the Motion would be talked out.

Loud shouts of "Divide! Divide!!" came from behind the grille.

"Order! Order!!", cried indignant Members.

"Divide, you liberty-loving Liberals!", a shrill voice retorted.

A white banner was thrust forth between the bars of the grille, bearing words which became the battle cry in countless demonstrations: "Votes for Women".

Orders were given by the Speaker to clear the Gallery. The disturbers of parliamentary peace were ejected, the Resolution was talked out and there the matter ended for that night only.

Chapter 22

PEERS AND EDUCATION
TRANSVAAL SELF-GOVERNMENT

WARNED by the experience of Mr. Balfour and the troubles of Sir Alexander Acland Hood, Sir Henry Campbell-Bannerman readjusted the rules. He abolished the much discussed adjournment for dinner and fixed the normal hour of rising at eleven o'clock instead of midnight. Each Member now dines at his own convenience—the Deputy Speaker taking the Chair when the Speaker is out. The popular time varies according to the Debate. The test of a Member's power to make his speech interesting is whether he functions as a "soup cooler" or as a "dinner bell". The old rule on the need for clearing the House during divisions was subsequently abolished. Members who do not wish to vote now remain in their seats, and one old form of "disorderly" protest has thus disappeared.

Mr. Birrell's Education Bill, after heated discussions in the Commons and exciting demonstrations in the country, eventually reached the House of Lords. The Upper Chamber devoted the whole autumn to it, and the lay peers gladdened the hearts of their episcopal brethren by remaining stubbornly at their posts, although the Debate ran into the hunting season. The Bishops, the only Members of the House, with the official exception of the Lord Chancellor, who sit in their robes, eloquently indicated their view as to the direction in which the Bill should be remodelled.

The Debates were controversial but decorous in this Assembly, where disapprobation never takes the form of articulate dissent and silent hostility generates an icy atmosphere more deadly than the fury of "another place" (the correct parliamentary reference by one House to the other).

For all practical purposes neither the orator nor his audience can at any moment be said to suffer from limitations by rules of order in the House of Lords, since it is presumed that disorder being unthinkable no necessity for such rules arises.

The Lord Chancellor, as the head of the Justitiary of Great Britain, presides over Peers chosen from Judges and great lawyers who constitute the Supreme Court of Appeal on litigation—in which phase of the work of the House of Lords ordinary non-legal peers of the Realm take no part. By virtue of his Office he is also Speaker of the House of Lords, but his sole duty in that capacity is to put the question and announce the decision of the House. If one or more peers rise together there is usually a mutual expression of willingness to give way, and, if necessary, the matter is decided by a subdued murmur of preference from the rest of the peers.

As Speaker of the House, the Lord Chancellor is indeed a less important personage than the Speaker of the House of Commons. In practice, however, though he has less responsibility, he has greater freedom. In the corridor leading from the House of Commons to the House of Lords is a painted panelling depicting an incident that occurred when Charles I went down to the House of Commons to arrest the five Members who had incurred his displeasure. The Members had meantime escaped on a barge to the City of London. When the King asked Mr. Speaker Lenthal where they were he received the answer inscribed on the panelling:

I have neither eyes to see nor tongue to speak in this place but as this House is pleased to direct me whose servant I am here.

This, in effect, has been the guiding rule for Speakers of the House of Commons for many generations. They interpret the will of the House and take no part in controversial affairs. The Speaker of the House of Lords, however, is invariably created a peer on, or very shortly after, his appointment as Lord Chancellor. As Speaker, he sits on the woolsack—the red divan, presumably stuffed with wool, which stands in front of the rails surrounding the steps of the Throne. By standing at the side instead of at the front of the woolsack he appears before the House

in his capacity as a peer, and, as he is also a Member of the
Cabinet, he takes a leading part in Debate.

The Lord Chancellor, as Lord Halsbury once expressed
it, possesses no greater right—but no less right—to call
a Member to order than the youngest peer in the House.
After a peer, jealous of this prerogative, had raised the
point on one occasion, Lord Halsbury, then Lord Chancellor, left his noble friends to themselves, and when, things
having become somewhat involved, an appeal was made to
him he grimly replied:

> Since you are good enough to ask me I should say we have
> been out of order for the last twenty minutes.

The freedom which, with mutual goodwill, works so well in
abstract Debate, presented many difficulties when Mr. Birrell's
Bill passed from the Second Reading to the Committee stage.
The Chairman of Committees who presides when the Peers,
like the Commons, sit as a Committee of the whole House on
the clauses of a Bill, possesses only similar powers to those of
the Lord Chancellor on matters of order, with the further
reservation that he never takes part in Debate.

Complicated amendments moved by various peers left
some of the clauses of the Education Bill still more complicated until marshalled and re-amended, and at times
the exact position was unrecognisable. One evening a
peer was carefully developing his arguments on a particular
point concerning which he had prepared a speech and was
determined to deliver it, when another peer asked what
was the question before the House.

"The question is", said the Chairman of Committees, "that
certain words be left out which have already been omitted in
order to put in certain words which have already been inserted."

After a few courteously administered rebukes of this
kind the House gradually attuned itself to the new class
of work. Under the Conservative Administration the
House of Lords as such had seldom found itself in conflict
with proposals of the Government of the day. The

majority among them were in effect now serving an appren-
ticeship to the duties of a parliamentary Opposition. A
very small number of followers sat behind Lord Crewe, who
was in charge of the Bill on behalf of the Government. Lord
Lansdowne (the Leader of the Opposition), as the Marquis
of Ripon (the nominal Leader of the House) shrewdly remarked, was the "Master of Legions".

The net result was that Mr. Birrell, from the steps inside
the rails of the Throne—where Privy Councillors and the
eldest sons of peers are permitted to stand—watched clause
after clause of his Bill transformed out of existence till,
as he subsequently declared, he cried within himself, like
MacDuff weeping for his children after the sack of his Castle
by Macbeth: "All gone! all my pretty ones!"

The Bill, as amended, went back to the House of Commons,
where it was decided that "This House doth disagree with
the Lords on the said amendments". The House of Lords,
when the measure was returned to them, decided that
"The Lords do insist on the said amendments".

At various informal conferences between leading Members of
both Houses attempts were made to arrive at some compromise.
The wags of the Lobby suggested that they were "pumping
oxygen" into the sinking Bill. Then finally came the announcement that in the absence of agreement between the two Houses
the legislative firstborn of the new House of Commons was dead.

Not so their first big administrative effort.

It had been well understood that Sir Henry Campbell-
Bannerman would take an early opportunity of granting
self-government to the Transvaal and the Orange River
Colony. This was in accordance with the clause in the
Peace Treaty which declared that "as soon as circumstances
permit representative institutions leading up to self-government will be introduced". There however grave
doubts in some quarters as to whether the time had arrived
when "circumstances permitted". Lord Elgin the Colonial
Secretary explained to the House of Lords at the end of
July the general terms on which it was proposed to set up

a Constitution for the Transvaal on somewhat similar lines
to the other self-governing Colonies.   Lord Milner and other
Peers strongly criticised the "precipitate haste".   Lord
Lansdowne as the Leader of the Opposition Peers said:

> We are bound to tell you that if these boons are to be given
> to the people of the Transvaal, they must be regarded as given
> by His Majesty's Government, and that we, at any rate, take
> no responsibility for the course you are about to pursue.

In the House of Commons Mr. Winston Churchill introducing the subject on the Colonial Office Vote had a more
stormy reception.   Members on the Opposition side condemned the policy of the Government and as a protest
opposed the Vote of Supplies to the Colonial Office which
was due to be divided upon at ten o'clock that night.   The
concluding words of the Debate are thus recorded:

> MR. BALFOUR : What security does he see that this abso-
> lute power given to the Transvaal will not be used to establish
> a condition of things which may make some future action
> against this country possible, probable, and dangerous ?   I
> see no such security, and because I see no security against
> this danger, I refuse to accept the invitation so kindly offered
> to us by the Under-Secretary for the Colonies that we on this
> side should make ourselves responsible with the Government
> for what I regard as the most reckless development of a great
> colonial policy.   [" Oh, oh."]   For this reason I look with
> alarm and distrust to the future, and only from a wisdom we
> can hardly hope or expect from the population in the Trans-
> vaal can the danger be avoided.   For these reasons I shall
> certainly give my vote against the Resolution about to be put
> from the Chair.

> SIR H. CAMPBELL-BANNERMAN, rising just before 10 o'clock,
> said : In the one minute left to me I will only say one thing,
> that never in the course of my Parliamentary career have I
> listened to a more unworthy, provocative, and mischievous——

The remaining words which the Prime Minister intended to
utter were drowned in angry protests during which the "minute"
expired and according to the rules the question had to be put.

Despite this hostile reception from Conservative Statesmen

and a poetic effort on the part of Mr. Rudyard Kipling—then at the height of his power as a virile and popular writer—to arouse feelings against the policy, public opinion at home and in the self-governing Colonies was generally favourable to self-government. The comments of some of the Conservative papers inferred that the Opposition were not taking a wise course in attacking it.

The Government pursued their policy and early in December the Letters Patent for the new Constitution for the Transvaal and Orange River Colonies were formally sealed. Mr. Winston Churchill towards the end of the Session moved a resolution giving the approval of the House of Commons. Concluding a general debate he said:

> It is the earnest desire of the Government to steer colonial affairs out of English party politics. . . . We do not ask hon. Gentlemen opposite to share our responsibility. . . . If by any chance our counsels of reconciliation should come to nothing, if our policy should end in mocking disaster, then the resulting evil would not be confined to South Africa. Our unfortunate experience would be trumpeted forth all over the world wherever despotism wanted a good argument for bayonets, wherever an arbitrary Government wished to deny or curtail the liberties of imprisoned nationalities. But if, on the other hand, as we hope and profoundly believe, better days are in store for South Africa, if the long lane which it has been travelling has reached its turning at last . . . if the near future should unfold to our eyes a tranquil, prosperous, consolidated Afrikander nation under the protecting ægis of the British crown, then, I say, the good as well as the evil will not be confined to South Africa ; then, I say, the cause of the poor and the weak all over the world will have been sustained ; and everywhere small peoples will get more room to breathe, and everywhere great empires will be encouraged by our example to step forward—and it only needs a step—into the sunshine of a more gentle and a more generous age.

The resolution was then carried without a division and the new era in South Africa commenced with the results to be recorded in later chapters.

THE CHAUFFEUR AT THE GATE OF PARADISE.

[Lord Watson stops the motor traffic in Hyde Park from four to seven P.M.]

AN INCIDENT OF THE EARLY DAYS OF MOTORING

Chapter 23

NEW SOCIAL FACTORS. ARMY REFORM

THE birth of the "taxi" was a landmark in traffic and street control.

Private motor cars had become familiar amongst well-to-do people, in spite of sturdy resistance from grooms and coachmen. The hansom and the four-wheeler, or "growler", held out longer than the dogcart and the brougham. The streets of London and the big cities were at first considered incorrect places for public motor vehicles, but the advance of the new form of traction was inevitable, and on January 21st, 1907, motor cabs fitted with the taximeter, which the old cabman with his "leave it to you, Sir" had stubbornly refused to adopt, were officially recognised as vehicles permitted to ply for hire.

At about the same time there was another indication of changing conditions. Hitherto it had been assumed that Trade Unionism and strikes were restricted to skilled or unskilled manual workers. Unions were however being formed by other people whose services were at the disposal of employers and in January 1907 a strike was declared of Music Hall artistes and musicians. This was eventually settled by arbitration.

Following upon a brief rest, political life renewed its activities. After his exciting and unsuccessful effort to solve the Education problem, Mr. Birrell was moved to another sphere of labour. He became Chief Secretary to the Lord Lieutenant for Ireland, and thus, as the adviser to the representative of the Sovereign in Ireland, was responsible to Parliament for all that happened in Irish administration apart from the ceremonial and social duties of the Lord Lieutenant.

Outwardly it would appear that a happier field had been found for Mr. Birrell. There were bonds of sympathy between him and the Irish Nationalists: he and they had a mutual sense of humour. Despite their differences on Education,

I

they agreed on most political questions, but a cloud no bigger than a man's hand hovered over Irish political life.

Sinn Fein was forming itself into a Party. The origin of this movement, fated to play so dramatic a part in Irish history, was in a sense literary and educational. The words "Sinn Fein"—"We ourselves"—were at first applied to Societies for encouraging the use of the Irish language and the study of Irish literature, which gradually developed into combinations of sentimental Irishmen pledged to wear clothing woven from Irish material by Irish hands. At about the time when Mr. Birrell became Chief Secretary the "Sinn Feiners" were advocating self-reliance in the agitation for Home Rule. They despaired of parliamentary action, and proposed that the Nationalist Members would withdraw from Westminster. Their programme included a form of government in Ireland controlled by voluntary National Councils, whose statutes should be enforceable by public opinion. They proposed to set up voluntary Tribunals for the settlement of civil disputes. Their ambitions also centred on the establishment of an Irish Consular Service. They proposed, further, to boycott English goods wherever possible and discourage Irish enlistment in the British Army. The consequences to Mr. Birrell of these new ideas were to come much later.

The next British Minister to appear in the immediate lime-light was the outwardly placid Mr. Haldane.

Army Reform had been the subject of many discussions in Parliament and the country since the conclusion of the South African War. Various schemes had been suggested and debated. Mr. Haldane outlined certain broad principles in 1906, and in February of 1907 he addressed the House of Commons for three hours. At a bewildering speed, in a high tone, with a smooth unemotional delivery, he went into full detail concerning his proposed reorganisation of the Forces. Now and then, to emphasise a point, he lifted his arms and comprehensively waved them over the House. Everybody who heard him was prepared to accept his asser-

tion that never before had there been such a stocktaking at
the War Office.   The speech gradually evolved itself into a
scheme under which a first line, or "striking force", of
Infantry, Cavalry and Artillery, should always be in an
efficient condition for mobilisation and should be able to
maintain itself in the field for at least six months.   The
second line, for Home defence, was to be composed of Militia,
Volunteers and Yeomanry.

The fundamental principle on which Mr. Haldane proceeded
was a military organisation formed into two lines based on
preparedness for war.   At the moment, he said, we possessed
a confused mass of troops—Army, Militia, Volunteers—having
no definite places in a definite military scheme.

The changes which attracted the greatest measure of popular
attention were those which affected the proposed second line.

The Militia were a quasi-regular force attached to the
Army but more closely connected with county life.   Normally
they served for some few weeks in the year and could be
called up in time of special emergency.   In the rigorous
campaigns of past wars they had done splendid work, but
they were the Cinderella of the Army.   They were without
first-class equipment, and had no effective supports in the
way of Cavalry or Artillery.   Still, county sentiment resented
their probable disappearance as an institution.   Eventually
Mr. Haldane, while converting the force into a special reserve
agreed to transfer to the first line those Militia Battalions
which were to be preserved, care being taken to preserve
also, as far as possible, the recognised names and traditions.

The Volunteers were a modern body.   In olden days
when there was a possibility of invasion Volunteer Corps
were formed but were disbanded after the danger had passed.
One distinguished and ancient Institution—the Honourable
Artillery Company, with traditions going back to the days of
Henry VIII—has an unbroken record of service through the
long centuries.   Generally speaking, however, the Volunteers
as Mr. Haldane found them were constituted under official
sanction in 1859.   Their actual birth dated from 1861.

They were liable to be called out and placed under ordinary military discipline in time of imminent national danger and great emergency. At other times the Force was controlled by its own officers. A Commanding Officer could dismiss a man, and a man, when not on active service, could terminate his engagement at any time upon a short notice.

Apart from a capitation grant towards expenses, each Corps depended for its existence on voluntary subscriptions. The officers undertook to obtain or give donations for this purpose. Local professional and business men who accepted commissions thus in many instances incurred a considerable sacrifice of time and financial responsibility.

The Yeomanry constituted a Cavalry Volunteer Force which had remained continuously in being since the Napoleonic Wars. As the name implies, the men were drawn largely from the sons of farmers, who provided their own horses, and the regiments were officered mainly by the county gentry. For the greater part of their history they were a power in reserve for maintaining order in their own counties, but they were liable to be called upon for any form of Cavalry service.

During the South African War Volunteers and Yeomen effectually demonstrated their value in time of need. An invitation to the Volunteers to supply a Service Corps for South Africa met with a ready response, and when a request was made for mounted troops the Yeomanry took a prominent part. These experiences created a more cordial appreciation of the reserve forces, but their recognition as an integral part of the military system was still vague and nebulous.

Mr. Haldane asserted that the organisation of the Volunteers was most confused and the financial position deplorable. Amidst loud cheers he announced that the financial liability on the officers would be removed. A new Home Army was to be constructed as a Territorial Force, in which enlistment would be for four years, during which attendance at drills and, so far as compatible with the men's responsibilities in civil employment, attendance at camp would be compulsory. The men would be enlisted to serve at home, but they might volunteer for service abroad. The Force was to be trained under the control and inspection of the Military Authorities, and the Regular Army would find the higher commands and staffs.

The new scheme was criticised from many points of view. Lord Roberts said it was a great step towards a National Army, but inadequate without compulsory drilling. Mr. Ramsay Macdonald said the Volunteers had never been appreciated by the War Office and had never had a chance of showing what they could do as a Civil Force. The present proposal, he contended, destroyed the civil character of their organisation. If the new scheme broke down it would be impossible to retrieve and reconstruct the Volunteer Force, and then there would be nothing between the country and conscription.

The Labour Party also objected to what Mr. Macdonald described as "the undemocratic nature of the training of the officers", which was largely in the hands of Cadet Corps associated with the Public Schools. Mr. Macdonald suggested that the Authorities should take a leaf out of the book of our late enemies in South Africa:—

> Let them put a man down twenty miles away from his home on a dark night and tell him to identify objects as far as he could see them. Let them give him the problem of bringing in twenty men to his own house on the assumption that an enemy was following up behind him, and if he did it then make him an officer.

"The Labour Party", continued Mr. Macdonald, "wanted a Force for fighting and not for show."

Objections to the proposals rained in from quarters where the subject was approached from an entirely different point of view to that of the Labour Party. An essential part of the new scheme was the formation of County Associations to encourage recruiting and to undertake the responsibility for the organisation of a new Force apart from military training. This appeal to the gentry met with a cold reception.

Mr. Balfour thought the people in the counties available and eligible for this kind of work already had their hands full. The Conservative Opposition put down a reasoned amendment declining to proceed with the scheme, but when this was defeated they did not oppose the Second Reading of the Bill.

A small minority consisting of Labour Members and a few Liberals who, by tradition and religion, were unable to associate themselves with military organisation voted against the whole principle, but it was ultimately carried.

The designation "Territorial Force" at first provided a subject for ridicule. Veterans, however, remembered how their own early efforts were favourite subjects for the cartoonist and the comedian, and the young men killed the sting of the nickname "Terriers" by cheerfully adopting this useful appellation as a term of comradeship.

The King invited the Lord Lieutenants of the Counties to Buckingham Palace and addressed them on their duties in connection with the Territorial Associations. In the course of a short but impressive speech he said he was confident that they would employ their best endeavours to carry out their high work.

Chapter 24

PROGRESS ON SEA AND LAND

A TRIUMPH was maturing for British Shipping.
Sailors watched with interest, landsmen with awe, the wonderful developments in maritime enterprise. There were still old skippers and seamen who had navigated the Oceans under sail. Some sailing ships were still upon the seas. In mid-Victorian days the first iron steamer was built for the Atlantic Ocean and put in service by the Cunard Company. Following that came the "Great Eastern" for many years accepted as the last word in marine construction. She was six hundred and eighty eight feet long; had a gross tonnage of eighteen thousand nine hundred and fifteen tons; and her speed was thirteen knots. For over forty years

she held the record as the largest vessel afloat. For speed
the "Campania" and the "Lucania", both Cunard liners
built in 1893, held the record in voyages across the Atlantic
until the big German ships took and held it into the first
few years of the new century.

British shipping took measures to regain the supremacy.
By agreement with the Government the Cunard Company
placed orders for two ships to be built for mail and
passenger service and to be available for the use of the
Admiralty, if required, in time of war. The "Lusitania"
was built by John Brown & Co. and the "Mauretania" by
Swan Hunter Wigham Richardson & Co. Both were ready
for service in 1907 and they regained for Great Britain
the Atlantic record. The "Lusitania" had a gross tonnage
of thirty one thousand five hundred and fifty tons, the
"Mauretania" a gross tonnage of thirty one thousand nine
hundred and thirty eight tons. The "Lusitania" attained an
average speed of 25.85 knots and the "Mauretania" an average
of 26.06 knots. They were both seven hundred and ninety feet
long or over a hundred feet longer than the "Great Eastern",
with a gross tonnage of some thirteen thousand tons more.

The launch of the "Mauretania", which by a few hundred tons
was absolutely the last word, was a great occasion for Tyneside.
Newcastle and the surrounding country celebrated the event
as a public achievement. Cheers re-echoed along the historic
banks as the huge ship, freed from the last restraining pile,
slid into the water and rode majestically upon the broad
river as though almost humanly conscious of her supremacy.

Skippers of cargo boats had been wont to speak of passenger
ships as "floating hotels". This latest effort of the marine
architect was a floating town. Men watching the new
vessels from ashore, or with still greater amazement exploring
the accommodation on board, asked each other if any bigger
thing could possibly sail the sea.

*   *   *   *   *

The Conservatives and Unionists in the House of Commons,
although in a hopeless voting minority, soon appreciated

the truth of the homely saying that work is the cure for most troubles.

The younger men acquired some of the arts of Opposition used against their own Leaders in the preceding Parliament. Lord Turnour (afterwards Lord Winterton), who came into the previous House at a bye-election and was then the "babe" of the House, had survived the General Election. Brimful of youth and vigour, he threw himself into the new work of his Party, and other young Conservatives also developed the faculty for parliamentary warfare. They had the benefit of advice and support from veterans who had known the days of Opposition when the Liberals were in Office years before.

Sir Frederick Banbury, who had been defeated at Peckham, was elected for the City of London in succession to Sir Edward Clarke. He brought into Opposition the stonewalling qualities which had been so useful to his Party when they were in Office. Lord Robert Cecil opposed the new Government with all the fervour of a man compelled by stern duty to strain every nerve in the struggle. Sir Alexander Acland Hood in Opposition, as in Office, gave battle at every opportunity, with all the fighting instincts of his race.

The little band had neither the debating power nor the picturesque touch of the Lloyd George/Churchill combination, but they moved together stolidly in their uphill march. They toiled through the weary watches of many a night, and one spring eve they contrived to beat the previous Parliament's record.

Among other subjects on the order paper that night was the Committee stage of the Army Annual Bill. As this measure, containing the regulations for the organisation and discipline of the Army, usually goes through as a matter of form, Chief Government Whips have a habit of saving Government time by bringing it on late at night, after the close of ordinary business, practically on the date on which it must be passed.

It has often proved a tempting opportunity for a fighting Opposition. In old times the Irish Nationalists had many a field night with the Government of the day on this Bill.

The Conservatives and Liberals in turn had occasionally given each other a strenuous time with it.

In 1906 the young men on the Opposition Benches tried their prentice hands upon it. After a year's practice on other subjects they were in first-class form. When they began to put complicated questions and to move amendments on intricate details, Mr. Haldane, with a whimsical smile on his face, complacently watched the old familiar tactics. Point after point was raised, countered and discussed. Clauses were declared to be ambiguous and a new phraseology suggested which the Secretary of State for War declared to be incomprehensible.

The hands of the clock travelled round, and the temper of the House followed its accustomed stages. Occasionally outbursts of anger from one side or the other succeeded equally vehement gusts of merriment. The day dawned, lunch succeeded breakfast, and a quiet afternoon was enlivened by a vigorous spurt from the tired combatants. Finally, after a sitting of twenty-six-and-a-half hours, the House adjourned.

On the Motion for the Adjournment Sir Henry Campbell-Bannerman formally announced that the Government could not give their sanction to a proposal for a tunnel to France under the English Channel. This pronouncement once more postponed for the time being the consideration of a project which had been advocated by its supporters for many years.

While the Conservatives were welding themselves into a compact fighting Opposition, the Liberal Party, under Sir Henry Campbell-Bannerman's genial leadership, was forgetting its differences. Mr. Ramsay Macdonald and others meantime were promulgating the ambitions of the Independent Labour Party. They declared that their policy was that of "moulding society into the Socialist State". This was still quite out of keeping with the policy of a very large number of the substantial Trade Unionists; but even at this early stage in the career of the new Party it was becoming evident that the energetic men of the I.L.P. intended to direct the policy of the party.

Various non-party reforms were steadily introduced and completed. The Court of Criminal Appeal was set up after careful discussion of the merits of this important change in legal procedure. It had often been pointed out that while in Civil cases a litigant dissatisfied with the decision of the Court had a right of appeal up to the highest tribunal, convicted criminals had no appeal from a Court and Jury, although in very special circumstances a case might be remitted for decision on a point of law to a special Court of Judges called the "Court for Crown Cases Reserved".

Under the new Act of Parliament machinery was provided by which a prisoner convicted of an indictable offence at Quarter Sessions or Assizes might appeal against verdict or sentence to a Tribunal consisting of three Judges of the High Court. If the Attorney-General certified that some special point arose requiring the decision of the highest tribunal, there might also be an appeal from the decision of the Court of Criminal Appeal to the House of Lords.

Another minor, but memorable, social change was the passage of an Act by Mr. McKenna, who had now become Minister for Education, providing for the systematic medical examination of children in the public Elementary Schools.

The Session of 1907 is also a landmark in legislation affecting women. An Act of Parliament permitting women to sit on local Authorities and to become Councillors and Aldermen was safely carried through both Houses.

This eventful year likewise saw the triumph of the importunate widower. A Bill legalising the marriage of a man with his deceased wife's sister had been tabled regularly by one Private Member and another, Session after Session, for more years than the oldest active parliamentarian could remember. Some of them had passed their Second Reading, but had failed to complete their further stages. They had been numbered among the victims at the "Slaughter of the Innocents"—a ceremony which takes place a week or two before the close of the Session, when the Leader of the House announces what measures are to be passed before the House rises and, by inference, what measures are to be dropped. Each Session being complete in itself and the Bill not having got through in one Session, it has to begin its journey over again the following Session. This year the Prime Minister adopted the Deceased Wife's Sister Bill. As the child of the Government it escaped the massacre, and after a brief struggle in both Houses ultimately became law.

The Session also marked the beginning of the greatest conflict in history between the House of Commons and the House of Lords. The Veto of the House of Lords had been a popular platform topic throughout the latter half of the XIXth Century. When Liberal legislation was rejected by the Upper Chamber, Liberal Speakers demanded the modification or abolition of the right of the House of Lords to reject a Bill passed by the House of Commons.

As the majority in the House of Lords was permanently Conservative, differences between the two Assemblies did not arise throughout the years of Lord Salisbury's Government, when there was a Conservative majority in the House of Commons. The relations between the two Houses thus became an abstract constitutional topic. A new generation had grown up since the Gladstonian days who did not realise the significance of the Veto.

When the Peers riddled the clauses of Mr. Birrell's Education Bill during the autumn of 1906, the old agitation was recalled. The men who had denounced the unfettered power of the Second Chamber in days gone by raised their voices again, and found an interested audience in their younger colleagues.

The agitation gathered force, and in June, 1907, Sir Henry Campbell-Bannerman proposed the following Resolution in the House of Commons:

> That, in order to give effect to the will of the people as expressed by their elected representatives, it is necessary that the power of the other House to alter or reject Bills passed by this House should be so restricted by law as to secure that within the limits of a single Parliament the final decision of the Commons shall prevail.

The Prime Minister explained that this Motion, even if it were tacitly accepted by the House, did not have the effect of law, but the Government desired to test the opinion of the House and make sure before any further step was taken that they had the House of Commons behind them.

The Resolution was carried and became the basis of more direct proposals at a later stage.

Chapter 25

SCOUTING.   ROYAL TRAGEDY.
TENSE PROBLEMS

THE Boy Scout was born in the year 1908.   His stature increased with wonderful rapidity.

Sir Robert Baden-Powell during the South African War commanded a stubborn and heroic resistance to a prolonged siege of Mafeking, an important trading town in British territory which the Boers endeavoured to capture at the beginning of the war.   When after holding out for two hundred and seventeen days the gallant garrison was relieved by a British force, the crowds in London were so enthusiastic in their demonstrations that the term "Mafficking" became the recognised description of extravagant exhibitions of popular excitement.   In Mafeking an experiment matured into the foundation of a great work which brought even more fame to General Sir Robert Baden-Powell than his historic military achievement.   During his earlier service as a Cavalry officer he came to the conclusion from a study of young recruits that there was something lacking in the way of practical training and the development of character between elementary school teaching and soldiering or civil life afterwards.   He therefore established classes of training in scouting and campaigning.   During the South African War Major Lord Edward Cecil as Baden-Powell's staff officer organised the boys of Mafeking into a corps of orderlies. This proved a great success, and Baden-Powell after he came home conducted experiments in training English boys mainly as a supplementary effort for the Boys' Brigades which were already associated with various religious and philanthropic bodies. The principle was to put the boys on their honour and make their training attractive.

Early in 1908 Sir Robert brought out a handbook of the training entitled "Scouting for Boys". The idea was immediately seized upon by people who were endeavouring to attract youths to healthy recreative training. Almost as if by magic troops of Scouts sprang into existence before the book, which came out in six fortnightly parts, was completed. The prospect of getting the boys into the open air and giving them a sense of individual responsibility was especially promising. It was felt that nothing modern would more surely appeal to the imagination of a high spirited youngster at that stage of his literary studies when books of travel and adventure are most popular with him. As a fact it has been admitted that in this—as in other respects—we acquired knowledge from the Zulus and the higher types of Africans, they having continued in their primitive life what our early ancestors in their cave and forest days instinctively practised for the physical development of the race. Sir Robert Baden-Powell may thus be said to have led civilisation back to its starting point, and induced it to re-adapt something which at some stage of its various forced marches it had left behind.

Obviously the new movement from the very commencement was growing too big to be tacked on to any existing organisation. Very quickly it became a self-contained institution. The cowboy hat, Khaki shirt, green tie and shorts— the uniform borrowed from a South African idea—soon became a familiar sight in the streets and country sides.

On the 1st February 1908 news arrived of an outrage in the Portuguese capital where political affairs were notoriously in a disturbed condition. As the Royal Family were driving in an open carriage to the Palace they were fired on by a group of assassins armed with rifles. The King and his eldest son—the Crown Prince—were both killed on the spot;

the Queen Mother with splendid heroism threw herself in front of her sons, and Dom Manoel the second son escaped with a wound in the arm. The escort and the police attacked and despatched the murderers who were led by a dismissed school teacher.

A Requiem Mass for the murdered King and Crown Prince was held at St. James's, Spanish Place, London. The King and Queen and the Prince of Wales, with a number of the Diplomatic body and many persons of eminence, attended. This was the first occasion on which an English King had been present at a Roman Catholic Service in Great Britain since the Reformation. A Memorial Service was subsequently held in St. Paul's, which was also attended by the King and Queen and by the Prince and Princess of Wales.

A case heard in the Criminal Courts called attention to the fact that the English law possesses procedure for the suppression of blasphemy. No prosecution under this power had been instituted for some twenty-five years, but it was held desirable to take action against a man who was alleged to have been guilty of blasphemous libel in open-air speeches. The precise nature of the libel was not published, but it was understood that the man's remarks concerning the Deity were couched in terms offensive to the public conscience. He was bound over to keep the peace on an undertaking not to repeat the offence but at a later date was sent to prison for non-observance of the terms laid down by the Court.

It is one of the facts in history that the efforts of any Parliament to undo the work of its immediate predecessor are usually unsuccessful. Two subjects upon which the Liberals had fought strenuously in the old Parliament were striking examples.

Mr. Birrell's Bill had gone beyond hope of resurrection. Mr. McKenna, his successor at the Board of Education, made another attempt to reform the Act of 1902. His proposal was that all public Elementary Schools should come under the full control of the Local Authorities and rent should be paid for those schools which had previously belonged to the

Denominations. Religious education similar to that which had been taught in the Board Schools was to be provided in all schools, and if denominational education were desired by a majority of the parents it could be given by properly trained teachers at the cost of the Denomination. Voluntary Schools might be continued, and if they came up to certain standards they would receive grants, but no rate aid, and they would not be recognised in parishes where there was only one school.

Mr. Balfour denounced the Bill as not an olive branch but a sword, and after various negotiations it disappeared.

The next effort at a reversal of modern legislation was a Licensing Bill brought in by Mr. Asquith mainly directed to an attempt at restoring the legal powers of the Licensing Authorities to renew, transfer or repeal a licence at their discretion. In order that this might be effected gradually a time limit of fourteen years was fixed during which compensation for the extinction of licences would continue to come from a levy on the Trade. After that, as the Chancellor of the Exchequer expressed it, "the country would recover unfettered freedom to deal with licences as it chose".

This part of the Bill was the crucial question for the Trade. Provisions as to Sunday trading, the supervision of Clubs, restrictions on the employment of barmaids, and other matters were inserted at the request of enthusiasts. Some of the friends of the Bill feared it had been over-weighted. Throughout the country agitation against it centred on what some people described as the "irritating details". On the other hand, demonstrations in favour of the Bill were attended by many thousands in different parts of the country. It went on its way through the House of Commons, and meanwhile other matters came on for consideration.

Mr. (afterwards Sir) George Toulmin, the Member for Bury and a well-known supporter of Social Reform in Lancashire, introduced the "Sweated Industries Bill", a measure destined to exercise an important influence on the lives of the very poor.

Since the days when the great divine and author of the Victorian era—the Rev. Charles Kingsley—wrote "Alton Locke" the conditions under which certain industries were conducted in the crowded districts of London and the great cities had given grave anxiety to men and women of both political Parties and all shades of religious thought. Harrowing tales had been told in works of fiction, in newspaper articles and in speeches, of work done upon brilliant uniforms and beautiful garments in insanitary slums at starvation payment.

Efforts had been made from time to time to deal with the situation by private effort, but it was urged that the evil required drastic treatment in the interest of properly established firms of fair employers as well as of the public and the employees. The Bill which Mr. Toulmin introduced was a re-statement of proposals previously put forward as a consequence of much thought and consultation upon the subject. It sought to establish Wages Boards with power to fix a minimum wage in trades scheduled as sweated industries. The Home Secretary had power from time to time to add to the Schedule. The Board was to be composed of representatives of employers and employed in equal numbers, with a Chairman chosen by the members or appointed by the Home Secretary. Payment of the minimum wage was to be enforced by the Factory Inspector.

Sir Frederick Banbury and one or two others thought they detected the thin end of the "Socialist wedge" in this, but other Members of the Unionist and Conservative Party, like Mr. Pike Pease (afterwards Lord Daryngton) and Mr. Goulding (afterwards Lord Wargrave), strongly supported the Bill; and Mr. Alfred Lyttelton said he rejoiced to notice that the sympathy of the House as a whole was with the objects which the promoters of the measure had in view.

The Bill was read a second time without a division and the principles thus approved were remitted to a Select Committee on home work for further consideration.

While the Liberal Party remained substantially intact on broad lines, there were still some differences on special subjects. Once again the General Committee of the National Liberal Federation at its Annual Meeting carried by a large majority, but amid some strong demonstrations of dissent, a Resolution in favour of the extension of the franchise to women. This was effectively followed by a Private Member's Bill introduced in the House of Commons by Mr. Stanger, upon which the Liberal Leaders went into different Lobbies when the Division was called. The Second Reading was, however, carried by two hundred and seventy-one to ninety-two. The Bill was referred to a Committee of the whole House, which meant that in the absence of Government aid there would be no time to deal with it, and it was thus shelved for another Session—a procedure indignantly resented by the active Suffragists.

Chapter 26

PARLIAMENTARY LANDMARKS. PENSIONS

THE Manchester School and advanced modernity came into very sharp conflict when Mr. P. W. Wilson, the Liberal Member for St. Pancras, a notable writer and parliamentary journalist, moved the Second Reading of an Unemployed Workmen's Bill, which was seconded by Mr. J. Ramsay Macdonald. Out of this arose the slogan "the right to work". The Bill placed upon Local Authorities the responsibility of providing employment at the standard wage for such work in the district, or providing the necessities of life for the unemployed person and his family.

The rejection of the Bill was moved by Mr. Fred Maddison, a Trade Unionist Liberal Member, who from his youth up had been closely connected with the Printing Trade, both as a printer and an editor. His strenuous and straightforward work for the principles of Trade Unionism and Liberalism, in both of which he believed with all his heart, had won him the admiration of opponents as well as of friends. Mr. Maddison could not move cheerfully along the

K

lines towards State control which Trade Unionists and many Liberals were adopting. He declared that the "right to work" would be followed by an intolerable State interference with individual life and liberty.

The motion for the rejection of the measure was seconded by Mr. Vivian, another Liberal Member, closely associated with co-partnership in housing, and one of the foremost pioneers of the Garden City movement.

Mr. John Burns, as President of the Local Government Board, came in for a fire of questions and interjections from some of the Labour Members when he expressed his determined opposition to the Bill. He declared that under it:

> the lanes in every country district would be black with people on their way to towns where the minimum wage was higher than that to which they were accustomed.

The Bill was defeated, but one hundred and thirty-six Liberals abstained from voting for or against it and seventy-four supported it.

Licensing now became the most exciting topic of the hour. A vacancy occurred in Peckham by the death of the Liberal Member. As a division of London the constituency was easily accessible from the headquarters of political Associations and kindred Societies. All kinds of "Leagues" and "Associations" who felt it desirable to inflict a defeat upon the Government Candidate converged upon Peckham. The Organisations connected with the Licensing Trade took a very active part, with the express purpose, as they avowed, of "emphasising the strong feeling of the country against the Licensing Bill". The Conservative Candidate happened to be a total abstainer, but he was opposed to the Government policy and anti-Government helpers flooded the constituency. It was said that there were almost as many canvassers as voters.

On the night of the election crowds flocked down to Peckham from all parts of London, and the scenes following the announcement of the poll, when the Conservative

Candidate was declared elected, excited unfavourable comment from responsible Conservative quarters.

When the new Member walked up the floor of the House of Commons with his sponsors the following day there were the usual cheers from his own side. Each "Hear, hear" from the Conservative Benches was met with cries of "Beer, beer" from the Liberal and Labour Benches. One Member sarcastically invited all total abstainers to give a loud cheer for their new recruit.

The most abiding interest of the election was that it initiated a general discussion on outside intervention at elections, which led ultimately to a legal provision to the effect that any expenditure in support of a person's candidature from any source must be included within the amount of his election expenses as limited by law.

The death of the Duke of Devonshire on the 24th March, 1908, severed one of the few remaining links with the Gladstonian period. Eloquent tributes to this great statesman were paid from both sides in Lords and Commons. The House of Lords, at the suggestion of Lord Rosebery, adjourned as a mark of special respect.

Although the Duke had never made any pretence to be an orator, historians recognised that he was the greatest force in the defeat of the two most effective public speakers of his time. It was common ground that his was the voice that influenced a sufficient number of Liberals to secure the defeat of Mr. Gladstone's Home Rule Bill of 1886. His example undoubtedly prevented Mr. Chamberlain from capturing the bulk of the Liberal Unionist Party for Tariff Reform.

Mr. Asquith expressed more vividly than any other statesman the source and secret of this commanding influence. Speaking in the House of Commons, he said:

> The Duke was a conspicuous example of single-minded devotion to duty, inflexible courage and tranquil indifference to praise or blame.

More bluntly it might be said that the man in the street always spoke of the Duke of Devonshire as a man who had no axe to grind.   His death was a severe loss to every cause he espoused.

On a Sunday afternoon in April of 1908 a rumour—incredulously received at first—circulated through the Clubs that the Prime Minister had resigned.

In this instance rumour had a truthful tongue.   A courier had actually arrived at Biarritz, where the King was staying, bearing a request from Sir Henry Campbell-Bannerman to be relieved of his responsibilities "on the urgent representation of his medical advisers".

After coming into his own at the end of a long period of patient, plodding public service, the homely Scottish gentleman found the burden too great.   No difference of opinion existed as to his successor.   The King sent for Mr. Asquith, whose acceptance of Office as Prime Minister was announced on the 8th April.

Sir Henry Campbell-Bannerman had worn his armour to the very close of his part in the fray.   He passed to his final rest only seventeen days after his resignation.   Touching references to the excellent qualities of a courtly, kind-hearted, honourable man were made in speeches from Members and Leaders of all Parties.

In accordance with custom, on the resignation of a Prime Minister all the Members of the Government tendered their resignations, leaving a free hand to the new Prime Minister in the choice of his colleagues.

There were few changes, and these were necessitated by promotions following upon the appointment of Mr. Lloyd George as Chancellor of the Exchequer in place of Mr. Asquith. In the case of heads of Departments moved from one Office to another no bye-elections were necessary, but when Mr. Winston Churchill, who, as Under-Secretary to the Colonies was till now merely the assistant to the head of his Department, became President of the Board of Trade in succession to Mr. Lloyd George, it was a new appointment to an "Office of profit under the Crown", and according to the Constitution he was compelled to seek re-election for North-West Manchester—which constituency he had represented since 1906.

The Conservatives concentrated all their energies in a determined effort to defeat Mr. Churchill. The Liberals were equally enthusiastic. Mr. Lloyd George spoke in the constituency, despite an old tradition that Cabinet Ministers should take no part in bye-elections. After a spirited contest Mr. Churchill was defeated and the seat won for the Conservatives by Mr. (afterwards Sir) William Joynson-Hicks. The victor declared that he had been returned by people who desired "to put a nail in the coffin of this miserable Government". Mr. Churchill was afterwards returned for Dundee.

Mr. Asquith, as Chancellor of the Exchequer, had already prepared his financial proposals. Before handing the Office over to Mr. Lloyd George he completed the first stage by a Budget speech that made history in that it outlined the scheme for Old Age Pensions.

Provision for the aged poor had been the dream for many years of politicians, orators and writers. In concise, unemotional business terms this practical man from Yorkshire gave shape and form to these cherished humanitarian visions.

The proposals were eventually embodied in a Bill which was carried by an overwhelming majority, composed of men of all Parties in the House of Commons. Exception was taken to it by some economists who contended that any scheme of Pensions should be based upon contributions by the pensioner. This view found a good deal of favour in discussion inside and outside the House, but was not translated into votes. Only twenty-nine Members of the Unionist Party and two old-world Liberals voted against the Second Reading of the Bill.

In the House of Lords some pessimistic utterances fell from a few peers, one of whom, Lord Lansdowne, described the measure as:

> one which will weaken the moral fibre of the nation and diminish the self-respect of our people.

The Lords, however, passed the Bill, and it received the Royal Assent on the 1st August.

Chapter 27

OLYMPIC GAMES. MINERS' HOURS
POLITICAL RECORDS

THE Marathon Race was a prevailing topic of interest in the summer of 1908. A Franco-British Exhibition was opened in London, thus developing the Anglo-French good relations. Some eighty French Senators and Deputies visited the Exhibition. They received the good wishes of the King and were entertained at the House of Commons. In connection with the Exhibition the Olympic Games were brought to Great Britain. This revival of the ancient Greek festival by delegates from different nations had been celebrated appropriately first in Athens, afterwards in Paris, and St. Louis. The games included every form of sport, but public excitement concentrated on the Marathon Race from Windsor Castle to the Stadium in the Exhibition grounds commemorative of the famous run of the Greek messenger to Athens with the news of the victory of Marathon. The first competitor to arrive was the Italian Dorando Pietri who collapsed near the winning post and had to be given assistance. This disqualified him, and J. Hayes, an American, became the winner; but Queen Alexandra presented a special prize to Pietri. The sports undoubtedly stimulated the public enthusiasm for Athletics.

Members of Parliament with alternating devotion to these interesting incidents outside and their duties at Westminster during the warm days and nights had been watching the progress of an event of considerable importance to the Labour party. Year after year the miners had held aloof, but at a meeting of the Miners' Federation of Great Britain it was now decided by two hundred and thirteen thousand, one hundred and thirty-seven votes to one hundred and sixty-eight thousand, two hundred and ninety-four that the Federation should become affiliated with the Labour Representation Committee. The Midlands and

North Wales showed majorities against the proposal, but eventually came into line with the majority.

Mr. John Wilson, the veteran leader of the Durham miners, was an old Liberal, and sturdily declined to join any other Party. Out of loyalty—so it was understood—to one who had served them well for so many years men in his area also refused to attach themselves to the Labour Party, but in later years they came into line with the other miners' unions.

In Parliament a further step in the direction of regulating conditions of labour was taken in the passage of the Coal Mines (Eight Hours) Bill. In former times the miners themselves differed acutely on the subject; the older leaders—more particularly from Northumberland and Durham—strongly objected to State interference. On the other hand, some mine owners—and Conservatives—had supported Bills brought forward from time to time for a legal eight-hours day in the interest of uniformity.

Mr. Herbert Gladstone, as Home Secretary, now introduced a Bill as a Government measure. It was opposed by several Conservatives, and one or two Liberals.

A feature of the Debate was a speech in opposition to the Bill from Mr. Stanley Baldwin, who had very shortly before this been returned at a bye-election as Member for the Bewdley Division of Worcestershire. The new Member mentioned as indicating the line he might be expected to take in Debates of this kind that although his family had been engaged for one hundred and thirty years in trade, the disputes they had had with their men could be numbered on the fingers of one hand. He himself, he said, had been in active business for twenty years and had never had the shadow of a dispute with any of his own men. In the sheet iron rolling trade his firm had already given their men an eight-hour day—long before the question had excited any interest in the political world. He, however, opposed the regulation of the hours in mines by legislation, and predicted that it would be prejudicial to trade.

This particular Debate was adjourned, but the Government

kept the Bill in being, and at a later stage it became an Act of Parliament.

All this while the Suffragist agitation had been carried on unceasingly in the country. On Wednesday, the 20th May, Mr. Asquith had met a deputation of Liberal Members, and to them he gave an undertaking that the Government intended to introduce during the current Parliament a comprehensive Reform Bill dealing with the anomalies of the existing franchise under which men were entitled to vote for Members of Parliament. A proposal for the inclusion of women as voters might then be made as an amendment to the Bill, and the decision would be left to an open vote of the House of Commons. The Deputation expressed their satisfaction, but the "militants" demanded immediate action by the Government.

Since the demonstration in the Gallery in 1906 there had been numerous incidents in the Lobbies and approaches to the House, and in October, 1908, the Chamber itself was again invaded. The women endeavoured to march in procession to the House of Commons, but were prevented by the Police under the ancient Orders of Parliament, by which it is illegal for any procession to approach within one mile of Westminster while Parliament is in Session. While this was going on in the streets a scene astounding to old parliamentarians was being enacted within the House. Just inside the outer door of the Chamber, leading off the Members' Lobby, there is a second door with a glass panel at the side. One of the special privileges of a Member was that he might bring a lady visitor to this panel, through which, by standing on a little stool, she might look at the House from a different point to that presented from the Gallery behind the Speaker's Chair.

This evening an ardent Suffragette was escorted to the panel by one of the Members. While the doors were swinging backwards and forwards as men passed in and out, the lady suddenly leapt off the stool and ran through the door. Rushing up the floor of the House, she shouted "Give justice to women". For a moment she stood there, before the astonished gaze of the startled House, but was very quickly hurried out by the attendants. According to the researches of capable authorities, this lady was the first "stranger" unbidden by the Speaker to cross the Bar with the House in full Session since the halberdiers marched up the floor on that momentous occasion when Oliver Cromwell, pointing to the mace, shouted: "What shall we do with this bauble? Here, take it away!" One or two people have since tried to copy the lady's example, but their efforts have been less dramatic.

A little while after the appearance of the invading Suffragist Mr. (afterwards Sir) J. F. Remnant, the Member for Holborn, who was addressing the House on the Licensing Bill, suddenly found himself in competition with a shrill voice from behind the grille. He continued to discuss licensing; the unauthorised orator discoursed on "Votes for women". Mr. Remnant held his own for a while, but his rival was backed by an improvised "claque". Officials rushed up to the Gallery and found that the undesirable visitors had come to stay.

By the satire of fate the iron grille, originally a symbol of security against feminine intrusion, had been converted into a rampart of Suffragism. The demonstrators had brought with them chains and padlocks, and secured themselves to the bars of the grille. Nothing could be done until the whole grating was removed from its socket, and then the bodies of the "disorderly strangers" were borne forth on the iron frames, to be detached therefrom in due course at a more convenient part of the building.

On the ninth of November the woman's cause scored a peaceful victory. Under the powers recently granted Aldeburgh elected Mrs. Garrett Anderson as Mayor and thus the first woman to hold that ancient office was duly installed.

A further stage in the struggle between the two Houses of Parliament was registered when the Licensing Bill went up to the House of Lords. The most interesting constitutional feature of the conflict was a meeting of Conservative and Unionist Peers at Landsowne House, at which a decision was arrived at that the Bill should be rejected on Second Reading in the House of Lords.   Lord Lansdowne, ordinarily the perfection of strict etiquette, whose courtly manners had made him an ideal Foreign Minister, created grave doubts as to the wisdom of calling a Conference at his private house. It was urged by people not usually opposed to the Conservative Party that in the circumstances the Debate in the House was reduced to a meaningless form. The Bill was thrown out by the Lords, and a few days later, speaking at the National Liberal Club, Mr. Asquith said:

> I invite the Liberal Party to-night to treat the Veto of the House of Lords as a dominating issue in politics—the dominating issue because in the long run it overshadows and absorbs every other.

One more effort was made to settle the Education question. A correspondence took place between Mr. Walter Runciman, who had succeeded Mr. McKenna as Education Minister, and the Archbishop of Canterbury as to the possibility of arriving at such an understanding as could be put into an agreed Bill. The attempt failed and the Education problem was left to Time's leisurely solution.

Chapter 28

BATTLESHIPS AND BATTLECRIES

ON the 1st January, 1909, men and women over seventy years of age, by the Bill passed the previous autumn, became entitled to pensions under conditions embodied in the following scale:—

"If the yearly means of the pensioner were under £21, the pension was 5s. per week; from £21 to £23 12s. 6d.—4s.; £26 5s. 0d.—3s.; £26 5s. 0d. to £28 17s. 6d.—2s.; £28 17s. 6d. to £31 10s. 0d.—1s. Over £31 10s. 0d., no pension.

The New Year saw the development of other social activities. The Tariff Reformers were beginning to think of the next Election, and a Confederacy was formed, directed by a Council of twelve, said to be well supplied with money, whose object was to prevent the return of any Free Trade Unionists to Parliament.

It was expected that a Unionist majority might be obtained at the next General Election of from thirty to fifty, and that fifteen or twenty Free Food Unionists, if returned, might frustrate its Fiscal aims. Sixteen well-known "Free Traders", including Lord Robert Cecil, were therefore "marked down". One of Lord Robert's meetings was broken up.

The Confederates in the House aimed at the more peaceful methods of securing the reduction of the "Free Fooders" through the Conservative Associations. The name of Mr. Bonar Law was given as the principal "Confederate".

Apart from Home politics, international affairs were growing in interest. King Edward went to Berlin, thus returning a visit which the German Emperor had made to Windsor the previous year. The British Sovereign was cordially received by the Kaiser and his subjects, but this interchange of hospitality had no lasting effect in combating a growing feeling that Germany had designs upon this country. An atmosphere of suspicion began to settle upon popular opinion. "An Englishman's Home", a play produced at Wyndham's Theatre written by Major (afterwards Lieut.-Col.) du Maurier of the Royal Fusiliers, aimed at advocating National Service in preference to games. The play presumed an invasion by the troops of the "Northern Emperor" and depicted a ludicrous failure on the part of the Territorial Forces to resist it.

The subjects for the coming Session of Parliament were thus, by the trend of circumstances, the Navy and the "Popular" Budget which Mr. Lloyd George had foreshadowed. In the previous Session the Chancellor of the Exchequer referred to the sources from which he might get the necessary money, and in the course of a speech in Committee on Old Age Pensions he said "I have no nest egg; I am looking or someone's hen roost to rob next year". Mr. Lloyd George endeavoured to modify this by referring to his "bad jest" and disclaiming any vindictive spirit in his financial plans. The jest had, however, been crystallised into a popular catch-cry which no explanation could silence or modify.

At the Opening of Parliament attention was again called to the distressing subject of Unemployment. A procession of wives and children of the unemployed, kept at the legal distance of one mile from the House, was accompanied by a car with the representation of a dilapidated cottage labelled "The Englishman's Home".

The demand for more battleships to repel a possible invasion—"Dreadnoughts", as they were called from the name of the latest pattern—grew week by week. It was stated that Mr. McKenna, who had become First Lord of the Admiralty in the reshuffle of Offices, was in favour of naval extension, and that certain other Ministers were in favour of keeping down the estimates. Mr. George Wyndham, speaking at Wigan, declared:

> We want eight,
> And we won't wait.

This couplet became the refrain of a song chanted at public meetings, especially around London, where the agitation for a bigger Navy was taken up enthusiastically, although it attracted less attention in the industrial districts.

In the course of a Debate upon a Vote of Censure on the Government for its Naval policy, Sir Edward (afterwards Viscount) Grey said no Government could pledge itself to eight: they had first to take stock, and then formulate their programme. He also urged that matters affecting the Navy should not be treated as Party questions. Mr. Asquith, winding up the Debate, declared that the Government would maintain unchallenged our command of the sea. There was no cause for anxiety, but there was ground for precaution.

Mr. Stanley Baldwin made his second speech in the House of Commons shortly after this. It was devoted to the ubiquitous Tariff problem—never absent from any question affecting either security or Social Reform. The suggestion was made that we were weakened by the departure of capital to other countries. Mr. Baldwin moved a Resolution calling attention to this subject, and asserted that investors were favouring foreign securities because of the foreign competition with which British producers had to contend.

Mr. Winston Churchill, in the course of a scathing speech in winding up the Debate, said:

> What a situation! What an exhibition of patriotism. At a moment when, according to the right honourable gentlemen opposite, supreme exertions are needed to maintain the safety of this country persons who have fortunes and whose wealth is great in this world are engaged in rapidly making investments in foreign countries in order that they may thereby be able to dodge the Income Tax Commissioners.

Tariff Reformers vehemently protested that the retort was merely an effort to turn the edge of the Debate, but Liberals in the country seized upon it and declared that the men who were demanding more battleships should, if consistent, be the most ready to make sacrifices in order to purchase them.

On one Social problem the Government found general support. The steps taken in past Sessions to deal with Sweated Industries now bore fruit. A Bill on similar lines to that for which Mr. Toulmin had secured approval in principle was brought in as a Government measure by Mr. H. J. Tennant, the Parliamentary Secretary to the Board of Trade, who had taken a deep interest in questions affecting the lives of the people and whose gifted wife (formerly Miss May Abraham) was a strenuous supporter of all movements for improving the lot of women workers. The measure was duly passed and thus a minimum wage was legally established in those industries where the greatest distress existed.

"Dreadnoughts" and Tariffs were for a while thrust into the background by a new religious controversy. Conflicting opinions as to the efficacy or the desirability of an Established Religion were recorded in the history of the Victorian period, but so far as the Church of England in England was concerned the subject had become one of those matters once described by Mr. Gladstone as "not within the range of practical politics". A very large number of people up and down the country were opposed to the principle of any particular Denomination being established and endowed by law, but the question was very seldom raised on public platforms or in ordinary political discussions.

In Wales, however, matters were entirely different. There, the Non-Conformists had never ceased to contend that the Church of England was not the Church of Wales; that the early centuries' endowments were national property; and that the tithes—the payment of a certain amount of money by the occupiers of the land as representing the last sheaf in every ten originally given to the Church—were if applied to one faith only an unjust burden upon people who voluntarily maintained their own places of Worship.

Church people replied that the Church in Wales, although under the same spiritual jurisdiction as the Church of England, was an ancient Welsh Institution, and that to deprive it of its ancient property or to its right to the tithes would be spoliation.

The Prime Minister brought in a Bill for the disestablishment of the Welsh Church and for vesting its endowments in public bodies, and although in the pressure of work its progress was not immediately expedited it was the source of another series of thrilling parliamentary situations.

Chapter 29

THE "BIG BUDGET". TRAGEDY AND HEROISM

M R. LLOYD GEORGE'S Budget of 1909 will never be forgotten by any politician of that day.

There are traditions of the great Gladstonian financial statements extending into hours, but there is no parallel in modern times to that spring evening when Mr. Lloyd George unfolded ream after ream of notes.

According to the Official Report, the Chancellor of the Exchequer rose at "six minutes after three of the clock" and sat down finally at "three minutes before eight of the clock".

Setting out with the enthusiasm of an orator accustomed to move multitudes in one thrilling hour, he discussed multifarious political problems with a glowing peroration to each section.

After a while it became obvious that he could not last the pace.   One of those incidents which make parliamentary life worth living relieved the tension.   Mr. Balfour, Leader of the Opposition, whose part it was to attack, harass and by all fair means defeat his opponent, observing that the Chancellor of the Exchequer was overstraining himself, quietly suggested that the House should adjourn for a while, in order to give the right honourable Gentleman an opportunity for rest and recuperation.   The Sitting was accordingly adjourned for half-an-hour.

In the course of his speech Mr. Lloyd George said the building of four Dreadnoughts represented nearly twopence, and the building of eight represented nearly fourpence on the income tax.   He added that whatever the cost, no great country could afford to shirk responsibility for the defence of its coasts against every possible invader.   To risk it in the present temper of the nations would be not Liberalism but lunacy.   He went on to speak of his hopes of extending the benefits of Old Age Pensions, of introducing legislation to deal with Unemployment and other social reforms.

Having thus skilfully prepared the "Imperialists" and Social Reformers for the necessity of finding more money, he began to enumerate the various sources from which he expected to get his increased taxes.

Every proposal in this direction touched some nerve spot. Motor cars, licences for the sale of intoxicating liquors, financial transactions for the purchase and sale of shares, leases of land, land itself—one interest after another heard its fate pronounced and wondered what would come next.

The Chancellor of the Exchequer reminded owners of property that the growth of property was due to security:

more money was required for security. He proposed a super-tax on all income over five thousand pounds, adjusted the duties on the estates left by deceased persons by increasing the burden on the big estates; he proposed a twenty per cent. tax on the unearned increment of land, a halfpenny in the pound on the capital value of undeveloped land. He raised the duty on spirits, tobacco, cigars and cigarettes. Brewers, distillers and wine merchants were all called upon to contribute more to the Exchequer, and after distributing his favours he concluded his five hours' speech with these words:

> This is a War Budget : it is for raising money to wage im-placable warfare against poverty and squalidness. I cannot help hoping and believing that before this generation has passed away we shall have advanced a great step towards that good time when poverty and wretchedness and human degra-dation which always follows in its company will be as remote to the people of this country as the wolves which once infested its forests.

When the full meaning of the taxes began to dawn upon all those influences affected, onslaughts rapidly followed from one source after another.

Lord Lansdowne declared the proposals to be a monument of reckless and improvident finance. The Conservatives and Unionists generally described the Budget as a colossal piece of Socialistic propaganda, and Tariff Reformers contended that there were now only two alternatives before the country —Socialism or Tariff Reform. Mr. John Redmond and the Irish Nationalists denounced the tax on whisky as prejudicial to a national industry. The Budget was condemned by an "All-Ireland" Meeting in Dublin, and the Corporation of Dublin City exercised one of their ancient privileges.

One afternoon it was observed that the brass rod at the bar of the House of Commons was drawn out. Before the commencement of business the doors were thrown open and the Serjeant-at-Arms announced:

"The Lord Mayor of the City of Dublin!"

"Let the Lord Mayor be introduced", said the Speaker.

The Lord Mayor, Sheriffs and Town Clerk, in the full robes of their Office, then advanced to the bar.

"What have you there, my Lord Mayor of Dublin?", asked the Speaker.

"A petition from the Lord Mayor, Aldermen and Burgesses of Dublin", replied the Lord Mayor.

Mr. Henry Campbell, the Town Clerk of Dublin, then read the petition, which represented "To the House of Commons of the United Kingdom of Great Britain and Ireland in Parliament assembled" *inter alia* that the proposals to raise increased revenue embodied in the Finance Bill now before Parliament "are calculated to seriously interfere with the trade and commerce and agriculture of Ireland".

"Let the petition be brought to the Table", said the Speaker, when the Town Clerk had completed his recital of the fifteen clauses and had concluded with the assurance that "your petitioners will ever pray".

Sir Courtenay Ilbert, the Clerk to the House of Commons, then "proceeded to the bar, received the petition and placed it upon the Table".

The Lord Mayor, Sheriffs and Town Clerk, after mutual bows, retired.

In ordinary circumstances a petition from any corporate body or group of persons would be formally handed in by a Member of the House, but, like the Corporation of the City of London, the Dublin Corporation had the privilege of presenting their own petition.

A "Budget-League" was formed by Liberal Members to conduct a vigorous campaign. This was countered by an equally determined "Budget Protest League" formed by the Conservatives.

The whole country was profoundly shocked at the news of the murder of Sir W. Curzon Wyllie, Aide-de-camp to the Secretary of India, at the India Office on July 1st, at the conclusion of a Reception. The murderer was a Hindu engineering student. The atrocity called forth very strong denunciation both in India and in England. A meeting

L

of natives of India in London, held at the Caxton Hall, expressed horror and abhorrence at the outrage. The assassin was eventually tried and hanged.

In the summer of 1909 Lieutenant Shackleton returned from a great achievement in the Antarctic Regions. Accompanied by Messrs. Adams, Marshall and Wild, he had come within ninety-seven geographical miles of the South Pole and made a series of useful explorations in the course of a return journey through terrible hardships and dangers. It was one of the most successful expeditions in the history of Polar exploration.

In the last stage of their progress towards the Pole Shackleton and his three companions, without any dogs or other help, pushed on, in grim determination, for nearly three hundred geographical miles and came nearer to either Pole than any other human beings in then recorded history. On his arrival home Lieut. Shackleton was knighted by the King.

Chapter 30

UNIVERSITY DEVELOPMENTS
TIRED LEGISLATORS

THE Charter of Incorporation granted to the University of Bristol in 1909 was a stage in a continuous advancement towards general University Education in England.

The Scottish Universities for very many years had provided instruction to students whose means would have precluded them from the advantages of University training in England. The University of Wales got its Charter in 1893. Generous scholarships had been provided at Oxford and Cambridge and good work had been done by Durham but this only met the case of the few. For the general body of middle class people in England London University up to 1900 was the source of scholastic awards. London however was a University in name rather than in fact until the end of the 19th century. Its degrees were a very high test of merit but it was really an examining body and in this capacity it provided a goal for students all over the world. In 1900 the University of London was reconstituted and brought into closer touch with those institutions engaged in higher education inside the " Greater London " area. The Senate was empowered to admit as "schools of the University" institutions situated within the administrative county of London, and not carried on for the private gain or profit of the owners, if they provided education of the university standard. The Senate also had authority to recognise as teachers of the University any members of the teaching staffs of Public Educational Institutions within a radius of 30 miles whether schools of the University or not. Matriculated students at schools of the University, or students under recognised teachers, were made eligible under certain conditions for recognition as "internal students". The linked-up colleges gave instruction to the internal students while the external students pursued their studies where they pleased. The degrees conferred upon internal and external students represented as far as possible the same standard of knowledge and attainments. The general scheme was in effect a compromise between the views of different schools of reformers. Many people would have protested strongly if the examining body—as such—had disappeared or been completely merged in the teaching university. It cannot be said that the controversy was closed at this date. There were still advocates of a residential university for London with all the communal life and mild discipline associated therewith. This topic came up again at subsequent stages of educational discussion.

More important even than the changes in London University was the progressive establishment of teaching Universities in the principal cities. The movement had some excellent University Colleges as a foundation. Birmingham obtained its Charter for a University in 1900. This was a development of the Mason College founded by Sir Josiah Mason in 1880. Owen's College Manchester named after a Manchester merchant, who bequeathed ninety-six thousand pounds for its foundation, was established in 1851 with the object of affording students unable to meet the expenses of Oxford or Cambridge the opportunity of obtaining something akin to the class of education provided at those centres. In 1880 Owen's College had been granted a Charter as the Victoria University founded and established with a kind of federal constitution under which Owen's and other provincial colleges were to form a University with the power to grant degrees.

The example of Birmingham was followed by Liverpool, then by Leeds. Sheffield also came into line and afterwards, as already mentioned, Bristol. Each one of these cities acquired a University of its own. Victoria University became the Victoria University of Manchester. Others followed in later years. University Education in Ireland at about the same time was undergoing a change. Many public men including Mr. Balfour, Sir Edward Carson and the Historian Professor Lecky had urged that some alternative should be provided to Trinity College, Dublin. The sons of Roman Catholic parents, for reasons which initiated lengthy discussions in Parliament and elsewhere, did not make use of Trinity College. Educationists, leaving aside the controversial arguments, saw clearly the need for encouraging University knowledge among the majority of the Irish people. In 1909 the problem was solved by the establishment of the National University of Ireland in Dublin and by the reconstitution of Queen's College Belfast as Queen's University.

Welsh students had the benefit of the well equipped and efficient University of Wales.

*   *   *   *   *

Through the long summer evenings the Finance Bill was fought clause by clause and line by line in the House of Commons. As "business arising out of Committee of Ways and Means" the Bill could come on after eleven o'clock, and discussion could continue till any hour. It *did* continue: night after night amendments were moved and discussed. The disposal of one set only made way for another batch. Weary men tramped the Division Lobbies through the small hours and wandered forth to their homes with the morning light unmercifully shining upon their grey faces and drooping figures.

On one of these nights in the middle of July a scene arose which led to a procedure of which there are very few examples in parliamentary history.

Throughout the evening speeches had been punctuated with continuous cross-firing and mutual interchanges of comment from both sides of the House. Between midnight and one o'clock, while Mr. Pretyman was speaking, there were some interruptions from the Labour Benches, where-upon Lord Winterton, rising to a point of order, said: "May I call your attention to the fact that the honourable Member for West Ham is not in a fit state to take part in this Debate?"

"I beg your pardon; I am as sober as you, my friend," said Mr. Will Thorne, the Labour Member for West Ham.

It is an old and accepted rule of the House that no Member may cast reflections on the sobriety of another Member. Lord Winterton was therefore called upon by the Chair to withdraw his observation.

"In my opinion," said the noble Lord, "the honourable Member is not in a fit state to take part in the proceedings, but as you, Sir, have ruled that the honourable Gentleman is in a fit state, I therefore withdraw."

The Chairman of Committees accepted this withdrawal, but other Members contended that it was not in correct form. The Chairman appealed to Members not to interrupt, and was proceeding with the business. Mr. Thorne declared that he had not interrupted anybody throughout the evening. The Chairman said he was not referring particularly to the honourable Member, but to interruptions generally. Members still persisted that the withdrawal was not sufficient. The Chairman ruled that the noble Lord had withdrawn.

"No: he repeated it", said some Members.

"There is no other possible meaning which can be attached to any words I used", replied Lord Winterton somewhat cryptically.

"If he is not prepared to withdraw, Mr. Chairman, I call him a liar", said Mr. Thorne.

"The noble Lord withdrew his statement, and the honourable Member for West Ham must not call the noble Lord a liar", said the Chairman.

"He is an absolute liar. I am as sober as any man in this House", retorted Mr. Thorne.

Following upon this, the Member for West Ham was called upon to withdraw from the House for "grossly disorderly conduct".

The incident was naturally discussed with considerable interest in the Lobby, and the Members of all Parties who had had occasion to observe Mr. Thorne, agreed that he certainly was not under the influence of liquor.

At a subsequent meeting of the House the Prime Minister moved that the record of Mr. Thorne's expulsion be "expunged from the Journals of the House".

Mr. Balfour, on behalf of the Opposition, cordially agreed that whatever steps were necessary to clear the character of the honourable Member should be taken. In the course of his brief speech on the subject he referred to the unfortunate habit that was growing up of running commentaries on speeches, but added:

I must say that of the offenders of all Parties in this House the honourable Gentlemen below the gangway [the Labour Benches] are the least offenders in this respect.

When Mr. Thorne appeared in the House at the next Sitting he expressed his appreciation of the handsome reparation made to him by the House, and added that he had received a letter from Lord Winterton which would be duly published. The letter which had been addressed to Mr. Thorne within a very few hours of the incident was published in the press. Lord Winterton wrote:

DEAR SIR,
        With reference to the incident that occurred last night, I am writing to say that I am quite satisfied as a result

of a talk with Mr. Keir Hardie that I was mistaken in making the allegation that I did against you last night, and, further, that you were not personally responsible for the continuous and disorderly interruptions upon which my allegation was based.

I fully recognise that my statement, even though subsequently withdrawn, was of a nature calculated to do your reputation harm, and I therefore have decided to express my sincere regret for having made it, and to give you permission to publish this letter, if you should so desire.

Yours faithfully,
WINTERTON.

As a consequence of the resolution of the House a reference to the Minutes of the House in any library where the Journal is kept will show on page 304 (1909) a line printed through the passage which recorded the fact that the Chairman ordered Mr. Thorne to withdraw, and in square brackets the note [This entry was expunged by the House on 16th July.]

In the whole history of Parliament very few instances can be found in which a record has been expunged, but in these strenuous days and nights still more exciting precedents were fated to be dwarfed as one new scene succeeded another.

Chapter 31

AN EPOCH. CONSTITUTIONAL PROBLEMS

ON a July day in 1909 a huge, strange bird alighted on the cliffs of Dover. People rushed down to the coast; the thing that had landed was triumphantly brought to London and exhibited to continuously passing crowds in one of the departments of Selfridge's big establishment in Oxford Street.

Newspapers enthusiastically recorded the achievement of M. Bleriot, announced to be one of the most intrepid flyers who had ever lived. Rising from the French coast in a mist, he had completed a flight in an aeroplane across the English Channel!

Millions of people had never seen an aeroplane. Thousands declared that no human contrivance could turn a man into a bird. Many of the old folk seriously thought it was blasphemous to defy the work of God by attempting it.

Balloons inflated with gas and sent up into the air to be carried whither the wind should take them were an old institution, comparatively. Aeroplane flight was only a very few years old. It was just beginning to prove itself a science. In December of 1903 Wilbur Wright was thrilled with hope when he flew for twelve seconds. The twelve seconds progressed to fifty-nine seconds. The flights became longer and longer. In 1908 Henry Farman achieved what was then a startling feat of flying from Chalon to Rheims.

These triumphs had been followed with the keenest interest by airmen. The great British public had not quite realised the possibility of mastering the air till a man in a machine heavier than air soared above the sea on the one side of the English Channel, and safely landed on the other side. For a while the stupendous victory over nature absorbed all other topics. It was accepted as a fascinating example of what might be done in this new form of sport. Very few people thought of it then as a stage in the growth of a dominating force in commerce and in war, although an Advisory Committee was actually sitting composed of eminent scientific men and representatives of the Navy and Army to superintend experiments in the construction of aeroplanes and airships. In the development of the latter, Count Zeppelin, the German inventor, had been making steady progress since his first effort in 1900, when his ship remained in the air for twenty minutes and was wrecked on landing. In 1906 he was more successful with flights at thirty miles an hour. It is said that when he first endeavoured to persuade people that the drifting balloon might be superseded by a ship that could be steered in the air his neighbours regarded him as a harmless crank.

The week before Bleriot landed on the cliffs of Dover—from the 17th to the 24th July—the grey ships of the British Navy lined the River Thames from Southend to the Houses of Parliament. The Fleet consisting of one hundred and

forty-nine vessels was one of the most imposing sights seen
in the world's greatest city for many years. The Embank-
ment was thronged with people. The Lord Mayor paid a
State visit to the Fleet and the following day twelve hundred
Bluejackets marched through the City and were entertained
at the Guildhall. The brilliant illumination of the Ships
on the 27th July was witnessed by crowds who came from
all parts of the country. The visit was a prelude to animated
discussion in and out of Parliament on naval affairs.

International relations were now attracting public interest.
In 1908 the Labour Party, recalling events associated with
"Red Sunday" had protested against an official visit to
Russia by the King. Mr. Arthur Henderson and other
members on the Foreign Office Vote, vigorously contended
that the projected visit of the Tsar to the waters of the Solent
should not be accorded any official recognition. Sir Edward
Grey called attention to the fact that under the present
Tsar an elected Duma had been set up, and went on to say:

> The House should understand what the hon. Member for
> Barnard Castle asks us to do. He asks us to refuse the civility
> of a welcome which would be given by all our neighbours in
> Europe. He asks us to do it at a time when Constitutional
> Government has recently been established in Russia and the
> Duma is in full activity criticising the Government and receiv-
> ing explanations from the Government of the day.

The Labour Party obtained support for their protest
from some Liberals, two Bishops and four clergy and ministers
of various Denominations, but the visit took place at the
end of July and the Tsar was accorded all the honours of a
Royal visitor, with mutual expressions of hope that the
friendly relations thus exchanged would bear good fruit.

In 1909 another Australian team arrived captained by
M. A. Noble. The English team was led by A. C. Maclaren
who had been playing in tests since 1896. C. B. Fry was still
scoring well and with Hobbs made a brilliant score that won
the first match. Australia however won the rubber by two
matches to one. Two out of the five matches were unfinished.

Within the Empire another bond of sympathy was woven by the South African Constitution Bill, which welded the various Colonies into one Dominion on similar lines to those adopted in Australia some years earlier. The most interesting feature of the scene in the House of Lords at the Second Reading of the Bill was the presence of General Botha. This distinguished member of the old Transvaal Republic had been in supreme command of the Boer Forces during the greater part of the South African War. He had accepted the decision of the three years' conflict, and his bravery as a soldier was equalled by his wisdom as a statesman. In the capacity of Prime Minister of the Transvaal he was present in this country as one of the Delegation from the Legislatures of the four Colonies—Cape Colony, Natal, the Transvaal and Orange River Colony. As a Member of the Privy Council, he took his place on the steps of the Throne to witness the completion of the process of consolidation, commenced some years ago, of which the inclusion of the Transvaal and the old Orange Free State as self-governing Colonies had been a culminating factor.

All diversions, pleasant or otherwise, now led back to the Budget. The country was adding new phrases to the political dictionary, and "Limehousing" became the familiar term for full-fledged platform oratory. Addressing a public meeting at Limehouse in the vicinity of the London Docks, the Chancellor of the Exchequer defended his Budget on the strategical principle that the best form of defence is attack. In glowing Celtic fire he denounced all the opponents of the Budget. He declared that the rich had demanded further expenditure on the Navy, but now they were "howling" against their share of the expense, while the workmen were willing to pay. They had promised Old Age Pensions, but the owners of mining royalties would not "spare a copper" for the miners' pensions. The Government, he said, were raising money by the Budget to pay for provisions against poverty, unemployment and sickness. He quoted instances of the rise in the value of land, the "fines" imposed for the renewal of leases, and declared that this was not "business", but "blackmail".

Mr. Winston Churchill, in a fighting speech at Leicester, ridiculed the opposition of the Dukes to the Budget. He pictured what he described as the gap between the poor and the rich—the absence of the minimum standard of life among the workers, on the one side, and the increase of "vulgar, joyless luxuries", on the other. The tax gatherer, he said, would, under this Budget, in effect ask, not "What have you got?", but "How did you get it?"

Strong language was also used on the other side. The agent of a great Scottish Duke refused a guinea to a Football Club, on the ground of the Budget, and a number of Liberal Members of Parliament made up the money by one-shilling subscriptions. The Duke of Rutland denounced the Ministry as "pirates". This recalled the couplet by a former Duke of Rutland:

> Let wealth and commerce, laws and learning die
> But leave us still our old nobility.

Summer glided into autumn, and found the House of Commons still fighting the Budget line by line. There was no recess—only one or two very brief adjournments of the Commons during which the Lords continued to sit. The Whips allowed men off in relays for casual leave.

The House of Commons passed the Finance Bill by three hundred and seventy-nine to one hundred and forty-nine.

All eyes were turned to the House of Lords. What would they do? The Conservatives strongly advised them to reject the Budget when it came up in the form of the Finance Bill. Mr. Lloyd George, speaking at Newcastle, warned them that if they did, they might be forcing a revolution. The question would be, should five hundred men "chosen accidentally from among the unemployed" over-ride the deliberate judgment of millions engaged in the industries which made the national wealth?

It was an accepted fact that the House of Commons alone could initiate financial proposals. If any measure coming to the Commons from the House of Lords happened to contain proposals involving the expenditure of public money, it was the duty of the Speaker to call the attention of the House of Commons to the fact, and the proposal, as a matter of course, then lapsed.

The question now arose whether the House of Lords possessed the right to reject financial provisions made by the House of Commons. Constitutional lawyers differed on the point.

Lord Lansdowne, when the Bill was formally moved in the House of Lords, proposed an Amendment to the effect that:

> this House is not justified in giving its consent to this Bill until it has been submitted to the judgment of the country.

A long Debate took place on this Amendment, which practically meant the rejection of the Bill. Some Peers who objected to the Budget were in grave doubt as to the wisdom of refusing the necessary supply of money: others held that if they believed the Budget to be wrong they should reject it whatever the consequences. In the end, Lord Lansdowne was supported by three hundred and fifty Peers of various ranks, and only seventy-five voted for the Bill.

The House of Commons, on the Motion of Mr. Asquith, promptly passed a Resolution declaring the action of the other House to be:

> a breach of the Constitution and a usurpation of the rights of the Commons.

The controversy very quickly spread from the Houses of Parliament to the country. Opponents of the Budget asserted that the Lords were right in demanding that the Government should submit their proposals to the electors. Liberals indignantly repudiated the claim of the non-elected House to decide when or under what conditions the representative assembly should be elected, and the Prime Minister decided to advise an Election in order to test this constitutional point.

LORD SALISBURY

Photo, Russell, London

SIR HENRY CAMPBELL BANNERMAN

Photo, Russell, London

MR. ASQUITH

Photo, Russell, London

MR. BALFOUR

FOUR PRIME MINISTERS

Chapter 32

PLAYS AND PLAYWRIGHTS
THE ELECTION AND AFTER

THE censorship of plays was a topic of animated discussion during the first decade of the century. Many
people were deeply concerned about the tendency of some of
the newer plays. The lighter productions were declared to be
frivolous to a point beyond healthy humour, and the problem
play was said to be travelling outside the bounds of wholesome
comment. It thus became a matter of debate whether the
powers of the Censor should be strengthened, or whether
questions of taste should be left to the decision of public
opinion.

The Lord Chamberlain as a principal officer of the Royal
Household has certain important powers with respect to
licensing theatres in and about London and places where the
Sovereign in Royal person "shall occasionally reside". He
also has authority over the allowance or disallowance of
plays produced and "acted for hire" throughout Great
Britain. In this task he has the assistance of an Examiner
of Plays—usually known as the Censor. Under the Theatres
Act 1843 it is provided that:

> It shall be lawful for the Lord Chamberlain for the time
> being, whenever he shall be of opinion that it is fitting for the
> Preservation of good Manners Decorum or of the public Peace
> so to do to forbid the acting or presenting any Stage play or
> Act Scene or Part thereof or any Prologue or Epilogue or
> part thereof.

The authority is thus very wide. It was urged by some
people that its very width was its weakness. Manners and
decorum are matters of times and customs. The "public
Peace" with respect to a play cannot be easily defined. In
the exercise of his power the Lord Chamberlain with the
advice of the Censor had forbidden some plays and the

authors of these prohibited works naturally disagreed with the opinion that the authority of the Censor should be strengthened. On the contrary, they contended, with the support of other playwrights, that the Censorship ought to be abolished, or that there should be an appeal from its decision to some other authority.

A Joint Select Committee of the House of Lords and the House of Commons under the Chairmanship of Mr. (afterwards Sir) Herbert Samuel was appointed to inquire into the subject. The witnesses included a long array of distinguished literary and dramatic talent, critics, managers, and members of the public. The inquiry was open to the press and the evidence provided some entertaining passages. There was a sparkling contest of mental agility between George Bernard Shaw and members of the Committee in the course of which G.B.S. matched his epigrams against the calm cultured shrewdness of such Examiners as Lord Gorell an ex-Judge of the High Court. Onlookers were amused to see that for once G.B.S. was out of his depth.

After holding many meetings during the summer the Committee presented a Report later on to the effect that the majority of the dramatic authors were in favour of abolition or appeal on the ground that the suppression of a play "hampers the possible growth of a great drama critical of contemporary life and of customary ideas". In this view the dramatists were supported by some writers of other schools of thought. The theatrical managers on the other hand were almost unanimously in favour of the retention of the Censorship. They preferred to know beforehand whether the play could be considered officially permissible rather than take the risk of prosecutions or control through local licensing bodies. The Committee found that the retention of the Censorship was desired by a large body of public opinion—for whom the Speaker of the House of Commons was a principal witness—on the ground that its abolition would involve serious risk of a gradual demoralisation of the stage. As a compromise between different opinions the

Committee suggested that the Lord Chancellor should continue the licenses of plays but that it should be optional to produce an unlicensed play subject to a possible indictment by the Director of Public Prosecution if the play was alleged to give grounds for offence. The Report was presented in due course. The Lord Chamberlain continues in authority and all plays must be licensed by him.

Parliament and the country became absorbed in other matters. A sharp contest in the constituencies at the General Election held in January 1910 resulted in the return of two hundred and seventy-five Liberals, forty Labour Members, eighty-two Irish Nationalists and two hundred and seventy-three Conservatives and Unionists.

The Liberals had thus lost their clear majority in the House and were running neck and neck with the Conservatives. As the Labour and Irish Nationalist Members were opposed to the Veto of the House of Lords, Mr. Asquith had a practical majority of one hundred and twenty-four on this question.

When the new House assembled the most touching human note was the entrance of Mr. Joseph Chamberlain. It had been known for some time that the health of the distinguished Unionist statesman was failing. Not until this information became public had people realised that Mr. Chamberlain was in his seventy-fifth year. His vigour and vitality had led most people to think and speak of him as an active, well-preserved middle-aged man. They forgot that he was already a man of forty when he first entered Parliament in 1874 after a strenuous Municipal career.

The electors of West Birmingham loyally re-elected their old representative, and, as this was a new Parliament, every Member was called upon to take the oath. When Mr. Joseph Chamberlain was led in by Mr. Austen Chamberlain and Lord Morpeth (afterwards the Earl of Carlisle) it was all too obvious that the House must reconcile itself to the thought that henceforth its greatest debater would take no active part in its discussions. As he sat on the front Bench, Mr. Chamberlain straightened himself, and for a few moments gazed around the House with something of his old alertness, as though watching for familiar faces. His son guided his hand, and he formally signed the roll.

As usual at the beginning of a Session the Opposition were anxious to draw the Government upon their intentions. On the 3rd of March the Prime Minister in reply to a question as to what would happen if the House of Lords refused to pass the Veto resolutions replied "We had better wait and see".

On the 4th April Mr. (afterwards Sir) Alfred Tobin asked the Prime Minister a question which led to the following dialogue:

MR. TOBIN : Is it still the intention of the Government to introduce the Finance Bill without the alteration of a comma, in the sense that no alterations of substance are contemplated, but only such formal changes as have been rendered necessary by the postponement of its introduction ?

THE PRIME MINISTER : A full statement of the alterations contemplated in the Budget of last year will be made before the House is asked to assent to it.

*   *   *   *   *

MR. PEEL (afterwards Lord Peel) : Will the contemplated changes affect the question of Irish finance ?

THE PRIME MINISTER : I am afraid that we must wait and see.

*   *   *   *   *

MR. LONSDALE (afterwards Lord Armaghdale) : Will the right hon. Gentleman on the Motion in respect of the Budget fix a date for the Third Reading ?

THE PRIME MINISTER : The hon. Member had better wait and see.

EARL WINTERTON asked the Prime Minister : If it is the intention of His Majesty's Government to introduce the financial provisions for the year 1910–11 immediately after the Spring Recess ?

THE PRIME MINISTER : I cannot at present name a date for the introduction of the Budget 1910–11.

EARL WINTERTON : Having regard to the natural anxiety of those about to be taxed, can the right hon. Gentleman say whether it is possible to give the date before the rising for the Spring Recess ?

THE PRIME MINISTER : I can only repeat the answer which I have already given.   The noble Lord must wait and see.

When the Prime Minister advised the honourable Members and the noble Lord to "wait and see" there was a general laugh.   The phrase was by no means new as a parliamentary expression but it made a catchy headline for the popular newspapers; it attracted the music-hall comedians; was chaffingly shouted across the floor of the House in Debate by both sides and repeated at meetings outside.   By the time it had circulated through various other channels, the context, and indeed the fact that it had arisen out of questions and answers had been forgotten.   After a few years no power on earth could dispel the popular delusion that Mr. Asquith had made the pronouncement "wait and see" as a general declaration of his own policy.

On the points referred to in the now historic dialogue, matters did not wait long.   Resolutions were carried asserting the rights of the Commons.   The Budget was amended in some respects, more particularly with regard to the duties on spirits, and sent up to the House of Lords.   This time the Budget was passed by the Upper House, but the problem of the relations between the two Chambers remained.   The Lords were prepared to admit that the possession of a peerage should not carry with it a seat in the House of Lords.   The Commons were not at the moment concerned with the composition of the "other place".   They were insistent upon withdrawing the right of the House of Lords to veto Bills from the Commons.

Chapter 33

DEATH OF KING EDWARD

ALL controversy was suddenly silenced at the beginning of May.   The death of King Edward VII was a shock

M

to this country, and, indeed, the civilised world. The universal popularity of the Monarch who, in a brief reign of nine years, made himself a foremost figure throughout all lands had been a beneficent influence in public affairs.

In accordance with customary procedure, a Privy Council Meeting was called on the 7th May, 1910, attended by Members of the Council and the Lord Mayor of the City of London. To them King George V said: "It is my sorrowful duty to announce to you the death of my dearly beloved father, the King". In the course of a brief address, and in a voice of deep emotion, the new King added: "I have lost not only a father's love, but the affectionate and intimate relations of a dear friend and adviser". King George declared that to follow in the footsteps of one so well beloved would be the earnest object of his life.

The Accession Proclamation was then signed by the Privy Council and the representatives of the City. Two days later the Duke of Norfolk, as Earl Marshal, attended by high officers of the Heralds' College, appeared on the balcony at St. James's Palace in official robes, with State trumpeters, and read the Proclamation as follows:

Whereas it has pleased Almighty God to call to His Mercy our late Sovereign Lord King Edward the Seventh, of Blessed and Glorious Memory, by whose Decease the Imperial Crown of the United Kingdom of Great Britain and Ireland is solely and rightfully come to the High and Mighty Prince George Frederick Ernest Albert:

We, therefore, the Lords Spiritual and Temporal of this Realm being here assisted with these of His late Majesty's Privy Council, with numbers of other principal gentlemen of quality, with the Lord Mayor, Aldermen, and Citizens of London, do now hereby, with one voice and consent of tongue and heart, publish and proclaim

That the High and Mighty Prince George Frederick Ernest Albert is now, by the death of our late Sovereign of happy memory, become our only lawful and rightful Liege Lord George the Fifth by the Grace of God, King of the United Kingdom of Great Britain and Ireland, and of the British

Dominions beyond the Seas, Defender of the Faith, Emperor of India ; to whom we do acknowledge all faith and constant obedience, with all hearty and humble affection ; beseeching God, by whom Kings and Queens do reign, to bless the Royal Prince George the Fifth with long and happy years to reign over us.

The Proclamation was next read at Charing Cross, and the Heralds proceeded towards the City of London.

Under the ancient custom and charter of London all persons however distinguished are "admitted into the City". Until quite late in the nineteenth century "Old Temple Bar", a huge gateway, stood at the boundary line outside the Temple between the City of London and the Strand. The Bar disappeared as the ever-increasing roll of traffic made it more and more a hindrance to business, but in order to maintain the old tradition a silken cord has since been drawn across the street at this point on ceremonial occasions.

The Lord Mayor, Aldermen and Sheriffs, in their scarlet gowns, approached the cord from the City side. The Heralds' procession halted on the outer side, and, having stated the nature of their mission, were duly received into the City by the Lord Mayor. The Proclamation was then read to the assembled crowds and the procession moved on to the Royal Exchange in the centre of the City, where it was again read. In Edinburgh, Dublin and the big provincial cities the Civic Authorities also read the Proclamation in public.

Addresses from both Houses of Parliament conveyed the profound sentiments of the people.

In one respect the procedure differed from that adopted on the death of Queen Victoria : when there was no recognised Labour Party in the House. On this occasion the new Party spoke through Mr. Enoch Edwards, a miners' Member, who, in a brief, effective speech, paid a touching tribute to the affection which the late King had inspired in the homes of the people.

The leaders of the two main political Parties desired to avoid a Constitutional struggle at the commencement of a new reign.

The advanced Liberals and the Nationalist and Labour Members were doubtful of the practicability of any effort to make terms with the House of Lords, but early in June a Conference, consisting of four Ministers and four of the Opposition Leaders, met in the Prime Minister's room behind the Speaker's Chair. An official statement was afterwards issued to the effect that other meetings would be held, that the proceedings would be strictly confidential and the discussions untrammelled.

While these meetings were in progress, ordinary Party debate was in effect muzzled, but the House of Commons obtained controversial exercise in some spirited Debates on a subject that cut across ordinary Party divisions.

A Conciliation Committee on Woman's Suffrage was formed, with the Earl of Lytton as Chairman, to draft a Bill which was expected to secure the widest possible number of supporters. It was understood that this Committee had the support of Mr. Winston Churchill, as well as of other leading men on both sides. The Bill was first moved by Mr. David Shackleton from the Labour Benches, who said he spoke for an Official Committee representing every section in the House. The short purpose of the measure was to make it possible that women who already had votes for the Municipal Elections—women who were householders in their own right—should also have the right to vote at Parliamentary Elections.

The subsequent Motion that "the Bill be now read a second time" was seconded by Sir John Rolleston, a well-known Conservative Member. Sir John referred to the suggestion that the movement was prejudiced by the methods of the militant Suffragists, but observed on this point:

> In every pack there are some hounds that run riot, and they are not the worst, either.

Mr. F. E. Smith had placed an Amendment on the paper "to leave out the word 'now' and at the end of the question to add the words 'upon this day three months'". Under this courteous formality the Second Reading of a Bill is never bluntly refused. The opponents take the course of moving that it be read "six months hence" if it be brought on early in the Session, or "three months hence" if towards the end of the Session, the point being that the House will not be sitting then and therefore the Bill cannot be read.

What would happen if, when an amendment of this kind had been carried, the House sat on longer than was expected and some wag claimed to have the Bill read a second time in accordance with the decision of the House has never yet been tested—at all events in this century.

The speech made by Mr. F. E. Smith in this Debate is accepted as one of his most brilliant efforts. He regarded the Bill as not a settlement but an irrevocable step towards a wider extension of Woman Suffrage. After discussing the subject in its various aspects he concluded:

> The honourable gentleman has spoken of many illustrious women writers and those of whom the whole sex and indeed the whole community, irrespective of sex, are proud. I do not wish to decry the claim of women to intellectual distinction. I have never in the course of my observations here or elsewhere founded myself on some assumed intellectual inferiority of women. I do not believe it, but I venture to say that the sum total of human happiness, knowledge and achievement would have been almost unaffected if Sappho had never sung, if Joan of Arc had never fought, if Siddons had never played, and if George Eliot had never written. At the same time without the true functions of womanhood faithfully discharged throughout the ages the very existence of the race and the tenderest and most sacred influences which animate mankind would have disappeared. Profoundly believing, as I do, that these influences are grievously menaced by the intrusion of women into the field of politics I move the amendment which I have on the paper.

The most dramatic moment in the Debate was when Mr. Winston Churchill rose to speak and announced: "Sir, I cannot support this Bill".

From what had been said outside it was fully expected

that he would vote for the measure. He proceeded to give reasons for opposing it which were diametrically contrary to those advanced by Mr. F. E. Smith. His complaint against the Bill was that it was too restricted in its scope.

In a subsequent correspondence on the subject Lord Lytton emphatically asserted and reasserted that he had been led to assume by Mr. Churchill's own attitude that he intended to support the Bill, although Mr. Churchill denied emphatically that he had given any pledge, actual or implied, to justify this assumption.

The Second Reading of the Bill was carried by two hundred and ninety-nine to one hundred and ninety, but by three hundred and twenty to one hundred and seventy-five it was committed to a Committee of the whole House, which meant that for yet another Session the bowl of Tantalus was held over those who thirsted for the Suffrage.

As usual, the vote showed a division of opinion between Leaders of both Parties. Mr. Asquith opposed the moderate Bill, as he had opposed others. Mr. Lloyd George, like Mr. Churchill, opposed it on the ground that it was too narrow and undemocratic. Mr. Balfour and Mr. Bonar Law supported the Bill, Sir Edward (afterwards Lord) Carson voted against it.

The Government found themselves involved in a triangular duel upon another question of immediate and vital importance. They were being pressed in various quarters to increase their naval programme and they were also called upon to defend it for its alleged magnitude by some of their own followers and supporters and by Members of the Labour Party. In his Navy Estimates Mr. McKenna made provision for an expenditure of some forty million, six hundred thousand pounds, as compared with some thirty-five million odd in the previous year.

This programme was condemned as insufficient by the Imperial Maritime League, who demanded a shipbuilding loan of one hundred millions, and also by those who opposed increased expenditure on armaments on the ground that they were wasteful and provocative. Mr. McKenna, defending the position of the Government, said:

> Our motto is to be safe and to be sober : if we asked the House of Commons for less than we are asking we should not be sure of being safe ; but I am certain that if we asked for more we should not be sober.

On a Motion to reduce the vote for shipbuilding by two million pounds, two hundred and ninety-eight Members supported the Government and seventy voted for a reduction.

Chapter 34

NORTH POLE DISCOVERED
SENTIMENT AND PROGRESS

COMMANDER PEARY was the hero of the British people in May and June of 1910 when he arrived in this country bringing with him the laurels of victory from the Arctic regions. Peary was born at Cresson, Pennsylvania in 1856. He held a commission in the United States Navy but his sea-faring career was principally directed to that dream of explorers through the long centuries—the discovery of the North Pole.

He conducted various expeditions. In one of these in 1891 he was accompanied by his wife. Mrs. Peary was the first white woman to join an Arctic exploration party. She returned again with her husband on a later expedition and their daughter was born at their Winter quarters. Valuable information was obtained in one journey after another. With the knowledge thus acquired and the complete confidence of the Eskimos who cordially co-operated with him Commander Peary set out in the "Roosevelt" for what proved to be his triumphal voyage.

When he reached the ice-field Peary, founding his plan on the lessons acquired in previous adventures, organised a lightly equipped advance party to find the best route. The main party followed on with sledges bearing provisions and all necessary articles. As the provisions were used up a small section was detailed to take back the empty sledges. The remaining party thus pushed on, fully equipped for their needs, and unhampered by superfluous baggage. On the march the advance party built snow houses and slept in them till the main party arrived. Then they started for another stage and the main party took their rest in the snow huts. Nursing the energy of his party and husbanding his resources the experienced leader approached the final stage in good form for the supreme test. Day by day the goal drew nearer and on the 6th April 1909 the Stars and Stripes floated over the North Pole.

The news of this triumph for our kinsman of the great English speaking race was received with sporting enthusiasm in Great Britain. The narrative of the journey, given by Commander Peary to a special meeting of the Geographical Society at the Albert Hall, was followed with glowing interest. In the hundreds of years of Arctic exploration men of many nationalities had approached this world-sought geographical spot. The pages of innumerable books of adventure have been filled with their exploits. Youth has gone forth in its pride and missed the goal. A weather hardened American fifty-four years of age won the coveted victory and he received a rousing British welcome.

*   *   *   *   *

The Auld Brig o' Ayr was a world wide topic. This ancient structure has played an important part in Scottish history and was closely associated with the life and work of Robert Burns. It is said to date from the reign of Alexander III who died in 1286. In 1786 a new bridge was commenced and the old one left standing. Burns was inspired by the spectacle to write the well known poem "The Brigs of Ayr" in the course of which he made the Auld Brig say to the New Brig:

"I'll be a Brig when ye're a shapeless cairn"

There was a weirdly prophetic truth in many of the sayings of the Scottish National poet, and in none more so than the prediction as to the bridges of Ayr. The new bridge was actually swept out of action by the floods towards the latter part of the 'seventies, while the more venerable stones and rude supports of the old bridge stood the test. The new bridge was rebuilt two years later and as time went on the ancestral brig began to give anxiety to its loyal admirers. It had to be closed in the interests of public safety but so faithful a monument to Scottish antiquity and poetry could not be permitted to become derelict. A public subscription was raised and at a cost of Ten thousand pounds the bridge was restored. It was opened in July of 1910 by the Earl of Rosebery. The enthusiasm associated with the restoration of this rugged old pile which had only its memories to commend it served as a happy reminder that in the rush and excitement of a new age sentiment was still a living force.

While Naval shipbuilding was the subject of animated discussion progress was still being made in the British Mercantile Marine. As stated in a previous chapter the world wondered when the "Lusitania" and "Mauretania" were launched. The White Star Company, whose ships—such as the "Oceanic" and "Adriatic" held high the reputation of British boats for efficiency and comfort, placed orders with Harland & Woolfe of Belfast for still bigger floating mansions. In the "Olympic" and "Titanic" built by this famous Belfast firm Ireland thus had the honour of eclipsing previous records. These two magnificent vessels showed a tonnage of over forty-five thousand, or some thirteen thousand greater than the "Mauretania".

Returning to social problems, Mr. Churchill, who had become Home Secretary shortly after the General Election, in a sympathetic speech, forecasted a scheme for reform in dealing with crime and prisons. One of the most important changes indicated was in connection with the question of permitting a period of grace before a defendant was imprisoned in default of the payment of a fine. Mr. Churchill mentioned that in the course of the year some ninety thousand persons who were fined had been sent to prison—many of whom could have paid if given time. He also remarked that there were persons who went to prison for offences containing "no element of moral turpitude", and under the new prison rules he proposed that it should not be necessary for such persons to wear the prison clothing or to be subject to other rigorous rules as applied to ordinary criminal cases. He had given instructions that all passive resisters and Suffragists should as a matter of course have the benefit of these rules. He also indicated new regulations for dealing with convicts out on licence.

His further suggestion that lectures and concerts would assist in improving the disposition of the prisoners towards reform was the subject of contemptuous humour in some quarters, but the idea was cordially taken up by experienced Prison Authorities.

For a while, interest in Home politics was diverted by a dynastic change in Portugal. The Republican Party in that country had been growing stronger and stronger, and eventually succeeded in obtaining such support from the Navy and the Army as enabled them to bring about a successful revolution. A Republic was proclaimed, and King Manoel left the country. He first went to Gibraltar and afterwards took up his residence in England.

As the year went on, rumours at home began to circulate that the conference on the House of Lords had broken down. On the day following the Lord Mayor's Show, after having been kept in existence for some five months, it held its twenty-first and final meeting. There had been times during the progress of the sittings when the guarded speeches of statesmen taking part in them suggested the possibility of good results, but an official report was now issued to the effect that the conference had come to an end without arriving at an agreement.

Mr. Asquith advised His Majesty to dissolve Parliament. This was regarded as a bold stroke in some quarters, a quixotic tempting of fate in others.

Before the dissolution was announced a Bill was formally brought in providing that the House of Commons should have complete control over finance and that any measure of general legislation passed by the House of Commons during three successive sessions spread over not less than two years should become law, irrespective of the House of Lords if they had refused meantime to pass it.

This Bill was the foundation and substance of the Liberal policy and upon this, in the main, the election was fought.

Tariff Reform and Home Rule were discussed in the campaign, and Mr. Asquith, in reply to a question at one of his meetings, pledged the Government to bring in a Home Rule Bill if they had a majority in the next Parliament. This was referred to by Mr. John Redmond in Dublin with approval, and attacked by Opposition Leaders. Mr. Balfour, speaking at Dartford, said the Parliament Bill was a device to get Home Rule through.

The result of the Election was strangely like that of the previous one: two hundred and seventy-two Liberals, forty-two Labour and eighty-four Irish Nationalists, as against two hundred and seventy-two Conservatives and Unionists (or two hundred and seventy-one, excluding the Speaker, whom everybody expected to see reinstated in the Chair as a matter of course) meant a practical majority against the House of Lords of one hundred and twenty-seven.

Having thus fought two elections in one year, older Members hoped for a settled period of existence at Westminster, little dreaming what stupendous problems would face them before they again consulted their constituencies.

Chapter 35

THE STATE ASSUMES CONTROL

FROM the Opening of Parliament in February 1911 onwards politics dominated the everyday life of the nation.

The Liberal majority of 1906 had been unwieldy. The Government, with the smaller but more compact majority, were preparing for the big and culminating conflict between the old Order and the new.

Forgotten pages of political records were unfolded, showing

the evolution of the House of Lords from ancient institutions. Historians recalled the fact that in the Assembly from which the present Parliament traces its descent, called together by Simon de Montfort in the reign of Henry III at the instigation of the powerful nobles, knights, citizens and burgesses all sat together and deliberated in common.

Incidentally Suffragists pointed out that women were an essential part of the original Assemblies. In the reign of Edward I the Abbesses of Shaftesbury, Barking, St. Mary of Winchester and of Wilton were summoned to Westminster. In the reign of Henry III too a number of ladies of high birth, including Mary, Countess of Norfolk, Alienor, Countess of Ormond, Anne Despencer, Countess of Pembroke, and Matilda, Countess of Oxford, were required by writ to give their attendance in the National Council Chamber.

Various reasons were given by historians for the separation of the burgesses from the nobility. In all the historical memories one fact remained. It was necessary that any Bill should pass both Houses before it became an Act of Parliament. The difficulty to be solved was as to what should happen when the two Houses disagreed. Hitherto a disagreement meant that the Bill was defeated. Against this virtual power of the House of Lords to decide the fate of any measure Liberals had continuously protested. The glowing oratory of Gladstone, the moving eloquence of John Bright, the declamatory protests of innumerable popular speakers at Liberal and Radical demonstrations, had proclaimed the gospel that the elected Chamber should possess the power to say the deciding word; but no working plan had been pressed to a definite conclusion.

Step by step Mr. Asquith proceeded to the task which so many men had attempted in the white heat of political fervour and left incomplete. Early in the Session of 1911 he reintroduced the Parliament Bill.

Before the Bill reached its further stages the Navy again excited attention. The estimates introduced were nearly a million pounds more than the 1910 estimates. A table was issued showing the progress of increases since 1901—when the figures stood at thirty million, nine hundred and eighty-one thousand, three hundred and fifteen pounds—to the present estimates of forty-four million, three hundred and ninety-two thousand, five hundred pounds. Still greater increases were indicated for succeeding years. There were those who thought still more money ought to have been spent, and there were others who viewed the increases with considerable disquietude. A Resolution was moved to the effect that:

This House views with alarm the enormous increases of expenditure of the Army and Navy in recent years.

An amendment to this was moved unofficially, but accepted by the Government, to the effect that:

This House views with profound anxiety and regret the continuance of the necessity for the maintenance by Great Britain of large armaments, and would welcome the establishment of international agreements for the simultaneous restriction of their armaments by the great Powers.

Sir Edward Grey, in a speech that created a profound impression upon the House, dealt with the Government's position. He declared that they must maintain "a fleet sufficient to hold the sea against any reasonably probable combination".

"Do not let it be supposed that because our estimates are increased this year our foreign relations are strained", the Foreign Minister went on to say. As to possible reductions in their futures, that, he said, must depend upon foreign naval figures. It was, he admitted, a paradox that the growing and enormous burden of military and naval expenditure in all countries was coinciding not merely with friendly relations between the Powers, but with the growth of civilisation as a whole. "It is a fact", he added, "that it is in the most civilised nations of the world that the expenditure is greatest". Replying to a suggestion that it was for us to find a way out of the evil, Sir Edward Grey said:

We certainly, I think, cannot be accused of having forced the pace. Our navy estimates for 1909 are said to have given provocation. They have not given rise to increased naval expenditure in Germany or, I believe, in any other country. The last addition to the German Naval programme was settled by law in 1908. This, further, has to be borne in mind: that though we maintain a strong navy and have announced our intention to maintain it, we do not maintain an army which can be regarded as an aggressive force, and, in my opinion, we are quite right in not doing so.

Sir Edward called attention to the fact that twice in the last twelve months the President of the United States had sketched out a step in advance towards arbitration more momentous than anything that any practical statesman in his position had ventured to say before. He quoted the following passages from President Taft:

Personally I do not see any more reason why matters of national honour should not be referred to Courts of Arbitration as matters of private or national property are. I know that is going further than most men are willing to go, but I do not see why questions of honour should not be submitted to tribunals composed of men of honour who understand questions of national honour, and abide by their decision as well as any other questions of difference arising between nations.

Sir Edward Grey went on to say:

I think it is not impossible . . . that the public opinion of the world at large may insist . . . upon finding relief in this direction. Some armies and navies would remain, no doubt, but they would remain then not in rivalry with each other, but as the police of the world. Some hon. Members say we should not live to see the day.

* * * * *

My attitude is one of encouragement, and even if our hopes may not be realised in our time that is no reason why we should not press forward in the direction in which we see a possible means of relief. What is impossible in one generation may be possible in another. It is rendered more possible in another by the fact that one generation presses in that direction, even though it fails to attain the goal. The great nations of the world are in bondage, an increasing bondage, at the present moment to their armies and navies, and it does not seem to me impossible that in some future years they may discover, as individuals have discovered, that law is a better remedy than force, and that all the time they have been in bondage to this tremendous expenditure, the prison door has been locked on the inside.

The amendment maintaining the position of the Government as opposed to the Resolution viewing the increases "with alarm" was carried by two hundred and seventy-six to fifty-six.

The speeches and the tone of the Debate were received on both sides of the Atlantic with general approval, and favourable comments were also heard throughout the Continent of Europe.

Excited Debates at Westminster and in the country on the Navy and the Parliament Bill were interspersed with more Social Reform, upon which there was a considerable measure of agreement between political Parties. The Shops Bill, introduced by Mr. Masterman (Under-Secretary for the Home Office), and ultimately carried into law, regulated the hours during which assistants might be employed in shops. The Bill, while making very little change in the state of affairs which had long pertained in the good establishments, imposed similar conditions by law on all shops.

The law of copyright was also revised. The great social effort of the Session was the National Health Insurance Bill, outlined by Mr. Lloyd George in his first speech after a long absence from the House through illness. This speech was only second in importance to that in which the Chancellor of the Exchequer had introduced his Budget of 1909. The scheme itself had more lasting results than the Budget. Under the Bill now proposed the State took powers to collect contributions from employers and employees, and, by adding a contribution of its own, established a fund out of which the insured person became entitled to free medical treatment and sick allowance. All wage-earners of both sexes employed in manual labour were compulsorily brought into the scheme; salaried employees up to a limit then fixed at one hundred and fifty pounds a year (subsequently increased to two hundred and fifty pounds) were also compulsorily included. Another part of the Bill made similar provision in certain specified industries for compulsory insurance under which temporary payments became due during periods of unemployment, under specified conditions.

The Chancellor of the Exchequer had a cordial reception from all Parties. Mr. Austen Chamberlain welcomed him back to the House personally and congratulated him on having "set the foundation stone of a work which every Party desires to see carried to a successful conclusion". Other Members on the Conservative side gave similar approval to the principle of the Bill. It was received throughout the press the following morning with such a chorus of praise that enthusiasts anticipated a speedy passage through Parliament and a unanimous welcome from the country.

Older hands gently murmured "Beware when all men speak well of thee!"

Chapter 36

MUSICAL HARMONY—POLITICAL DISCORD

ONE of the most attractive features of the first decade of the New Century was the development of British music. Mr. (afterwards Sir) Henry J. Wood in alliance with Mr. Robert Newman at the Queen's Hall in London had established a movement for bringing good music within the means of all classes by his popular promenade and symphony concerts, at which to a degree of perfection hitherto unattained in England, high-class orchestral music was rendered.

The example was followed not only in London but in other great cities. The taste for good music was declared by all competent observers to be spreading throughout the country. The local choral societies—long an interesting element in the social life of the towns—were growing stronger. Musical festivals had become a firmly established institution.

Mr. (afterwards Sir) Thomas Beecham whose father, the first baronet subscribed liberally to musical enterprises in the North inherited a love for music. He studied the art himself and became a conductor in the North. In 1905 he gave his first concert in London and afterwards founded the Beecham Orchestra. Four years later he founded the Beecham Opera Company, consisting entirely of English speaking singers and in 1910 produced classics that had not yet been heard in London.

By these and other influences,—the spread of higher education and the improving facilities for intercommunication—the extension of musical interest and the love for good music had reached an encouraging standard by the end of 1910. The general advancement found a sympathetic response in the work of the experts and it was a favourable juncture for the assembly of the first Musical Congress ever held in this country which was opened in May 1911. The King signified his good will by becoming a patron and the Government also gave its support. The Congress was the fourth of its kind promoted by the International Musical Society. Two of the preceding congresses were at Leipsig, coinciding with a Bach festival, and at Vienna during the Haydn centenary. Mr. Balfour who now presided observed that we alas! in this country could not boast of names like that, but there was a time when Britain bore its full share in the output of music. Mr. Balfour went on to say:—

> I think there are signs, I think there have long been signs, much more than signs, that this state of things is not only coming to an end, but has come to an end. I certainly can look back over the period of my own life, and see how year by year more men of original productive capacity have come to the front in this country until we can look our continental friends in the face and say that Britain is at last in process of taking its place among the great creative musical communities.

*   *   *   *   *

Facing the new parliamentary position the Lords made continuous efforts to put their own House in order. A

N

Bill for that purpose was introduced by Lord Lansdowne in which the hereditary right to a seat in the Second Chamber was formally surrendered, but the stern prophet of Radicalism —Lord Morley (better known in the House of Commons as Mr. John Morley)—refused to accept this as a substitute for the Parliament Bill. He told the Peers that they had brought the present trouble upon themselves by rejecting the 1909 Budget and now their Veto must go.

Mr. Asquith's Bill reached its final stage in the House of Commons on the 15th May. An animated Debate was wound up in a vehement speech by Mr. Winston Churchill in the course of which, speaking on behalf of the Government, he said:

> We have acted throughout upon notorious and intolerable provocation. We have acted upon grave injury and open challenge. We have marched only by the rules of strictly constitutional procedure. We even subjected ourselves to the ordeal, exertion, and risk of a second General Election. We have carried the policy of the Parliament Bill through three successive Parliaments. We have never varied or departed from it in any way since it was first proposed in this House by a Leader whose memory we revere and honour. We have never increased it, and we should never reduce or abate it.

After this, the Third Reading was carried by three hundred and sixty-two to two hundred and forty-one. The House of Lords, on the advice of Lord Lansdowne, passed the Second Reading of the Bill, with an indication that there would be grave Amendments in Committee.

The strictly parliamentary problem gave way temporarily to a social question with a direct bearing on parliamentary representation. At the end of May the Attorney-General, Sir Rufus Isaacs (afterwards Lord Reading), moved the Second Reading of a Bill which the Government had framed to deal with a situation created by what is known in legal history as the Osborne Judgment. In the course of his speech Sir Rufus concisely and comprehensively dealt with the matter. He pointed out that when, in 1871 and 1876,

Trade Unions were recognised as lawful institutions nobody thought of them as organisations taking part in political action and no special provisions were made in that respect. Some of the older Unions had supported Members of Parliament out of the Union funds, and their action, although discussed, had not been held to be outside their legal rights.

When the Labour Representation Committee was formed, a new question arose. The Amalgamated Society of Railway Servants passed rules under which levies were made for the purpose of providing money for the maintenance of Members of Parliament elected under the constitution of the new Labour Party. There was a dissentient minority, and Mr. Osborne, one of the Members of the Society, brought an action to restrain the Society from enforcing the rules.

There were over eleven hundred Trades Unions registered with the Board of Trade, with a membership of two million, three hundred and fifty thousand. The Unions which had passed rules to enable them to take part in political activity and levy money for the purpose had a membership of one million, five hundred thousand.

The highest legal tribunal ultimately gave a judgment on the legal position, to the effect that a Trade Union had no power to collect or to administer funds for political purposes, and any rule to that effect was not permissible.

The Attorney-General admitted that it was extremely difficult to know what was and what was not covered by the Osborne Judgment. A good many opinions had been taken from the legal experts, and Sir Rufus said he was not at all sure that the Unions had any certain guide from these gentlemen, as to how far they might go or as to what, legitimately, they might do.

Sir Frederick Banbury here drily suggested that this applied to most things.

The Attorney-General, accepting the interjection in good humour, said it might be a meritorious thing to contribute towards the incomes of the lawyers by litigation on the subject. Trade Unions, he added with a smile, had done their part nobly in this respect in recent years, but it was a very unsatisfactory way to spend money paid in for other purposes, and they were entitled to ask the House to say definitely how far they might go and what would be the future legitimate sphere of their activities. The Bill now proposed gave the Unions power to carry out objects understood to be legitimate before the Osborne Judgment, while giving any member the right to claim exemption from contributions to the political activities of the Union, on giving due notice to the officials of the Union that he objected to the payment of this part of his subscription.

In the course of the debate there was some strong criticism from the Conservative Benches, although the Opposition as such did not contest the Bill.

Mr. Macdonald quoted a previous judicial decision, not carried to the highest tribunal, that the miners of South Wales were legally justified in transferring money from their Union funds to Liberal Organisations.

A breeze sprang up later when Mr. Churchill referred to the litigation on the subject, and on this he said:

> It is not good for trade unions that they should be brought in contact with the courts, and it is not good for the courts. The courts hold justly a high and, I think, unequalled prominence in the respect of the world in criminal cases, and in civil cases between man and man, no doubt, they deserve and command the respect and admiration of all classes in the community, but where class issues are involved, and where party issues are involved, it is impossible to pretend that the courts command the same degree of general confidence. On the contrary, they do not, and a very large number of our population have been led to the opinion that they are, unconsciously, no doubt, biassed.

This was received with loud shouts of "No, no" and "Withdraw!" and general expressions of indignation on the part of several Members. Mr. Churchill said he was quite indifferent to these interruptions, and contended that he had not attacked the judges.

The point was raised the following day on a question of parliamentary procedure. Under the Rules of the House restrictions are placed upon observations involving censure upon certain persons. The point is dealt with in a book by Sir Erskine May, one of the recognised authorities on parliamentary procedure:

> Unless the discussion is based upon a substantive motion drawn in proper terms reflections must not be cast in Debate upon the conduct of the Sovereign, the heir to the Throne and members of the Royal Family, the Viceroy and Governor of India, the Lord Lieutenant of Ireland, the Speaker, the Chairman of Ways and Means, Members of either of the Houses of Parliament and Judges of the Superior Courts of the United Kingdom, including persons holding the position of a Judge, such as a Judge in the Court of Bankruptcy and in a County Court.

Under this Rule if a Member desire to question the conduct of any of the personages enumerated he must frame a definite Motion, and if the Motion be deemed by the Leader of the House of sufficient importance a day may be set apart for a discussion upon it.

Judges are specially protected in the interests of the independent administration of justice. A Judge of the High Court, once appointed, can only be removed by a Motion made and carried through both Houses of Parliament.

The Deputy Speaker when the point was raised as to Mr. Churchill's speech said a great deal depended upon the force of the words "unconsciously no doubt biassed". In any case he held that he could not give a ruling on the incident of the previous night, which had now passed.

Mr. Alfred Lyttelton submitted that giving full weight to the word "unconsciously" which the Home Secretary used, there was a distinct imputation that in matters of class, or what the Home Secretary called "Party issues", the Judges were incompetent to divest themselves of partiality.

The Deputy Speaker again held that the incident of the previous night must be regarded as closed.

When Mr. Churchill rose he was greeted with shouts of protest. Ultimately he said the words which he used had been misrepresented and he asked leave to read the exact words to the House.

The Deputy Speaker held there could be no discussion and that the right honourable Gentleman could only make a personal explanation.

"It is a monstrous misrepresentation", said Mr. Churchill. There the incident closed.

Chapter 37

CONSTITUTIONAL ISSUES

THE Coronation of George V and Queen Mary in Westminster Abbey, on the 22nd June, 1911, with all the regal dignity and picturesque splendour of this historic ceremony, provided a respite from parliamentary strife.

Surveying the cheering crowds as the Royal coach passed through the streets of London, or watching the festivities in any big city or in the towns and small villages throughout the country, an intelligent foreigner would have found it impossible to imagine that these enthusiastic people were divided into contending political factions.

In some measure the innocence of the unsophisticated stranger would have been justified. Political argument was fierce and sometimes bitter. There were also instances of very bad feeling in some quarters. The great body of the general public were interested but good humoured and "made allowances for" extreme politicians.

When Parliament returned to its daily round the House of Lords began to alter the Parliament Bill. Lord Lansdowne and his big following inserted Amendments reaffirming their claim to call in the electors. A Joint Committee of both Houses was to be formed which should be entitled to decide that certain Bills of great gravity which had not been "adequately submitted to the judgment of the people" should be approved or otherwise by a referendum.

The idea of taking a vote upon one particular subject had often been suggested, but there were no actual precedents for it in modern politics. Lord Haldane, who had recently come up to the House of Lords from the House of Commons, reminded their Lordships that the referendum was "if not as old as the hills, as old as the most ancient democracy". Smiling benignly on his new colleagues, the versatile War Secretary gave rapid quotations from mediæval history.

Had noble Lords ever heard of Themistocles? When he wanted ships to sail against his enemies Themistocles called the people together and, by a speedy referendum, obtained their consent to build a navy, but Themistocles was dealing with a democracy "enclosed within a wall of no great ambit". Athenian orators found it possible in one speech to address the whole of the electors and thus to "make the people hear and understand". Every modern country in Europe had found it necessary by reason of its dimensions to regard the voice of the people as best expressed through representatives. The ancient method with all its charms was impracticable.

Lord Salisbury was not daunted by Lord Haldane's lecture. He was not quite sure how far it was relevant, but, assuming that it had some reference to the question, what was the moral to be drawn from the experience of Themistocles? Obviously the referendum in his case proved a success!

A whirring noise accompanied Lord Salisbury as he proceeded to defend the traditional powers of the House of Lords. Thoughts were for the moment diverted from old-world politics to modern science. Eyes were strained in the hope of catching, through the open window, a glimpse of the aeroplane floating serenely by—a novel sight at this time of day.

Flying machines were still outside the ordinary calculations of mankind. Experiments were continuously made in the War Services, and private flights were undertaken in more or less secluded places. It had only occurred to Parliament just a month ago that a time had come for passing an "Aerial Navigation Bill" giving the Home Secretary power to regulate conditions under which flying pilots might be permitted to navigate the air over the heads and homes of the people.

When the Amendments to the Parliament Bill proposed by Lord Lansdowne were duly inserted and the measure was sent back to the House of Commons, the short answer again was that the House of Lords had no right to decree any form or any time by or at which the constituents should elect the House of Commons or the House of Commons consult the electors.

The crisis had now reached a stage when argument had, for all practical purposes, ceased; one side or the other must give way. Constitutional historians, seeking a precedent, went back to the year 1832.

It was recalled that Earl Grey (who was then Prime Minister) first brought in a Bill in 1831 which extended the power of voting to classes hitherto unrepresented, and carried its Second Reading in the House of Commons by a majority of only one; shortly after which he appealed to the country and coming back from the General Election with the Reform Party strengthened carried another Bill by a House of Commons majority of one hundred and thirty-six, which Bill was twice rejected by the House of Lords and then amended by them in what was regarded as a vital principle. The stages in that contest between the two Chambers were thus almost identical with those which had occurred upon the Parliament Bill.

One further step remained to complete the analogy. The Sovereign, in exercising the prerogative of recruiting the House of Lords from time to time by Peers specially created, has for centuries acted upon the advice of the Prime Minister. Earl Grey intimated that if the House of Lords persisted in emasculating the Reform Bill he would advise His Majesty to create a sufficient number of new Peers to ensure a majority for the Bill in the Second Chamber.

King William IV gave Earl Grey written permission to say that he would accept this advice if tendered. Upon this fact being communicated to the Peers they gave way, under the advice of the Duke of Wellington, who was then the Leader of the Conservative Opposition.

In political circles the popular question now was "Will history repeat itself?".

Some people urged that if Mr. Asquith adopted the course followed by Earl Grey it would be impossible for him to find a sufficient number of new Liberal Peers. The more general contention in Conservative quarters was that the Peers would not be created if the Lords resisted. Another line of argument was that even if nominated their influence could be discredited. Mr. F. E. Smith, in an article to the "Morning Post", urged the House of Lords on no account to surrender. He declared that the Peers who would be created would be "harlot" Peers and "batches of infamy", whom the electors would in due course cause to be expelled from the House. Similar advice was given by other leading Conservatives who declared that Mr. Asquith and the Government were playing a game of bluff. Historians reminded them that in 1832 Earl Grey had been accused of "playing a game of brag".

On all these points a discreet silence was observed among the most influential circles of Conservatism.

Excitement on the 22nd July, 1911, reached a climax. Mr. Asquith's supporters were jubilant over what they regarded as a master stroke; their opponents looked upon it as something far different.

The Prime Minister had written to the Leaders of the Opposition a letter dated the 20th of which a copy now appeared in the newspapers. It was to this effect:

When the Parliament Bill in the form which it has now assumed returns to the House of Commons we shall be compelled to ask that House to disagree with the Lords' amendments. In the circumstances, should the necessity arise, the Government will advise the King to exercise his prerogative to secure the passing into law of the Bill in substantially the same form in which it left the House of Commons, and His Majesty has been pleased to signify that he will consider it his duty to accept and act on that advice.

Over the week-end the letter was the one topic of discussion throughout the country. Members of the House of Commons came down to Westminster on Monday with a lively anticipation of a fuller statement from the Prime Minister. When Mr. Asquith advanced to the table for this purpose the concentrated fury of feuds ancient and modern entered into the souls of his opponents.

"Traitor! Traitor!!", shouted Lord Hugh Cecil from his corner seat on the front Bench below the gangway. The cry was taken up by other sons of peers and by their political sympathisers.

Stolidly waiting for the turmoil to subside, the man at the Table stood for a few minutes silently watching his opponents. He resumed his seat when the Speaker rose to appeal for order. Immediately he came back to the Table the storm burst forth afresh. White with passion, the young Conservatives below the gangway incited their middle-aged companions above the gangway. Not a word from the Prime Minister could be heard.

Pointing to a prominent Member whose gesticulations were as wild as his language, Mr. Will Crooks, who, as a Magistrate, sometimes performed the unhappy duty of sending people to mental hospitals, shouted "I have seen men certified for less than that".

The Speaker appealed to the Opposition generally, and to one or two Members in particular, but the discipline of modern civilisation had once again lost its hold upon that assembly. The gulf that separated primitive instinct from reasoned argument was bridged and recrossed.

Some of the Government supporters below the gangway protested against the attack on their Leader; Members on the other side retorted. Mr. Asquith still stood by the Table. The interest of the spectator was attracted from point to point by such rapidly successive incidents that it was impossible to concentrate on any given spot.

Suddenly a picturesque figure shot up from the Irish Benches. Mr. William O'Brien, with pointed beard and

delicately chiselled features—a modern replica of what
Charles I might have looked like had he lived another ten
years—lifted his right hand to the heavens and screamed:
"Who was the ruffian that said 'McNally'"?

It was discovered subsequently by research into Irish
history that somewhere back in the beginning of the last
century or thereabouts a man dwelt in Ireland named
McNally who became an "informer"—the Irish colloquial
equivalent of "sneak", or the French "agent provocateur".
In the course of the interchange of compliments it appeared
some person near the Irish Benches had mentioned the hated
name apropos of something or somebody, and this was more
than the O'Brien patriotism could endure.

A stage had now been reached when all hope of securing
any semblance of order had to be abandoned. After a few
disjointed sentences, broken up by interjections and jeers,
Mr. Asquith finally resumed his seat.

Mr. Balfour rose to reply to the speech which had not been
delivered. He obtained an orderly hearing and was
obviously embarrassed thereby. He admitted that he was
being treated well by his opponents, but in mitigation of
what occurred he recalled the fact that his old friend and
colleague, Mr. Alfred Lyttelton, had on one occasion received
far different treatment to that which Members of the Liberal
Party were now according him.

Mr. Balfour contended that the course adopted by the
Prime Minister was contrary to the spirit of the Constitution,
and he proceeded to answer arguments which he assumed Mr.
Asquith would have used had he been given the opportunity.

The usually placid Sir Edward Grey, in tones of burning
indignation, now declared that since the Opposition had
refused to hear the Leader of the House not one of his
colleagues would take his place. He refused to discuss Mr.
Balfour's speech, and concluded by moving the adjournment
of the Debate.

Mr. F. E. Smith now leapt up on the Opposition side
ready with epigrams which were never coined. The uproar

burst forth afresh and the Speaker ruled that a situation of grave disorder having arisen the House stood adjourned.

Having made their protest in such a form that it must appear in all parliamentary records, the opponents of the Government were uncertain what steps they ought to pursue. The more vigorous amongst them who still urged that there should be no surrender were known as the "Die-Hards" or "Ditchers". Years before the Unionists of the North of Ireland had declared that they would "die in the last ditch" rather than accept Home Rule. The declaration had been adopted since then by all non-compromising opponents of any new proposal.

In contrast, the men in the Conservative Party who counselled discretion were nicknamed "Hedgers".

All the inspiring and traditional political memories were with the Ditchers. They were led by the Earl of Halsbury, the former Conservative Lord Chancellor who had seen many storms weathered by the House of Lords in the nineteenth century. They had men like Lord Willoughby de Broke— the sporting lords adored in their own counties. In the Commons they had captured the kind of Conservatives who were in demand at public meetings throughout the country.

The quiet, solid men in the Party awaited a definite word from the Leaders. It came shortly after the scene in the House of Commons. Mr. Balfour, as Leader of the Party, and Lord Lansdowne as Leader of the Conservative and Unionist Peers, wrote letters declaring that further opposition would be futile, and advising the acceptance of the Parliament Bill as the only course now open to the House of Lords.

Chapter 38

HOVERING WAR CLOUDS

AT a moment when the constitutional crisis was at its fiercest stage an incident on the north coast of Africa brought the disputants into one unbroken line.

Morocco, the farthest west of the Mohammedan world, had long been a subject of animated interest among the European Powers. Outside diplomatic circles Morocco suggested tales of Moorish pirates in far-off centuries who made descents upon the coasts of Europe, reaching even as far as Devon and Cornwall, and carried back Christian slaves whom they offered to their Prophet as potential converts to Mohammedanism. The sufferings of these unhappy captives and their heroic devotion to the Christian Faith filled some of the most pathetic pages of history.

The records of those days were occasionally revived by popular writers as subject matter for excellent stories. Outside works of fiction Morocco meant very little to the general public. Its importance was brought home to everybody in July of 1911 by the possibility of a European war.

Political writers reviewed the history of unstable Governments of successive Rulers in modern Morocco. The fact was recorded that after various dynastic changes money was borrowed from France at the beginning of the century and French aid was called in with a view to establishing a regular system of administration. In 1904, as part of the Entente Cordiale, Great Britain and France came to an understanding with respect to Morocco.

Germany viewed with concern the increasing influence of France in Europe and elsewhere, and in 1905 the German Emperor landed at Tangiers, where he had conferences with the representatives of the Sultan of Morocco. The Sultan, soon after this, rejected the scheme of reforms proposed by France, and, at the instigation of Germany, issued invitations to the Powers to meet his representatives and advise him concerning the reforms needed. The conference met at Algeciras, and, as a result a general Act of Agreement was signed which empowered France to supervise the conduct of certain reforms considered necessary.

In October of 1910 there was a general rising of troops round Fez. The City was besieged in the spring of 1911, and French troops were sent to occupy the City and pacify the district. This was resented by Spain and also by Germany, who had never been quite satisfied with the agreement made with France. Public interest throughout Europe was stimulated a little later by the despatch of the German gunboat "Panther" to Agadir. The alleged motive of this was the protection of German subjects. The only German subjects in the neighbourhood of this port were the agents of the German firms, and they were in no way molested. The "Agadir incident" was thus taken as a challenge to the extension of French influence in Morocco. It was very strongly suspected, and even broadly stated, that the German intention was to acquire a German port on the Morocco Coast.

Questioned in the House of Commons as to the situation, Mr. Asquith said:

> I am confident that diplomatic discussion will find a solution, and in the part that we shall take in it we shall have due regard to the protection of those interests and to the fulfilment of our Treaty obligations to France, which are well-known to the House.

The Chancellor of the Exchequer, speaking at the Annual Dinner of Bankers and Merchants in the City of London, advocated specific settlement of International disputes by arbitration but declared it essential to the highest interests of the world that Great Britain should at all hazards maintain her place and prestige among the great Powers.

The meaning of this pronouncement was more fully realised on the 27th July, when, in reply to a question in the House of Commons as to the progress of events in Morocco, Mr. Asquith, while expressing the hope that a settlement by mutual agreement would be arrived at, went on to say:

> But we have thought it right from the beginning to make it quite clear that failing a settlement such as I have indicated we must become an active party to discussion of the situation. That would be our right as a signatory to the Treaty of Algeciras; it might be our obligation under the terms of our Agreement of 1904 with France; it might be our duty in

defence of the British interests directly affected by further developments.

This was just three days after Mr. Asquith had been shouted down in a discussion on Home politics. Mr. Balfour, speaking with that impressive deliberation which characterised his utterances on great occasions, thus summed up the position of himself and his Party on the International question:

> If there be any observers or critics outside these walls who have counted upon our differences and our absorption in the bitter home disputes of the moment, in the hope that they will make easy a policy which they, under other circumstances, thought this country might object to; if there are any who suppose that we are wiped out from the map of Europe because we have our own differences at home; it may be worth while saying, for the benefit of those whom it may concern, that they have utterly mistaken the temper of the British people and the patriotism of the Opposition— whether the Opposition be drawn from one side of the House or from the other side of the House.

These memorable pronouncements were the all-absorbing subject of immediate public interest. A feeling had been growing strongly that the relations between Germany and this country were not cordial; there had been more strong talk in some quarters about German designs upon this country. This was the first definite and official incident that brought a war with Germany within the range of things that might happen. For a few days the parliamentary conflict was a topic of very minor importance. The tension was relaxed when it became known Germany had found it possible to enter into an agreement with France. There were rearrangements of spheres of influence elsewhere than in Morocco. France was satisfied, our interests were not involved and our responsibility for the time being ended.

Just about this time the Naval Defence Scheme was published, showing the arrangements for co-operation between the Mother Country and the Dominions. It was provided under this plan that the Naval Services and Forces should be under the control of their respective Governments, the training and discipline to be generally uniform with those of the Fleet of the United Kingdom, and arrangements were made for the interchange of officers and men. The ships of each Dominion were to hoist the Royal Navy White Ensign by the stern, and the flag of their Dominion at the jackstaff, as symbols of the authority of the Crown and the Dominion's responsibility.

Returning to the prevailing domestic topic, the "Die-Hards" continued to urge resistance at all costs. The "Observer", which came out Sunday after Sunday with vehement appeals for a stubborn defence, was supported by speeches and letters. It was even suggested in some quarters that Unionist Peers who voted for the Parliament Bill should be "blacklisted" by the Party. The "Die-Hards" themselves determined definitely that they would refuse to follow the advice of the Unionist Leaders.

Without any alteration in the principle of the Bill, the proposed referendum was rejected by the House of Commons.

Chapter 39

THE OLD HOUSE OF LORDS PASSES

ON the 10th August, 1911, the old House of Lords assembled for the last time clothed in full legislative powers and privileges.

The ostensible question before the House was that Lord Lansdowne's Referendum Amendment be not insisted on. In reality the fate of the Parliament Bill, and thereby the fate of the constitution of the House of Lords itself, hung in the balance. The Debate had commenced on the Bill the evening before; throughout the day the "Die-Hards" had openly boasted that they were gathering adherents.

At a crucial moment Lord Rosebery advanced slowly to the Table and, observing that it had been stated only a few peers would be created, just as a warning, asked for some official pronouncement upon the intentions of the Government. Lord Lansdowne made a similar appeal.

Lord Morley, the cultured man of the people, born amid the hum of machinery in Blackburn, a colleague of Gladstone's, a Radical of the old school, who had come up from the House of Commons at this crisis by one of those strange coincidences which occur in the lives of public men, replied:

> If the Bill should be defeated to-night His Majesty would assent to the creation of Peers sufficient in numbers to guard against any possible combination of the different Parties in opposition by which the Parliament Bill might be exposed a second time to defeat.

Following upon an interjection by Lord Willoughby de Broke, who apparently still maintained that the Government were bluffing, Lord Morley, his pale, scholarly face stern and resolute, said:

> That is a pure and absolute delusion. All I have to say on this part of the matter is that every vote given to-night against my motion not to insist upon what is called 'Lord Lansdowne's amendment' is a vote given in favour of a large and prompt creation of peers.

He twice repeated this fateful pronouncement, rapping the table with his knuckles and raising his voice so that each syllable pierced every corner of the building.

Lord Rosebery, speaking in solemn tones, reminded their Lordships what the declaration thus made on behalf of the Government meant. Whatever happened that night, the Bill must pass. Lord Halsbury interjected a word of doubt; Lord Rosebery, turning towards him, asked how long did noble Lords suppose the Bill could be kept off.—Forty-eight hours? A week? A month? "What is a month in the life of a nation?", he asked, and answering the question in effect he added that the only difference between the two sections of the opponents of the Bill was whether it should pass with an enormous creation of peers, or whether it should pass "without that scandal and constitutional strain". He quoted the example of the Duke of Wellington, whose courage

o

none of them could doubt, and who, he said, by yielding in 1832, preserved the House of Lords for eighty years.

Still the "Die-Hards" were not convinced. Hour after hour the Debate went on. It was a struggle within the Conservative Party; the Liberal Peers left them to settle their differences. As an example of the tone and temper of the House, an exciting scene occurred when Lord Heneage and Lord St. Leven rose together. Under ordinary circumstances each noble Lord would have offered to give way to the other and the moral advantage would have been to the one who induced the other to accept his offer. On this occasion each held his ground, and conflicting shouts of "Heneage" and "St. Leven" were so insistent that at first the Lord Chancellor did not hear Lord Halsbury move "that Lord St. Leven be heard".

Eventually, on this motion, Lord St. Leven was heard first and declared himself a "Die-Hard". Lord Heneage, who spoke afterwards, said he would vote with the Government rather than see the new peers created.

The official Conservative plan obviously was to abstain from voting, and place upon the Liberal Peers the responsibility of rejecting the Referendum, but the "Die-Hards" would have none of it. They attacked the Government, they heaped scorn upon their own Leaders.

Lord Curzon pictured the arrival of four hundred new peers, and, turning to the "Die-Hards", said in an imploring tone "Let us realise what is before us"!

"It is because four hundred peers are going to run away to-night", shouted the Marquess of Bristol, an ex-naval officer, in a voice that could be heard from the foretop in a gale of wind.

"I would sooner run away with the Duke of Wellington than stand with the noble Lord", retorted Lord Curzon.

Promptly came the answer: "I would rather fight with Nelson at Copenhagen than run away with you!"

Thoughts of Nelson in that historic naval fight, with the telescope to his blind eye, and of the victory won that day in spite of the signalled orders, which the blind eye could not read, presented fascinating possibilities, but it was unlikely that history would in this case repeat itself.

Lord Rosebery, in a very brief and, as he expressed it, painful speech, made a final appeal. So impressed was he with the dangers of the situation that although he had intended to abstain from voting, he now declared his intention of voting for the Bill.

Lord Selborne, winding up the Debate for the "Die-Hards", summarised the situation in uncompromising terms :

> The House of Lords, as we have known it, as we have worked in it, is going to pass away. We ourselves, as effective legislators, are doomed to destruction. The question is, shall we perish in the dark by our own hand or in the light, killed by our enemies?

Late at night the division bells rang. The wives and daughters of peers, in beautiful evening frocks, leaned over the balconies which run along the two sides of the Chamber, and watched their family chiefs moving slowly towards the division lobbies. Ambassadors from various lands, diplomatically unmoved, sat side by side in their special balcony. Members of the House of Commons thronged the seats reserved for them on either side of the crowded strangers' gallery.

From a small turret just behind the Throne Lord Lansdowne, Lord Curzon and Lord Midleton gazed down upon those of their colleagues who had remained for the division. The "Contents"—that the Lords Amendments be not insisted on—filed to the right of the Throne; the "Not-Contents" to the left of the Bar.

Two Bishops were observed to be voting with the "Die-Hards". Thirteen Members of the Episcopal Bench joined the "Contents", their white robes conspicuous among the sombre black coats of the laymen.

When the House was cleared the lobby doors were closed, and after a pause reopened. In tense silence two single lines of men came forth. That from the Opposition lobby kept level with the procession from the door of the "Contents" almost to the end.

When the records were brought to the table the Clerk handed the slip to the Government Teller. A deep sigh of relief from some, a groan of disgust from others, greeted this sure indication that the "Die-Hards" were defeated.

The figures carried by the Teller to the Lord Chancellor showed that the Government proposal was carried by one hundred and thirty-one to one hundred and fourteen.

The Members of the House of Commons who had been watching the division rushed across the lobbies to "the other place", and loud cheers burst from the Liberal, Labour and Irish Benches there as the result was passed round.

The "Die-Hards" made no effort to conceal their disappointment. The Unionist Peers who voted for the Government were denounced in Conservative quarters as "traitors" and "rats". One was said to have been hooted as he entered the Carlton Club. A suggestion was made in some quarters that a "black list" should be hung in the principal Unionist Clubs.

How near the "Die-Hards" came to victory—a sufficient explanation perhaps for their disgust at the actual result—was related afterwards.

Lord Willoughby de Broke later on commenced a book "The Passing Years", but the narrative was broken by the author's untimely death. An anonymous biographer who completed the work thus writes:

As Willoughby foresaw, there was certain to be a few who would try and break away at the last moment. He was right. The debate closed; half-a-dozen 'ditcher' peers as if by magic suddenly vanished. Two I know he headed off, but one, a noble duke, was more fortunate. A good deal of whipping had been necessary to get him to the House at all, but to keep him there was quite another proposition. And so Willoughby de Broke adopted the silent precaution of hiding his Grace's hat and coat. But it was no good, the noble owner bolted off without either and was never seen again! . . . It was not until the next morning that the whole truth was known. Meanwhile it was clear that there had been some very unexpected cross-voting. Willoughby had, as I have said, definite promises from one hundred and twenty-three peers to support Lord Halsbury; nine at least must have "run out" at the last moment. And they had. On the other hand, eight had unexpectedly "run in". The Duke of Norfolk was very largely responsible for the latter move, and if only all Lord Halsbury's followers had stood their ground from first to last, the Bill would have been thrown out by a majority of eleven.

The tragedy of that "if" was doubtless realised by the "Die-Hards" when eight days after the division five Lords Commissioners, in their full robes, sitting on a Bench in front of the Throne, announced the Royal Assent to the Bill.

Chapter 40

THE SOUTH POLE—M.P's REGAIN SALARIES

POLAR exploration, always a thrilling subject, had been rendered more intensely attractive by the success of Commander Peary. The achievement of this great explorer at the North Pole gave additional stimulus to the ambitions of other travellers. Captain Ronald Amundsen the son of a Norwegian Ship owner had been following in the footsteps of his fellow countryman Dr. Nansen, whose expeditions had fascinated people of all lands in the concluding years of the Nineteenth Century. Amundsen now turned his attention to the South Pole where there was still an undiscovered world to conquer. He set out in January of 1911 in Nansen's famous ship "The Fram". When he reached the point of the main south journey he adopted the plan of forming depots of provisions for the return journey and thus lightening the load for the outward journey. Climbing mountains and reaching plateau after plateau at high altitudes, his party made swift progress. They pushed on more slowly for awhile, temporarily blinded by blizzards and walking over thin ice that at times gave way under foot. Ultimately the travelling became more easy and they arrived at the

South Pole on the 14th of December. After making useful observations Amundsen and his companions set out for home picking up the depots on their way and finally arrived at Hobart on the 7th of March. Thus within a short while of each other the two Poles were reached leaving future travellers to seek further fields of discovery.

*   *   *   *   *

On the day the House of Lords assented to the Parliament Bill the Chancellor of the Exchequer moved a Resolution in the House of Commons to the effect that a salary of four hundred pounds a year be paid to all Members of Parliament —except Ministers and other Members of the Government in receipt of salaries attached to their respective Offices.

The revival of a very old practice naturally called attention to the history of Members and their emoluments. In the early days attendance in Parliament was not a great privilege. The journey to Westminster was negotiated under difficulties, and no particular dignity seems to have been attached to the position. Indeed, according to some records the representative, especially if he sat for a town, excited compassion rather than envy. He was called upon to perform a public duty for which, like other public servants, he had his wages. These apparently were not fixed upon a particularly liberal scale, even allowing for the fact that money in those days had a far greater purchasing value. In the middle of the fifteenth century the "standard rate" was two shillings a day, although there are cases of "blacklegs" who undertook the job for "twelvepence a day". A century later the Members, with or without the aid of the ancient counterpart of a Trade Union, had succeeded in getting the price raised to five shillings a day, and there are instances of very generous burgesses who brought the emoluments up to ten shillings a day.

Sometimes the Member compromised for a payment in kind, as in the case of Sir John Strange, the Member for Dunwich, a seaport town, who consented to take "a cade and half a barrel of herrings" for his fee. A "cade", it might be explained, was a barrel or cask of five hundred herrings.   The legislative value of the Member for Dunwich was therefore fixed at seven hundred and fifty herrings.

Very occasionally a constituency had the good fortune to discover an "amateur", but, like some other amateurs, he received an honorarium not far short of the professional fee.   It is related of Sir Robert Hitcham, who eventually became Attorney-General and Judge of the County Palatine of Ely that early in the XVIIth Century he undertook to serve the Borough of Kings Lynn gratuitously, "in consideration of which tender care for their pecuniary resources the Corporation, on the occasion of his passing through the town on his way to Ely in July, 1610, entertained him handsomely and gave him a gratuity of twenty pounds".

The payment of a salary was an enforceable contract.   In the year 1681 Thomas King brought and won an action against the Borough of Harwich for arrears of salary as Member.

There seems to have been no direct cleavage between the days of payment and the days when Members ceased to have any pay.   The assumption was that if any modern Member chose to emulate the example of Mr. Thomas King, he might sustain his legal claim to a "reasonable wage".

The old Radicals always advocated payment of salaries to Members of Parliament.   They contended that it was a well-known fact that men of political ability without ample private means were only able to sit in Parliament by aid from Party funds or support from well-to-do patrons. It was urged that either of these courses was detrimental to the independence of the House of Commons.   The opponents of payment of Members contended, on the other hand, that the independence of Parliament was based upon voluntary service, and instead of enabling men of exceptional ability and modest means to become Members of Parliament, the salaries would enable men who were already well off to spend more money in "nursing" their constituencies.

Although the principle had been adopted as part of the Liberal programme, the situation arising out of the Osborne Judgment had really forced the subject into the region of practical politics. It was felt that some means must be found of enabling men from the wage-earning classes to serve in Parliament. Indeed, Mr. F. E. Smith and some other Conservatives suggested that in the circumstances payment of Members was the way out.

Mr. Lloyd George, in proposing his Motion, urged that the existing system meant that, apart from Nationalist and Labour Members, election to the House of Commons was confined to men of means with unearned incomes: barristers practising in London; men engaged in well-established businesses with accommodating partners; and City men. He pointed out that attendance in Parliament was now a serious and continuous duty, very different from the days of the last century when sessions were short and there were comparatively few divisions.

Mr. Arthur Lee (afterwards Lord Lee), who was well known as an opponent of the proposal to pay salaries to Members of Parliament, declared the Resolution to be a violation of the principle of gratuitous service.

The proposal was received without very considerable enthusiasm by the Labour Members; it was well known that they were more keen on the complete re-establishment of the position as it existed before the Osborne Judgment, with a perfectly free hand to use Union funds for the support of their Members. They accepted the Resolution, however, and Mr. Ramsay Macdonald remarked with approval that the salary was not sufficient to be coveted. At a later stage Mr. Philip Snowden gave an interesting balance sheet showing how the two hundred pounds a year which he had received from a certain organisation had failed to cover his out-of-pockets as a Member of Parliament.

Mr. F. E. Smith explained that his original support of payment of Members had been contingent upon the maintenance, without qualification, of the Osborne Judgment, and he now opposed the Resolution. The Motion of the Chancellor of the Exchequer was carried by a large majority. It required no confirmation by the House of Lords, and thus took effect forthwith.

An all-round rise in the cost of living now began to make itself felt amongst other people besides Members of Parliament. It led to higher charges in clubs and restaurants and reached the larders of the workers. An epidemic of labour unrest broke out in which dockers, shippers and railwaymen were included with others, and as a consequence there were serious riots in Liverpool, which occasioned an exciting Debate in Parliament with the Government exposed to criticism from two points of view. They were attacked by the Labour Members for failing to grasp the situation, and it was suggested that unnecessary steps had been taken in the preservation of order. The Conservatives, on the other hand, indicted that the Government were not sufficiently firm in applying strong and severe action for the maintenance of law and order.

Mr. Ramsay Macdonald retorted by scathing comments on the different attitude of the Conservative Party towards disorder in this country and threats of disorder in Belfast. Undeterred by criticisms of this kind the Ulster Unionists, through the Orange Lodges and the Unionist Clubs of the North of Ireland, announced their determination to resist every decree of an Irish Parliament if Home Rule ever became law.

A passing incident indicated that religious thought had its influence on everyday life. Jack Johnson, a negro pugilist of enormous strength, had defeated a "white champion" in America. Arrangements were made to match him against an English boxer. A "Black" versus "White" agitation which followed upon the American fight seemed likely to be intensified, and the contest was opposed on this account by many people. The most vigorous objection came through the religious Societies, in which the Reverend F. B. Meyer, an eminent South London Free Church Minister, took the foremost part. The Home Secretary decided to interfere, but official action became unnecessary in consequence of an injunction obtained by the Metropolitan District Railway (the owners of the freehold on which the match had been arranged) preventing the lessee from using it for that purpose.

In the political world a persistent crusade against Mr. Balfour was gathering force among some Conservatives. The Tariff Reformers contended that a strong lead from a stout believer in Tariff Reform would have rallied their forces; the "Die-Hards" resented Mr. Balfour's surrender on the House of Lords. He was described by one of his disgruntled followers as a "champion scuttler". A section of Die-Hards and their supporters in the more aggressive sections of the Press insisted that "Balfour must go", and "B.M.G." became the popular catch cry of the hour.

The attacks on another public man somewhat relieved the pressure for a while. Mr. Lloyd George was realising that the initial welcome given to his Insurance Bill was all too sweet to be wholesome. The blessings showered upon the principle of the measure when the Bill was introduced had been discounted or forgotten. A violent campaign against the whole Bill started by certain newspapers found its most fruitful soil amongst the middle classes.

It was represented to small employers, particularly of domestic servants, that it was an intolerable imposition that they should be responsible for the machinery of the scheme under which a stamp was each week to be stuck on a card supplied for the purpose, as a record of the necessary weekly contributions.

"We won't lick stamps" became the battle cry of protesting drawing-rooms. Passive resistance was again threatened—this time from a different quarter to that which Mr. Balfour had to face over his Education Bill—and, by the grim humour of coincidence, the Minister now to be resisted was the man who, about nine years ago, was the principal antagonist of Mr. Balfour's proposals.

The more substantial men of the Conservative Party contented themselves with pressing Amendments upon the attention of the Government without committing themselves to any definite disapproval of the principle.

Mr. Lloyd George's chief difficulty in the practical working of the scheme was with the Doctors. The system under which each Doctor was to have a certain number of patients

on his "panel" for which he was to receive a fixed payment
per head was an extension of a plan that had been in force
by arrangement with the various Friendly Societies and also
in accordance with the course privately adopted by some
medical men in the industrial districts. It was contended,
however, that this was a much bigger thing. It was opposed
in principle by some leading men as an attempt to lay the
foundation of a nationalised Medical Service. Others took
the more immediately important objection that the terms
and conditions proposed by the Government were inadequate.

A very important step towards the smooth working of the
scheme had been taken by an agreement with the Friendly
Societies. These Organisations, dating back many years,
were among the most influential institutions of industrial
life. The Oddfellows, the Foresters, the Hearts of Oak and
other Societies in England, and the Shepherds (to quote one
example) in Scotland, had developed a huge voluntary
method by which Members, in return for regular contributions, received benefits in the shape of medical attendance
and weekly payments of money in time of sickness. The
funds were well invested, and further accumulating benefits
came to the members therefrom.

Early in the history of the Insurance Bill it had been
obvious that any system of State sickness insurance must
work in co-operation with the Friendly Societies. One after
another they agreed to come in, and this fact was Mr. Lloyd
George's stoutest bulwark against the storm of protests
now showered upon him.

Chapter 41

UNREST AT HOME AND ABROAD

A RUMOUR spread through an excited Lobby one November afternoon in 1911 that Mr. Balfour had determined
to resign.

Many people had felt that the limit of human endurance

must be reached sooner or later if the campaign against the Leader of the Conservative Party continued. Faced now with the actual prospect of losing the Leader of the Opposition, men of all Parties spoke of the impending event as though mourning a personal loss. The skill, the literary charm, the polished sword-play of this master of debate took prominence among the treasures of Parliament.

When the authentic news came matters were not quite so bad as they seemed. Mr. Balfour announced to a meeting in the City that he must withdraw from the leadership of his Party but he would remain a Member of the House of Commons.

At the Lord Mayor's Banquet Mr. Asquith expressed unfeigned regret at Mr. Balfour's resignation, which he described as an irreparable loss to the daily life of Parliament.

The Members of the Conservative and Unionist Party now applied themselves to the problem of finding a new Leader. The name of Mr. Austen Chamberlain was freely discussed; Mr. Walter Long as a country squire of the good type, public spirited, straightforward and generally esteemed, would have pleased many people, but other ideas were influencing the descendants of the old Tory Party. Mr. Bonar Law, the commercially trained Scottish-Canadian, was chosen to lead the new generation.

Foreign policy claimed the early attention of the Conservative Leader. For a long time the feeling of unrest had been simmering in Great Britain and in Germany as to existing and probable future relations between the two countries. The tide of excitement ebbed and flowed. Expressions of mutual goodwill from high official quarters and also from the ranks of the workers relieved the tension periodically. In 1908 a big deputation representing Trade Unions in all parts of Great Britain visited Berlin and was enthusiastically received at huge demonstrations in favour of mutual goodwill. At other times statements of a contrary character found public expression in certain quarters and though the Morocco incident had passed, its effect upon public opinion was not dispelled.

Towards the end of November it was thought desirable to make the position clear, and to this end Sir Edward Grey formally moved "that the foreign policy of His Majesty's Government be now considered." The Foreign Minister traced in detail the whole of the circumstances of the Morocco incident. There had been some criticism of the speech made by Mr. Lloyd George at the Bankers' Dinner. Sir Edward said this speech was made with the approval of himself and the Prime Minister. He added:

> Its point is that where British interests are affected, we must not be treated as if we are of no account. If the time ever comes when this cannot be said by a Minister speaking in the position the Chancellor of the Exchequer is in now, we shall have ceased to exist as a great nation.

Coming to the more general question the Foreign Minister said an agreement had now been reached between the French and German Governments in which both sides had made substantial concessions and substantial gains, and in spite of that agreement this was the moment chosen by some people to excite themselves—and as many others as they could in Germany or here—by discussion of how near we came to war. On this, Sir Edward went on to say:

> Really it is as if the world were indulging in a fit of political alcoholism, and the best that can be done by those of us who are in positions of responsibility is to keep cool and sober.

After reviewing the foreign policy of this country, past, present and future, Sir Edward said:

> Any support we would give France and Russia in times of trouble would depend entirely on the feeling of Parliament and public feeling here when the trouble came, and both France and Russia know perfectly well that British public opinion would not give support to provocative or aggressive action against Germany. And the same considerations *mutatis mutandis* apply to France and Russia.

*   *   *   *   *

One of the essential conditions of the friendship of ourselves with France and Russia in the last few years has been the certain knowledge that neither they nor we wish to pursue a provocative or aggressive policy.

He pointed out that one does not make new friendships worth having by deserting old ones. We desired to do all we could to improve the relations with Germany, but it must be a cardinal point of improved relations with Germany that we did not sacrifice friendships which had lasted now for some years. As to future relations, Sir Edward said:

> Do not let us imagine that we can force the pace at this moment in improving relations with Germany. We cannot compel suddenly, after the friction of the last few months, the favourable breeze of public opinion, either in Germany or here. . . . Though public opinion may be adverse at the present moment, excited as it recently has been, in some ways one can already see that the horizon is brightening.

Mr. Bonar Law observed that the year now drawing to a close had been so crowded with great events that it almost seemed as if our power of sensation were dead. We had been living under the shadow of a volcano from which lava had been already flowing. He assured the House that the change in the leadership of his Party did not imply a change in their attitude on foreign politics. On the immediate topic he went on to say:

> I can imagine few, if any, calamities which would seem so great as a war, whatever the result, between us and the great German people. I hear it also constantly said—there is no use shutting our eyes or ears to obvious facts—that, owing to divergent interests, war some day or other between this country and Germany is inevitable. I never believe in these inevitable wars. Prince Bismarck once said, and said truly, that no man can overlook the hand of Providence. I am myself old enough to remember that twenty-five or thirty years ago the same thing was said far more persistently about our relationship with Russia. It is never said now. Why? For one reason, because the whole perspective of the world has changed. It is constantly changing, and I see no reason to think that ten or fifteen years hence it may

not completely change again. If, therefore, war should
ever come between these two countries, which Heaven forbid!
it will not, I think, be due to irresistible natural laws; it
will be due to the want of human wisdom. But neither men
nor nations are always wise, and in my belief the best, perhaps
the only absolute security for peace, is that each country
should realise always the strength of the other, and should
realise, too, that whatever may be the domestic differences,
from whatever party in either country the Government may
come, each nation is prepared to defend to the last her rights
and her honour.

*   *   *   *   *

We all rejoice that this Morocco settlement seems to be
going to be carried through. . . . We do not grudge Germany,
to use an expression which is constantly found in statements,
her place in the sun. We do not wish to stand in the way
of her legitimate aspirations.

The Leader of the Opposition thus concurred with the
Foreign Minister in asserting that we had no desire for
accessions of territory:

Our responsibilities are great enough already. We have
no wish to increase them. The one wish by which all my
Friends behind myself are actuated, and I believe it is true
of every man, it is true of the whole nation, our one desire,
our one ambition, is not to enlarge but to build up our Empire.

The Prime Minister acknowledged "with gratitude though
without surprise" the very weighty endorsement of the
Government's position on Foreign affairs which fell from
the lips of the Leader of the Opposition.

Mr. Asquith assured the House in another part of his
speech that there was no secret arrangement of any sort or
kind which had not been disclosed, and fully disclosed, to
the public, and, endorsing the tone adopted by Sir Edward
Grey and Mr. Bonar Law, he concluded:

We have no cause to quarrel with any of the great Powers
in the world of any sort or kind. The first of all British
interests remains, as it has always been, the peace of the

world, and for the attainment of that great purpose our diplomacy and policy is with single-mindedness directed.

These speeches were received in the country and throughout the world with profound interest, and it was hoped that the international atmosphere had thereby been rendered clearer and fairer.

Returning with unabated controversial zeal to domestic affairs the House of Commons found in the Insurance Bill a topic for an animated Debate towards the close of an eventful year.

When, after going through many spirited nights of discussion in Committee and Report Stage, the Bill came on for the Third Reading, the Opposition put down an official Amendment in which they declared that the Bill had been neither adequately discussed in this House nor fully explained in the country.

The Government looked upon this as a wrecking Amendment, and strenuously opposed it. In the course of the discussion Mr. Ramsay Macdonald, while refusing to support the Opposition Amendment, admitted that in detail the Bill was not what the Labour Government would have introduced. He called special attention to the fact that an Amendment had been introduced by which, in addition to the Friendly Societies, the Insurance Companies and "Collecting Societies" were to take part in the administration of the Bill. As to the Doctors, Mr. Ramsay Macdonald from his point of view thus summed up their attitude:

> I do not quite know what position the medical man is in. One day we are told he is satisfied, and the next day we are told that he is profoundly dissatisfied. There is one thing I should like to congratulate the doctors upon, and that is their trade union methods.

*   *   *   *   *

> The doctors have threatened that if they do not get the wages they want they will throw down their tools, have a strike, and refuse to work the Bill. Not only that, but they have got together a strike fund among themselves from which they are going to supply strike pay, should that be necessary.

The Chancellor of the Exchequer admitted that he could not say that the Doctors were satisfied. If they were to express satisfaction it would weaken what Mr. Ramsay Macdonald described as "their 'Trade Union' position".

The Amendment was defeated and the Bill read a third time. It received the Royal Assent in due course, but that was by no means the end of the Chancellor's troubles. He had not yet come to terms with the medical profession.

A servants' protest meeting was called in the Albert Hall, attended by some ten thousand women, presided over by the Dowager Lady Desart, and a Resolution was passed in favour of organising resistance to the Act when it came into operation.

Completing the general commotion the militant Suffragettes during the latter weeks of the year renewed their activities. As a protest against the Government and the House of Commons for concluding the Session without taking further practical steps towards the enfranchisement of women, they endeavoured to reach the House in an organised procession but were repelled by the police. Many of them were arrested and sent to prison in default of payment of fines. They also set out on a window-breaking crusade with hammers and stones, and altogether within a few days some two hundred and twenty-three charges were dealt with in the Police Courts. Mr. Lloyd George was assaulted in his carriage on the way from a public meeting.

Women of all ages and drawn from all classes of society had by this time thrown themselves into the militant movement. Foremost amongst them was the widow of Dr. Pankhurst, a member of the Bar and an authority on municipal law, who in his lifetime had taken an active and self-sacrificing part in social efforts of various kinds. His wife had always been enthusiastically associated with him in this work. As the two daughters grew up they inherited the passion for "forward" movement.

Among other leaders in the militant crusade was Mr. Pethick Lawrence, a member of an influential city family and a relative of Sir Durning Lawrence, who sat as a Unionist

P

Member of Parliament for many years. Mr. Pethick Lawrence also was spoken of as a Unionist Candidate in his younger days, but after travelling a good deal he returned to England in the early years of the century with decided leanings towards the then newly formed Labour Party. His wife supported him in his advanced views, and together for the time being they concentrated their energies on the militant suffrage movement. Like other enthusiasts they came into direct conflict with the law on several occasions.

The militant Suffrage movement generally had now become one of the recognised facts of everyday life.

Home affairs and those Foreign affairs which directly concerned us were so absorbing that the general public in Great Britain would hardly have noticed that war had broken out between Italy and Turkey but for the usual formal proclamation declaring the strict neutrality of this country.

Chapter 42

HOME RULE AND OTHER CONTROVERSIES

THE year 1912 brought with it more topics of fierce Parliamentary controversy.

It was common knowledge that the next legislative effort of the Government would be a Bill re-establishing a separate Parliament for Ireland. The Irish "Home Rulers" had never ceased to agitate for this. For over a quarter of a century Home Rule for Ireland had been a Liberal doctrine. It was at one time the single dividing line between the Liberal Party and the "Liberal Unionists". Many of these latter had now returned to their old Party either convinced that Home Rule was inevitable or accepting it as a lesser evil than the abandonment of Free Trade. The rest were now blended into one Party with the Conservatives, with one organisation, under the joint designation of the "Conservative and Unionist Party".

Mr. Gladstone, with all his eloquence and genius, twice— in 1886 and 1893—failed to carry Home Rule Bills. The first one was thrown out by the House of Commons; the second by the House of Lords. Once again Mr. Asquith was venturing where his illustrious chief had met disappointment little removed from despair.

The most perplexing aspect of the problem was the racial, religious and social division between the South of Ireland and that portion of the Northern Province, once the most Celtic part of Ireland, now peopled largely by descendants of Scottish Presbyterians who drifted into Ulster in circumstances which form an old chapter of history.

On the 12th July of each year the story of the defeat of the Irish and Catholic supporters of the dying Stuart dynasty on the banks of the River Boyne by the Protestant Prince of Orange—William III—has been retold by the celebrations in honour of the anniversary of the battle. The enthusiastic processions have become an institution in the streets of Belfast and other towns of the North of Ireland. The custom has extended to the west coast of Scotland and to parts of Lancashire.

The annual demonstration is the more firmly established by reason of the fact that in course of time the Orangemen—as the followers of King William were designated—became not merely a political body but also a powerful benevolent Order with the ritual and passwords of a secret Friendly Society.

In the old days a very large proportion of the Protestants of the North, like their Scottish cousins, were Liberals who held strong views on Land Reform and other questions, but they held fast to the Act of Union. Older parliamentarians remembered the days of Mr. Gladstone's first Home Rule Bill, when the Unionists of Northern Ireland declared their determination to resist by force any attempt to place them under an Irish Parliament.

The old battle-cry, said to have been coined by Lord Randolph Churchill, was revived by the new prospect of Home Rule:

> " Ulster will fight
> And Ulster will be right."

In the first week of 1912 twenty thousand Ulstermen marched past Sir Edward Carson at Armagh, County Tyrone, and declared their determination to defy the authority of an Irish Parliament if and when it should be established.

An announcement was made that those Liberals of Belfast who had remained supporters of the policy of the Liberal Party were organising a demonstration in favour of Home Rule and that Mr. Winston Churchill would address a meeting in the Ulster Hall. This building was associated with memories of Lord Randolph Churchill's attack on Mr. Gladstone's Home Rule proposals, and the news that the son of their former champion would speak there in favour of the hereditary foe aroused bitter resentment among the Orangemen. Their leaders publicly asserted that Mr. Churchill would not be permitted to speak. It was stated that five thousand men would occupy the Ulster Hall for some days before his arrival and that the approach to it would be blocked by seventy-five thousand men. Conservative and Unionist papers like "The Times" and the "Morning Post" deprecated these threats. "Punch", by a cartoon headed "A Silly Game", depicted Sir Edward Carson standing with his back to the door of Ulster Hall trampling upon the placard of Mr. Churchill's Meeting and shouting "Ulster will fight". Mr. Punch, standing by, is represented as saying "What! against Free Speech? Then Ulster will be wrong."

It was asserted by a correspondent of the "Daily News" that a leaflet had been circulated at an Orange Meeting in Ulster calling on Germany, as the great Protestant Power, to come and save Ulster from being ruled by the Pope.

In spite of friendly advice, the Ulster Unionists continued their preparations for preventing Mr. Churchill from addressing the meeting in the Ulster Hall. A correspondence took place between Lord Londonderry and Mr. Churchill, from which it appeared that the main objection was to the use of the Ulster Hall. Mr. Churchill said he could not ask the Ulster Liberals to abandon their Meeting, but ultimately it was agreed that he should speak in another hall, and " Punch ", in a further cartoon on the subject, pictured " our one and only Winston " in various attitudes deciding that he would go as Daniel in the lions' den and adding "for all I care, let 'em choose their own den ".

The Meeting in the substituted hall passed off quietly.

In international affairs efforts were being made to bring about a better understanding with Germany, but feeling was irritated by the arrest and conviction of a British subject charged with an attempt to obtain military secrets.

In Home politics there was further trouble over the Insurance Act. The Doctors were still by a vast majority opposed to it, and the Unionists predicted that it would break down.

The temper of Parliament was indicated on the first day of the Session. After congratulating, according to custom, the Members who in non-partisan speeches moved and seconded the address in reply to the Speech from the Throne, Mr. Bonar Law said :

> Now, Mr. Speaker, I have done with compliments, and I am sorry to say that I do not think they will be very frequent during the Session upon which we have now entered.

Following upon this, he delivered a rattling, all-round attack upon the policy and administration of the Government.

From parliamentary conflict public attention was diverted to another serious condition of labour unrest. An impending strike in the coal trade overshadowed all other problems. The situation became so tense that the Archbishops issued the following prayer for use in the churches :

> O God Who art the Father of all, and Who alone makest men to be of one mind in an house, we beseech Thee, at this time of strife and unrest, to grant to us, by the inspiration of Thy Holy Spirit, a fuller realisation of our brotherhood man with man in Thee ; allay all danger and bitterness, and deepen in us a sense of truth and equity in our dealings one with another for the sake of Thy Son our Lord Jesus Christ, AMEN.

While this trouble in the industrial world was spreading the militant Suffragettes again became active. Anti-Suffragist Societies had been formed and a big demonstration was held in opposition to Woman Suffrage at which letters in opposition to the Suffrage were read from leading statesmen, including Mr. Asquith. One of the most effective speeches of the evening was made by Miss Violet Markham, a member of a powerful family in the industrial districts of the North Midlands; a strong supporter of Social Reform generally, and an ardent opponent of Woman Suffrage.

As a counter-stroke the militants, in order to impress the Government with the importance of dealing with Woman Suffrage in the coming Session, sallied forth once more with hammers concealed in their muffs, and broke plate glass windows to the value of between four thousand pounds and five thousand pounds. Mrs. Pankhurst drove up to the Prime Minister's residence in a private motor car, handed in a letter and then broke some of the windows with stones. In this "foray" one hundred and twenty-four women were arrested. Mrs. Pankhurst was sentenced to two months' imprisonment.

A counter-demonstration was made by anti-Suffrage medical students, who, in the presence of cheering crowds, smashed the windows at two of the offices of the Suffragist movement. The Women's Social and Political Union Offices were raided by the police and some arrests were made.

Trouble for the Government was continuous from all sides. The medical opposition to the Insurance Act was reaffirmed by a representative Meeting of the British Medical Association, who claimed as a minimum capitation fee a figure which the Government were not disposed to grant. The Doctors and students joined in active opposition to Government candidates. At a bye-election in Manchester the local Medical Staff worked hard against the Liberal who was defeated.

By the second week in March the coal strike was affecting trade in a very serious degree: eight hundred and fifty thousand miners and nearly one million, three hundred thousand workers in other industries had ceased work. Prayers in the churches were again offered. Eventually Mr. Asquith announced to the House of Commons that negotiations for a settlement by private arrangement had become hopeless and the time had arrived for Parliament to intervene.

As a consequence of investigations and enquiries the Prime Minister told the House of Commons that there was overwhelming evidence of cases where miners working underground were prevented, from causes for which the individual miner was in no sense responsible, from earning what they were willing and able to earn. The scale of a minimum wage which should be guaranteed to the miner had been agreed to by the miners and a large percentage of the mineowners, but other owners refused to come in. A Bill was therefore presented establishing the guaranteed minimum wage by law.

By more or less graphic illustration the process of coal mining was explained. The miner was depicted getting the earth or stone, through which the seam of coal runs, hewn out above and below the seam, so that the coal may be dislodged and sent to the pit shaft. It was shewn that one man might be in a "soft hole", where the earth came out with comparatively small effort on the part of the hewer, but another man, by the accident of circumstances, might find himself in a stony working place where, by reason of the conditions of the "seam", he could not secure a living wage though he might be working harder than his neighbour. It was further urged that there were other chances outside the control of the miner himself, such as imperfect roadways or shortage of "tubs" for carrying the coal away, which rendered his wage uncertain.

Members of the House who still clung to the principle of strict individualism contended that all these varying circumstances were matters for private negotiation but did not justify State interference between employer and employed to the extent of fixing a compulsory minimum wage for adults.

Mr. Balfour made an impressive reappearance on the front Opposition Bench to move the rejection of the Bill, but it was eventually carried and the strike came to an end.

Chapter 43

INCREASING TROUBLES—A TRAGEDY AT SEA

AMONG the general public Suffrage was becoming more exciting as a topic for discussion than either the Home Rule Bill or the Bill for Welsh Disestablishment.

On purely political questions people took sides with their own Parties, and in mixed company each person had a fairly clear idea as to his neighbour's opinion. Woman Suffrage had adherents and opponents among Liberals and Conservatives. Labour was the only Party really united on the subject. Their Members were unanimously in favour of Woman Suffrage.

The problem was a source of acute division in family circles; at every social gathering at some moment someone invariably introduced the prevailing topic.

Special facilities were given for the Second Reading Debate on what was known as the "Conciliation Bill" very early in the new Session. The proposal for all practical purposes, as in the Bill of 1910, was to give the parliamentary vote to women who, as ratepayers, already had a vote at Town Council Elections.

Sir Edward Grey, Mr. Lloyd George, Mr. John Burns and other well-known Liberals were supporters of the Bill. Sir Alfred Mond seconded the motion for the Second Reading. Mr. Bonar Law was in favour of it, as was Mr. Balfour. The whole of the Cecil family had been and continued to be consistent supporters of Woman Suffrage. They brought all the traditional zeal of their House into the constitutional side of the struggle. Mr. Asquith, as a consistent opponent of the movement, concluded his speech on this occasion with a declaration which became historic:

I am bound to take what I believe to be—what I have always believed to be throughout the whole of my political life—the only sound and prudent attitude with regard to this question and vote against any proposal of this kind, which I have no doubt would in the long run prove to be injurious to women and fraught with the gravest possibilities to the future good government of this country.

Some Members who had been steady supporters of Woman Suffrage asserted that they felt constrained to vote against all Bills of this character until the militants ceased their unlawful tactics. As against this point of view Sir Edward Grey said ·

I have a natural reluctance to be driven out of my course and out of a vote of which I approve by outbursts of violence. Just as, naturally, I object to be driven into a vote of which I do not approve by outbreaks of violence.

The deciding voice came from Ireland. No official intimation had been issued to the Irish Members as to how they were to vote, but it was whispered in the Lobbies that Mr. Pat O'Brien, the cheeriest and most popular of Whips, had been heard to say that the boys could do what they liked so long as they did not jeopardise Home Rule by embarrassing the Government.

The interpretation was fairly clear to all parliamentarians. If the Suffrage Bill passed its Second Reading, time for its further stages would undoubtedly be demanded. This meant more domestic differences in the Government and more parliamentary time consumed which might be badly needed for the Home Rule Bill. The Irish Nationalists' devotion to Home Rule was as the mother's instinct which subjugates all else to the life of her child.

The majorities for previous Suffrage Bills still suggested that supporters of this one were safe and it would only be a question of numbers. Right up to the moment when the last man emerged from the "aye" Lobby this assumption prevailed.

Mr. (afterwards Sir) James Agg-Gardner, a veteran Conservative, beloved by all men in the House—repre-

senting genteel Cheltenham—as the mover of the Second
Reading and the principal Teller for the Bill, walked slowly
up the floor of the House from the door of the "aye" Lobby.
When he arrived at the Table, the "no" Lobby Tellers were
not there. He looked round him perplexedly; the Benches
were crowded with excited men who, as usual, shouted
"Order! Order!!", because at the moment they had nothing
else to do. Technically Mr. Agg-Gardner was out of order:
he had no function to perform at the Table until the other
Tellers arrived. The most unassuming of men, he looked
painfully self-conscious in the midst of the seething multitude.
Every seat was occupied and he could not escape that way.
A colleague on the front Opposition Bench touched his arm
and signalled to him to go back to the Bar. He turned in
that direction and meantime the "No" Tellers made their
way to the Table.

The result was by this time evident: the "No" Tellers
were late because they had more men to count. When the
figures, two hundred and twenty-two against the Bill and
two hundred and eight for, were announced the anti-Suffragists
burst into uproarious cheers; several of them standing at
the Bar triumphantly waved their handkerchiefs.

The result was a surprise all round: this was the first
occasion in modern times that the House had actually rejected
Woman Suffrage on a direct vote.

An analysis of the division showed that many Irish Nationalist Members had voted against the Bill and the rest had
abstained. The abstention of those who voted, or the
favourable votes of those who abstained, would have won
the day for the Suffragists. This fact was the subject of
excited comment among the friends as well as the opponents
of the Irishmen. Somewhile afterwards Mr. Walter Roach,
a fervent supporter of Home Rule and of Woman Suffrage,
gave expression to current conversation. Quoting the
fate of the Conciliation Bill, he said:

  Every Member sitting as a Nationalist Member for an
  Irish constituency who was against Woman Suffrage voted

against the Bill, whilst of those who were supposed to be in favour of the Bill not a single one was found in the Lobby! I say to the Irish Members my faith is quite as strong and undimmed in Irish Home Rule as it is in Woman Suffrage, but they will forgive me for saying that they then played a selfish game. It is just as well to talk quite frankly and not to say one thing in the Lobby or the Smoke Room and to use soft words to the Irish Members in the House. They have played a selfish game. I can assure them—not by way of making any threats—that selfish games react upon the people who play them.

Meanwhile, the way was clear for the discussion on Home Rule. Mr. Asquith introduced his Bill on the 11th April. In the Debate on the First Reading there was a bitterness and a passion hardly ever known at this preliminary stage of a parliamentary measure. Mr. Asquith referred to what he described as the "new style". Mr. Bonar Law had been speaking up and down the country in terms that delighted his more enthusiastic followers but were in striking contrast to the usual tone of Mr. Balfour's speeches. The Prime Minister quoted one passage from the Leader of the Opposition to the effect that:

"The present Government turn the House of Commons into a market place where everything is bought and sold. In order to remain for a few months longer in Office His Majesty's Government have sold the Constitution."

Following upon this quotation came a smart dialogue across the Table:

The PRIME MINISTER: Am I to understand that the right hon. Gentleman repeats here, or is prepared to repeat on the floor of the House of Commons—

Mr. BONAR LAW: Yes.

The PRIME MINISTER: Let us see exactly what it is: It is that I and my colleagues are selling our convictions.

Mr. BONAR LAW: You have not got any.

The PRIME MINISTER: We are getting on with the new style. The right hon. Gentleman said that I and my colleagues are selling our convictions—

Captain (afterwards Sir James) Craig: You have sold them to Mr. John Redmond.

The Prime Minister: That we are producing a Bill which the right hon. Gentleman said, elsewhere in the same speech, does not represent our views—

Mr. Bonar Law: Hear, hear.

The Prime Minister: In order that for a few months longer we may cling to office. Does he really believe that? What have I to gain? [An Hon. Member: Office.] What have my colleagues to gain—[An Hon. Member: Office]— by a transaction to purchase for us—

Captain Craig: Eighty Nationalist votes.

The Prime Minister: To purchase for us a short further spell of the burdens and responsibilities which we have borne in very difficult and troublous times, now for the best part of seven years, at the price of surrendering our convictions and soiling for all time our personal and political honour. How many people, I wonder, in this House really believe that?

Mr. Redmond, speaking later, said it might be considered in the interest of some people to engender passion in Debates and to endeavour to overwhelm the issue by personal attacks. He appealed to his friends not to be tempted to retaliate— to conduct the Debate with self-restraint and good temper. He concluded a fervent speech with these words:

I pray earnestly that this Bill may pass; that it may achieve all the objects which its promoters have in view; and that, in the beautiful words of the prayer, with which the proceedings of this House of Commons are opened every day :— 'the result of all our counsels may be the maintenance of true religion and justice, the safety, honour and happiness of the King, the public health, peace and tranquillity of the realm, and the uniting and knitting together therein of the hearts of all persons and estates within the same, in true Christian love and charity'.

The Bill received its First Reading and went forward to its further stages. Its proposals, in brief, were that Ireland should have a Parliament consisting, under the King, of a Senate and House of Commons with power to make laws for the peace, order and good government of Ireland. The Crown, war and peace, the Navy and Army, treaties and other matters of a similar character were left under the control of Imperial authority. The Irish Parliament was to have no power to make laws, either directly or indirectly, for the establishment or endowment of any religion or for prohibiting the free exercise of any religion or giving preference to or imposing disability on any religious body. The Lord Lieutenant was empowered to withhold the Royal Assent to any Bill under certain conditions, and the Imperial Legislature could nullify, amend or alter any Act of Parliament under certain conditions, for which purpose the supremacy of the Imperial Parliament was to be preserved. Members for Irish constituencies, to the reduced number of forty-two, were to be returned to the Imperial Parliament.

The Debate was adjourned in passion, and meanwhile the thoughts of the nation and the whole world were centred on news from the freezing seas which reminded man with tragic directness that he had not yet subdued the forces of nature.

On the 16th April, just before the Debate on the Home Rule Bill was resumed, Lord Charles Beresford asked for authentic information concerning the news that the passenger ship "Titanic" had been wrecked. This triumph of swiftness and strength—the nearest to perfection in ship-building craft that modern science and human skill could attain—had been supposed to be unsinkable and the disaster had shocked all calculations.

Ordinarily, the President of the Board of Trade would answer questions relating to the Mercantile Marine. When the Prime Minister advanced to the box it was obvious that a statement of grave importance was about to be made. He asked the House to permit him to answer the question. As he proceeded to read the message received by the Board of Trade to the effect that the ship had foundered, Members in all parts of the House removed their hats. In tones of deep emotion Mr. Asquith continued:

I am afraid we must brace ourselves to confront one of

those terrible events in the order of Providence which baffle foresight, which appal the imagination and which make us realise the inadequacy of words to do justice to what we feel. We cannot say more at this moment than to give necessarily imperfect expression to our sense of admiration that the best traditions of the sea seem to have been observed and of the willing sacrifices which were offered to give the best chance of safety to those who were least able to help themselves, and the warm and heartfelt sympathy of the whole nation to those who find themselves suddenly bereft of the nearest and dearest in their desolated homes.

Further information which came to hand showed that the "Titanic" left Southampton for a maiden voyage to New York, and struck a submerged portion of an iceberg with a glancing blow which tore open a number of her watertight compartments below the waterline.

The accident happened about half-past-ten on Sunday night, the 14th April, and some four hours afterwards the vessel sank with a loss of one thousand, six hundred and thirty-five lives. Of the total number of souls on board, seven hundred and eleven were saved. Amongst those who went down was Mr. W. T. Stead, one of the best-known journalists of his time—the founder of the "Review of Reviews" and other periodicals.

On both sides of the Atlantic thoughts of the terrible calamity dominated public interest. An Inquiry was held in America. A Commission of Inquiry in London, presided over by Lord Mersey, formerly President of the Admiralty Court, while finding nobody to blame made certain recommendations for future guidance which led to a revision of the regulations affecting passenger ships.

Chapter 44

SAVING ART TREASURES—MORE ACUTE CONTROVERSIES

AN event of importance as an encouragement of the popular taste for art was the opening of five new rooms at

the National Gallery in the Spring of 1911.   This fine building on the North side of Trafalgar Square, facing the fountains
and the Nelson column, has for very many years been highly
appreciated by visitors to London though frequented perhaps less generally than it should be by residents in the
Metropolis.   Founded in the early part of the Nineteenth
century and assisted by a parliamentary grant of some five
to ten thousand pounds, with occasional increases to permit
of special purchases, it collected works of the Great Masters.
The National Art Collection Fund, a society of private sub-
scribers, made many additions to the collection.   In the early
part of 1906 the Council of the fund were able to announce
that negotiations for the famous Velasquez "Venus and
Cupid" were practically completed, and shortly afterwards
the picture was hung in the Gallery.

In September 1911 it was announced that the trustees of
the National Gallery had bought from the Countess of Carlisle the picture by Gossaert Mabuse "The Adoration of the
Kings".   The purchase price of forty thousand pounds was
declared by experts to be much less—some said by one half
—than might have been obtained for it from American collectors.   Of the forty thousand the Government contributed
fifteen thousand and the duty payable; the balance coming
from the National Art Collections Fund and the National
Gallery Fund.

At the Royal Academy Banquet in the following May the
Prime Minister referred to the fact that it had been the privilege of the Government to help in securing the retention of
this picture by this country.   Mr. Asquith went on to remark
that the picture might have been lost but for the intervention
of the Tax payer and he added that only in the course of the
last few years they had read that two great Masterpieces by
one of the greatest painters had passed at enormous prices
to foreign collectors.

The question of retaining art treasures was becoming a
topic of considerable anxiety to art lovers.   The Prime
Minister with these examples before him felt called upon to

express his views to such an authoritative body as the Royal
Academy. He observed that there were countries which
had adopted drastic means legislative and administrative to
preserve their "art patrimony". Upon this aspect of the
matter he said:—

> I do not think public opinion in this country is ripe for
> the imitation of these forms of procedure nor can you expect
> the British Tax payer to enter into unlimited competition
> for this purpose with the millionaires of the world.

The Prime Minister paid a tribute to the public spirit of
owners of pictures and said he thought it was a very rare
thing for the possessor of a great picture here not to be ready
and willing to give the first refusal of it to the Nation when
he was about to part with it. Referring to the future he
said the remedy was to be found in increased co-operation
between private generosity and State aid and, lest he should
be supposed to hold out improbable prospects, he added
that, as had been the case with the formation of the Great
National Collection in Trafalgar Square, private generosity
might be expected to play a most active and a most important part.

Another Welsh Disestablishment Bill on similar lines to
that which was introduced in 1909, and then dropped in the
pressure of parliamentary business, was introduced by Mr.
McKenna towards the end of April, 1912.

A few days afterwards Mr. Winston Churchill moved
the Second Reading of the Irish Home Rule Bill, thus bringing
the two great controversial measures of the Session into the
arena for alternating demonstrations of furious gladiatorial
combats.

Mr. Churchill, in the course of a comprehensive speech
reviewing the whole Irish situation, leant across the Table
and, addressing the Opposition, said:

> Can you say that you are satisfied with the existing con-
> dition of things?

*   *   *   *   *

What position and what status do you accord to four-fifths of her [Ireland's] representatives? They are to remain here, but they are to be regarded as political pariahs. [Several hon. Members: 'Why?'] Anyone who co-operates with them or who accepts their co-operation in the ordinary working of parliamentary business—[Several hon. Members: 'Oh']—we are told is guilty of dishonourable and contemptible conduct, of paltering with the unclean thing.

The Irish position from both points of view was put in impressive speeches. Mr. Thomas Scanlan, the Member for North Sligo, in the course of a reasoned argument on the general problem, said:

We look forward to a time when those who have fought against one another as Protestants and Catholics will join hands and stand shoulder to shoulder and fight together to exterminate religious differences, and to bring about the peace and prosperity and happiness of Ireland and the greatness of the Empire.

Mr. Charles Craig, the Member for South Antrim, on the other hand, said:

You may call it what you like, but we in the North of Ireland believe that a Parliament in Dublin would be dominated by the Roman Catholic Church, and the Roman Catholic Church, being what it is, we do not believe, to use a colloquial phrase, that the Protestants would have a "fair show". Protestants are not going to allow themselves to come under the domination of that Parliament.

A feature of the Debate was a maiden speech by Mr. Samuel Young, who, amid loud and general cheers, mentioned that he was ninety-one years of age. As a Protestant and an inhabitant of Ulster, in business in Belfast,—representing the Catholic constituency of East Cavan—he warmly supported the Bill.

For several days the Debate went on with eloquent speeches on both sides. One Ulster Unionist, Mr. R. Thompson, whose remarks were greeted with interruptions by a "stranger"—promptly removed—from the gallery, made

Q

a somewhat cryptic reference to the possibility of international complications if troops were sent to Belfast to
repress the opponents of Home Rule. He said it had come
to his knowledge that Germany had taken the measurements
of the Docks in the Port of Belfast, and the depth of the
water in the Channel, and he concluded:

> Further, I may say, that Germany has actually named
> her officer to take charge of an expedition against Belfast
> if and when called upon to do so. If by this Bill you get
> up a state of civil war in Ulster and Belfast, see where you
> are. Germany did not take all this trouble for nothing. I
> will conclude by impressing upon the right hon. Gentlemen
> representing the Government and the House to beware before
> sending Government troops to Ulster.

Ultimately the Second Reading was carried by three hundred
and seventy-two votes to two hundred and seventy-one.

The Second Reading Debate of the Welsh Disestablishment Bill came swiftly upon the heels of the Home Rule
discussion. The rejection of this measure was moved by
Mr. F. E. Smith in one of his eloquently contemptuous
speeches which drew several Liberal Members into excited
interruptions. In his concluding passage he said:

> This Bill will leave behind it the memory of unforgettable
> wrong. It will revive antagonisms happily declining. It
> will give satisfaction to none except those who say: 'How
> these Christians love one another.' The Government will
> be well advised, even at the eleventh hour, to withdraw a
> Bill which has shocked the conscience of every Christian
> community in Europe.

The most exciting moment in the discussion came at a
later stage when Mr. Lloyd George dealt with the charge
that the financial proposals were an act of sacrilege. Especially referring to the attack made upon the Bill by the Duke
of Devonshire, he said:

> The Duke of Devonshire issues a circular applying for
> subscriptions to oppose this Bill, and he charges us with the
> robbery of God. Why, does he not know—of course he

knows—that the very foundations of his fortune are laid deep in sacrilege, fortunes built out of desecrated shrines and pillaged altars.

*   *   *   *   *

Look at the whole story of the pillage of the Reformation. They robbed the Catholic Church, they robbed the monasteries, they robbed the altars; they robbed the almshouses; they robbed the poor, and they robbed the dead. Then they come here when we are trying to seek, at any rate to recover some part of this pillaged property for the poor for whom it was originally given, and they venture, with hands dripping with the fat of sacrilege, to accuse us of robbery of God.

In this atmosphere the ordinary amenities of life at Westminster were suspended.

More Labour troubles now occupied the attention of the Government and the public. A strike of transport workers at the London Docks was the subject of heated scenes in the House and protests from two points of view against the action of the Government. The official Opposition contended that the Government had not taken sufficiently firm steps or given sufficient support to the firms who endeavoured to continue their services in spite of the strike. The Members of the Labour Party took the opposite view and called for some measures by the House and the Government to effect a settlement. Terms were suggested by the Government but refused by the employers.

Forcible feeding of Suffragist prisoners on hunger strike became a subject of repeated questions to the Government. An undertaking had been asked from some of the women then in gaol that they would refrain from further breaches of the law. Towards the end of June Lord Hugh Cecil and other Members suggested a special Debate on the subject.

A question was put one afternoon to the Prime Minister by Mr. Tim Healy as to whether he could see his way, as a number of these prisoners were to be discharged on the following Saturday, to make a slight concession and have them discharged at once. "Why keep up this endless torture?" asked Mr. Healy.

The Prime Minister replied that it was not for him to interfere with the action of his colleagues, that it was purely an administrative matter for the Home Department. He added:

> I must point out that there is not a single one of these women who could not come out of prison this afternoon if they gave the undertaking that has been asked for.

"You know they cannot", shouted Mr. George Lansbury, the Member for Bow and Bromley.

Loud shouts of "Order!, Order!!" greeted this interjection. Raising his voice, Mr. Lansbury cried:

> It is perfectly disgraceful that the Prime Minister of England should make such a statement.

Proceeding with his remonstrance, the protesting Member was greeted with further shouts of "Order! Order!!" which partially drowned his voice. Leaving his place from below the gangway, he rushed up the floor of the House and stood opposite the Treasury Bench. Sweeping his arm comprehensively at the Members of the Government, he said:

> You are beneath contempt. You call yourselves gentlemen and you forcibly feed and murder women in this fashion. You ought to be driven out of Office.

Above vigorous cries of "Order! Order!!" the voice trained to addressing outdoor crowds in Bow and Bromley was heard:

> It's perfectly disgraceful. Talk about protesting! It's the most disgraceful thing that ever happened in the history of England.

Shaking his fist in the face of Mr. Asquith, Mr. Lansbury finally shouted:

> You will go down to history as the man who tortured innocent women: that's what you'll go down to history as.

Then the irate Member returned to his place and addressing the Speaker said:

I have had my say, Mr. Speaker. [Cries of 'Sit down!' and 'Order! Order!!'] It is disgraceful that the Prime Minister of this country should tell women in prison on principle that they can walk out. The hon. Member for Cork knew he could walk out of prison, but he did not, and the Liberal Party for the sake of votes defended William O'Brien when he refused to wear the prison clothes.

This was an allusion to an exciting period when the Liberal Opposition of that day protested with the Nationalists against the prison treatment of Mr. William O'Brien in Ireland under a Conservative Government. When Mr. Lansbury sat down the Speaker, in a calm voice, asked the hon. Member to leave the House in consequence of his "grossly disorderly conduct".

Again Mr. Lansbury burst forth in protest:—

I am not going out while this contemptible thing is being done. Murdering, torturing and driving women mad and telling them they can walk out! You ought to be ashamed of yourselves. You may talk about principle and fighting Ulster. You ought to be driven out of public life. You don't know what principle is. These women are showing you what principle is. You should honour them for standing up for their womanhood. I say, for the Prime Minister to say they could walk out is beneath contempt, and I shall stick to it. I tell him it is beneath contempt to tell the Commons of England that and to laugh at the sufferings of these women. You ought to be ashamed of yourselves!

The Speaker, in a tone that had a subduing effect, said:

I must point out to the hon. Member for Bow and Bromley that in refusing to leave the House he is disregarding the authority of the Chair.

Mr. Lansbury, in a softened voice, replied:

I have no intention in any sort of way of being dishonourable to you, Sir, but I can't contain myself when men sitting there say these women can walk out, when they know very well they cannot walk out. They are fighting for a principle and Members would be better employed if they were doing the same.

The Speaker reminded Mr. Lansbury that it was his duty to defend the House against disorder.

Apparently unaware of what was expected from him under the circumstances, Mr. Lansbury asked:

What is it you want me to do, Mr. Speaker?

Then, looking along to the corner seat of the next Bench, where Mr. Macdonald, now the Leader of his Party was sitting, he asked:

What am I to do Mac?

It was intimated to the hon. Member that what he had to do was to withdraw from the House during the remainder of the Sitting. When this became clear to him he rose and, addressing the Speaker, said:

All I want to say, Mr. Speaker, is that I make that protest against the statement made by the Prime Minister.

He then walked out, and very shortly afterwards the House was busily discussing woods and forests.

Chapter 45

TRIUMPHS IN AIR AND AIR WAVES

WHILE some women were struggling for the Vote, others were making still more daring incursions into realms hitherto reserved for the strongest of men. They had soared into the air as passengers, and had taken an active part in aviation. Miss Harriet Quimby in April 1912 crossed from Dover to Hardelot in a Bleriot monoplane— covering the distance in forty minutes. Miss Quimby was the first woman to fly across the English Channel.

This feat was a milestone in the extremely rapid development of aviation. For all practical purposes the public interest in the science may be said to date from somewhere about the time that Bleriot swooped down upon the English coast. The earlier years were experimental. When the airman found his "air-legs" his progress was incredibly swift in design, construction, and execution. Flying meetings were arranged in continental centres and in England.— Blackpool and Doncaster were among the first to provide flying-off places. Very soon flights were undertaken from London to Manchester. Then came Paris to London and other distances that had seemed impossible a few years earlier. In 1911 the aeroplane was first tried as a war machine. During the Mexican rebellion an American named Hamilton carried out a reconnoitring flight over a Mexican town. The aeroplane was also used for purposes of reconnaissance by the Italians in their Tripoli campaign.

Seaplanes were a later but a quick development. The first English flight from the water was by Commander Swarm and S. V. Sippe at Barrow in November 1911. Airships grew almost before the eyes of a startled public. Zeppelin's persistent experiments in Germany were recorded and travellers had seen his rigids floating in the air. British rigid airship No. 1 was started in 1909 and others soon followed.

*   *   *   *   *

Candidates supporting the Government had a trying experience at bye-elections with the Insurance Act. The bigger industrial concerns, with more important matters to occupy the administrative heads, simply put the Act into operation through the ordinary executive process of office organisation. Smaller employers of more or less casual labour, and especially people with general servants, were stirred to resistance and in some cases to defiance of the law by a strong Press campaign.

A firm of London Solicitors wrote to the Chancellor of the Exchequer to the effect that they would take the decision of a Police Magistrate as to the penalty proper for a firm refusing to observe the Act, which they described as an "obviously unfair scheme". Mr. Lloyd George replied that this theory of obedience to the law would apply to dockers and Suffragists, and indicated that in all cases the Government intended to apply the law. A second protest meeting in the Albert Hall was attended by titled ladies and domestic servants.

The subject occasioned far more excitement than Home Rule. It was remarked by a leading Conservative paper that the "burning question" of Home Rule would not burn. So far did the ordinary public leave the Irish question to parliamentarians that as a protest it was suggested in the "Observer" that the Unionists should stop all business in the House of Commons by a "disciplined storm" consisting of continuous cries of "Dissolve! Dissolve!!", and thus endeavour to rouse the country.

Meantime, Mr. Asquith visited Ireland, where he was received with tremendous enthusiasm and escorted by a torchlight procession, though the militant Suffragists followed him here as elsewhere.

An impressive Naval Review in the Solent, as an example of what the nation was obtaining for its expenditure, preceded the introduction of a supplementary Naval Estimate by Mr. Winston Churchill, who had become First Lord of the Admiralty.

Mr. Churchill dwelt specially on two points—the increase in the German naval strength and the British Dominions' naval activity. Summing up the situation, he said:

> The task of maintaining the Naval power of the Empire under existing conditions is a heavy one. All the world is arming as it has never armed before. . . .
>
> There is an earnest disposition on the part of the self-governing Dominions to assist in the common defence of the Empire.

Mr. Balfour and other Members on the Conservative side expressed their gratification at the statement by the First Lord as to the attitude of the Dominions. Referring to the increases of armaments that were going on in the world,

and to the fact that our expenditure in this department had
increased by twelve millions during the last few years Mr.
Balfour said:

> We, at all events, have this consolation : we do not build
> for ambition; we build for peace and security.

The general atmosphere in this Debate was a striking
contrast to that in the more controversial discussions of
domestic legislation. Criticism was on minor points.
Between the two Front Benches and their immediate supporters there was general agreement on broad principles. Some
Independent Liberal Members protested against the increase,
while some Conservative Members (including Admiral Lord
Charles Beresford) were not satisfied that the provision
made was adequate.

In Home affairs the most dramatic incident was the
collapse of the London Dock strike after a long struggle,
with some pathetic scenes and some disorderly incidents.
A visit of the King to the Albert Docks to cut the first sod
of the new extension had been abandoned on account of the
unrest occasioned by the strike in that part of London.
The dispute left behind it a feeling of bitterness which had a
lasting effect upon social and political questions along the
busy banks of the Thames.

In the House of Commons a Bill was again brought in by
Sir Rufus Isaacs, the Attorney-General, similar to that
introduced in 1911, for permitting Trade Unions to use
their funds in support of movements for parliamentary
representation.

Vigorous efforts were made to create animation in the
country on the Irish question. A Unionist demonstration
was held at Blenheim, the seat of the Duke of Marlborough,
when Mr. Bonar Law, Sir Edward Carson and Mr. F. E.
Smith addressed some ten thousand people. Mr. Bonar
Law said he could imagine no length of resistance to which
Ulster could go in which he would not be ready to support
them.

On this Mr. Asquith declared:

> The moment you lay down, as the leaders of the Con-
> stitional Party lay down, the doctrine that a minority—I
> do not care what minority, if you like a majority,—are entitled
> because a particular act of legislation is distasteful to their
> views, and as they think, oppressive to their interests, to
> resist it by force, there is an absolute end to parliamentary
> government.

In the same Debate reference was made to serious riotings
that had taken place in Belfast. Mr. Winston Churchill, in
a letter to Sir George Ritchie, the Chairman of the Liberal
Party in Dundee, described the speeches of the Conservative
Leader as:

> doctrines from which every street bully with a brickbat and
> every crazy fanatic who is fumbling with a pistol may derive
> inspiration.

To this Mr. Bonar Law replied that Mr. Winston Churchill
was begging the question, and suggested that the attacks
which he had made upon the Leaders of the Conservative
Party for their resistance to Home Rule might very well
have been applied to his own father. Enthusiastic demonstrations were held in the North of Ireland in which Sir
Edward Carson was the chief figure and was escorted by
mounted bodyguards carrying dummy wooden rifles. At
Portadown Sir Edward was presented with a blackthorn
cudgel adorned with orange and pink ribbons, and, finally,
at the Ulster Hall came a presentation of the yellow banner
under which William III had marched to victory at the
Boyne. Sir Edward Carson marched under the banner to
Ulster Hall and a covenant was signed which concluded
with the words:

> 'In the event of such a Parliament being forced upon us
> we further solemnly pledge ourselves to refuse to recognise
> its authority.'

Sir Edward Carson, whose practice at the English Bar was

at this period probably the most extensive amongst all the eminent advocates of the day, relinquished his legal work in order that he might devote all his energies to the struggle. His strenuous and continued parliamentary opposition at various stages of the Home Rule Bill was one of the most brilliant efforts in the records of West-minster. His Nationalist fellow-countrymen, while they fought him inch by inch with the intensity of century-old passion, were nevertheless proud of him, more especially as he was a son of Dublin City. A graduate of Dublin Univer-sity and in his younger days at the Irish Bar a personal friend of Mr. John Redmond, who practised on the same circuit, he had nothing but politics in common with the dour men of Antrim and Armagh; yet, he fought with them and for them and was the one man for the leadership.

All Members of the Conservative and Unionist Party in Great Britain did not go so far as Mr. Bonar Law in their encouragement of active resistance. Although Sir Edward Carson and his Ulster colleagues aroused some parliamentary excitement, the general public still remained unimpressed. Home Rule was discussed at Debating Societies and in bye elections, but the political interest of the man in the street was directed to other matters, and one subject in particular was engaging the attention of the Government and Parlia-ment. Wireless telegraphy was new—the Irish question was old.

Gugiliemo Marconi was born at Bologna in 1874. At this time of day it may sound incredible that until the present century was in its 'teens little or nothing was known of wireless messages by the general body of the people in any country of the world. When quite a boy young Marconi began making experiments in his father's house with the transmission of messages by utilising air waves. After several attempts he succeeded in the summer of 1895 in obtaining telegraphic signals through space over a distance of one-and-three-quarter miles. This, at the time, was a wonderful achievement, though Mr. Marconi, in a speech

made many years afterwards, thus modestly disclaimed
absolute originality:

> I must confess being at times amused by the discussions
> which occasionally take place as to who is the real inventor
> of wireless. To my mind wireless existed when the prehistoric
> man first understood or felt the meaning of a smile of encourage-
> ment from the prehistoric girl.

To the youthful Italian engineer, nevertheless, may be
traced the system of utilising electric waves. He came to
England and has since paid an eloquent tribute to the
welcome and assistance he received here, more particularly
from Sir William Preece, the Engineering Chief to the Post
Office, who, according to Mr. Marconi, was one of the very
few scientists to realise some of the enormous possibilities of
electric waves at that date. In 1897 Mr. Marconi was able
to demonstrate the system by sending messages over Salisbury Plain. Two years later he transmitted messages across
the English Channel, and in 1902 from England to Canada
and the United States.

In this early stage of the science a person here and there
with an engineering bent who set up weird instruments in
his garden, by which he professed to send messages from one
point to another, was regarded by his neighbours as a bit
more cranky than the man who, a few years earlier, thought
he had a conveyance that could travel on the highroad
without steam or without horses.

Scientists who took the subject seriously realised that the
theory was sound, and Marconi went on improving and
inventing. The great strides towards the perfection of
wireless transmission began in the second decade of the
century. There were other inventions, and controversy
utterly beyond the capacity of the ordinary layman raged in
scientific circles as to the relative merits of particular
systems. The "Marconi" method so far succeeded that
when people thought of sending a message through the air
they called it a "Marconi".

SENATORE MARCONI

A Company was established to put the system into practical effect as a means of communication for general use. As in the case of ordinary telegraphy and the telephones, both of which began with a private Company, a large body of opinion considered it desirable that the State should control the new method of communication. Accordingly, a contract with the Company was proposed, the terms of which Mr. (afterwards Sir) Herbert Samuel, the Postmaster-General, explained to the House in August 1912. Mr. Samuel suggested that on two points there would be no disagreement: first, that the erection of long range wireless telegraph stations at suitable points throughout the Empire was in itself desirable for commerce in time of peace and for communication in time of war. He continued:

> However little we may anticipate war, it is of course the primary duty of the Government to make provision for Imperial defence.

The second point with respect to which he thought there would be no controversy was that these stations when erected ought properly to be in the hands of the Government in the different parts of the Empire. Many incidental scenes were destined to arise out of " wireless ".

*   *   *   *   *

On the 20th of August 1912 General Booth passed away at the ripe age of 83. He continued his wonderful work practically to the end. During the year before his death he made a motor car speaking tour in Great Britain. In the organisation of his beloved Army he had travelled throughout Europe several times. He was five times in America and Canada. He visited South Africa three times and India twice, and also made a journey to Japan. He had been made an Hon. D.C.L. of Oxford and a freeman of the City of London. His funeral was made the occasion of reverential tributes to his great service to humanity. After lying in State at Olympia the remains were buried at Abney Park cemetery. Fifty-one brigades of the Salvation Army

escorted the funeral cortege. Members of the public lined
the streets and the Lord Mayor saluted the coffin as it passed
the Mansion House. The General having been in supreme
command for so many years some anxiety had been expressed
as to the succession, but all doubts were set at rest when
Mr. Bramwell Booth the son of the dead founder took control
as General.

Chapter 46

A "SNAP"—MORE DISORDER

ONE of the most effective "snaps" in parliamentary
history was scored on an autumn day in 1912.

The Financial Resolutions necessary for the Home Rule
Bill were at the Report Stage, Sir Frederick Banbury quietly
and unostentatiously dropped in a Resolution limiting the
total payments with respect to the Bill to a sum which the
Government regarded as quite inadequate. The matter
came up on a Monday and was treated as a casual affair by
the Liberal Party managers. According to their arrangements, the division should take place somewhere about
seven in the evening, but the Conservative Members showed
no disposition to talk.

Liberal Members who had strolled into the Lobby wondered
why the division bell was ringing at about four o'clock.
Light dawned when Conservatives flooded in from all points
of the compass. Old parliamentary hands realised that
the Government Whips were "snapped". Only the possibility of the Opposition Whips having miscalculated their
reserves, or the chance that more Liberal Members than
appeared on the checkers' lists were within hail, could save
a defeat.

With anxious eyes Members on either side watched the
Tellers counting their men through the respective Lobby
doors. A mighty shout went up from the Opposition Benches
when the Clerk at the Table handed the significant sheet
of paper to Sir Frederick Banbury. The figures, two hundred

and twenty-eight to two hundred and six, did not show a big majority, but it was sufficient.

When the triumphant cries to the left of the Chair at last subsided, the Prime Minister and Mr. Bonar Law rose together. As Leader of the House the Prime Minister got the call. In one sentence he moved that "further consideration of the Resolution as amended be now adjourned".

At twenty minutes past four Members flocked out to the Lobby and hung about in little groups. The prospect of another General Election loomed on the horizon. A special meeting of Ministers and Government Whips was understood to be in progress and everybody remained in the neighbourhood of Westminster awaiting news of their deliberations. A Member was seen rushing to the Post Office to despatch a telegram; others followed, and then word went round that the Government had decided they would not resign. Their supporters drifted off to their Clubs cheered by the thought that sufficient unto the day was the evil thereof.

The following afternoon Mr. Asquith gave notice that on the Wednesday he would move a Resolution to the effect that the decision of the House on Sir Frederick Banbury's Amendment be rescinded.

On the Wednesday Mr. Asquith opened quietly by quoting precedents, going back to Sir Robert Peel and coming down to Mr. Balfour, who was sitting modestly by the new Conservative Leader. The classical case, Mr. Asquith said, was in 1905, when the Government were defeated on a very important Vote in Supply but did not resign. Mr. Bonar Law in turn quoted precedents as showing that in those earlier instances the decision of the Government was condemned by the Opposition. Other speeches were made in a similar tone and the Debate grew more and more excited as it proceeded. While one Member was speaking there were shouts of "Traitor! Traitor!!" at the mention of the Prime Minister. The Speaker asked who made use of that expression.

"I did", said Sir William Bull, a cheery and good natured, but obviously enraged, Member of the Conservative Party.

Another honourable Member desired to share the blame. The Speaker told them both that they must not do it again. Before many minutes had passed, the word "Traitor" rang out once more, and again the Speaker asked who said it.

Sir William Bull this time monopolised the responsibility and was speedily called upon from the Chair to leave the House during the remainder of the day's sitting.

"I don't think it will be very long, Mr. Speaker, before you will be required to send other Members out", interposed Mr. Charles Craig.

"The hon. Member is not in possession of the House", replied the Speaker calmly.

"When the hon. Member is finished I will give it them even more strongly", responded Mr. Craig.

After a series of speeches from the Opposition side, Sir Rufus Isaacs rose to reply on behalf of the Government. A hurricane of shouts drowned his very first words.

"Hon. Members on that [the Opposition] side of the House who have spoken have been listened to in silence and they ought to hear what is said from the other side", observed the Speaker.

"Mr. Speaker, you have said——" began the Attorney-General.

Shouts of "Adjourn! Adjourn!!" prevented the right hon. and learned Gentleman from commenting further on what the Speaker had said.

Once again an appeal was made from the Chair: "I would remind hon. Members who are in the corner [to the immediate left of the Chair] and who are calling out 'Adjourn'", said the Speaker, "that an appeal has been made over and over again for fair play".

"We want fair play on both sides, and they [the Government] will not give it us", ejaculated Mr. Austen Chamberlain.

"I express no opinion with regard to that", said the Speaker. "Those who appeal for fair play ought to show it."

"It is civil war," cried one right hon. Member.

Sir Rufus Isaacs once more returned to the despatch box.
What followed is thus officially recorded:

> Sir RUFUS ISAACS: You have ruled, Mr. Speaker—[Inter-
> ruption]— . . . The hon. and learned Member has
> challenged us—[Interruption]—to quote precedents—[Inter-
> ruption]—for the course we are pursuing—[Interruption].
> I desire—[Interruption]— . . . Mr. Speaker, you have
> pointed out——[Interruption].
>
> Mr. RONALD M'NEILL: Why do you not sit down?
> [Interruption]. . . .
>
> Mr. SPEAKER: In my opinion grave disorder has arisen,
> and, under Standing Order No. 21, I adjourn the House and
> suspend the sitting for an hour.

The hour's adjournment did not bring peace. When the
Speaker resumed the Chair, Sir Rufus Isaacs once more
began—

"Mr. Speaker——"

"Sit down", shouted Members opposite.

"There is your parliamentary machine broken," cried one
hon. Gentleman.

When the Attorney-General did sit down, Viscount Helms-
ley rose from the Conservative Benches below the gangway.
His own friends shouted "Adjourn! Adjourn!!".

The Speaker made another appeal to hon. Members.

"No more business in this House", shouted Sir Edward
Carson. This was the signal for a continuous chant from
the Conservative Benches. It began with individual shouts
in different keys. Then the voices blended in unison and the
refrain "No more business! No more business!!" drifted
into a consolidated drone of "Adjourn! Adjourn! Adjourn!!"

Eventually the Speaker, rising when the volume of sound
was like the never-ceasing roar of many waters, said:

> It is quite obvious to the House that it is useless to continue.
> If hon. Members confine themselves to Parliamentary cries,
> I have no power to treat them as creating disorder. Therefore,
> in the circumstances, it is quite obvious that the Opposition

R

having determined not to allow further business, I am compelled to say that a state of grave disorder has arisen, and,
under the Standing Order, I must adjourn the House until
To-morrow.

The official record then proceeds :

> " Adjourned accordingly at Twenty-four minutes
> before Nine of the clock, till To-morrow (Thursday) at a
> Quarter before Three of the clock."

Members lingered for a while in the Chamber, discussing
the incident. As Colonel Seely and Mr. Winston Churchill
moved along the Treasury Bench to go out some of their
former colleagues in the Conservative Party shouted "Rats!".
Mr. Churchill smilingly waved an acknowledgment.

Mr. Ronald M'Neill, a stalwart and genial Member of the
Conservative Party, suddenly picked up a book and, flinging
it across the Table at Mr. Winston Churchill, hit the First
Lord of the Admiralty on the side of his face.

By a happy coincidence the book was a manual containing rules and advice for the observance of good order in
parliamentary proceedings.

Mr. Churchill paused for a moment. Other Members
began crowding towards the Table. Matters were looking
serious when Mr. Will Crooks, with his inimitable cockney
good humour, shouted cheerily "Should auld acquaintance be
forgot". The quaint intervention raised a laugh and before
it subsided the two crowds had gone their separate ways.

When the House met the following day Mr. Ronald M'Neill,
addressing the Speaker, said when political feeling was very
high and taunts were exchanged between Members on both
sides of the House he regretted to say that under the influence
of a momentary loss of self control he discharged a missile
which struck the First Lord of the Admiralty. As soon as the
heat of the moment had passed he fully realised his action
was entirely reprehensible and returned to the House, and,
with the assistance of the President of the Local Government
Board (Mr. John Burns) endeavoured to find the First Lord

of the Admiralty, in order to express regret and ask his pardon.   Mr. M'Neill went on to say that he was unsuccessful in his effort to find Mr. Churchill, and added:

> I am anxious to take this, the first, opportunity of saying how extremely I regret having lost my temper and of tendering to the right hon. Gentleman and to the House a full and unreserved apology.

Mr. Churchill thanked the hon. Gentleman for what he had said, and added:

> I can assure him I have not, nor had I at any time, any personal feeling in the matter, and if I had any personal feeling the observations he has thought proper to address to the House would have effectually removed them.

Between these two Members all was well, but the broad situation remained.

Members had arrived at the House in ominously "select" groups: Conservatives walked down with Conservatives. The ordinary everyday intermingling and good-humoured banter between men of different Parties as the converging streams of Members met at the outer gates was tacitly suspended.

After Mr. Ronald M'Neill had done the courteous thing, personally, Members sat up in expectation of developments. The Speaker found the way out for both sides.   Commencing his observations with the dictum that it was rather unusual for a Speaker to intervene in a case of this kind, he remarked that the circumstances were somewhat unusual.   He thought nobody in the House would desire to see a repetition of the scenes which had occurred the day before.   He suggested that another solution of the difficulty might be found after a little reflection and consideration.

Acting upon this advice, the Prime Minister and the Leader of the Opposition concurred in a Motion to adjourn the House till the following Monday.   After a week-end of careful thought all Parties agreed upon a course which for the time being relieved the tension.

A new Money Resolution was introduced and discussed
de novo. The Government thus got the original Resolution
on a second time of asking. The Opposition, on the other
hand, had their satisfaction in the fact that the amendment
which they had carried was not directly rescinded. Moreover, the Government had lost much parliamentary time.
On the assumption that the controversial legislation proposed by the Government of the day is wrong, an Opposition
naturally assumes that a day lost means a day's less mis-
chief, and several days wasted the abandonment of bad Bills.

The Government certainly wanted the time very badly,
but they consoled themselves with the philosophic assurance
that it might have been worse.

And so the Bill went on its way, through storm and stress,
with other problems intervening to vary the sources of excitement.

Chapter 47

TRIANGULAR BRITISH CRICKET—
IRISH BILL CARRIED

THE Summer of 1912 was exceptionally interesting to
cricketers. The Australians arrived for their triennial
visit and a Team came from South Africa. There was thus
an opportunity for a British triangular contest. Nine
Tests in all were played and the English Team proved themselves the champions. They won four matches—three
against South Africa and one against Australia. Two
matches with Australia were drawn on account of bad weather.
The Australians beat the South African Team twice. The
English Team, captained by C. B. Fry, gave some very fine
exhibitions of cricket. Hobbs made a century at Lords.
The triangular duel, however, was somewhat marred by
bad weather. It did not receive the public support which
had been expected, and the experts predicted that the
experiment, while well worth the trying, was not likely
to be repeated for some time. They little thought then how

long it would be before a test match of any kind was again played in England.

The Olympic Games were held at Stockholm in July 1912 when the Marathon Race was won by Mr. K. M. McArthur of South Africa. This completed the fifth of the meetings originally arranged to take place at intervals of four years. By what proved to be one of life's grim ironies the sixth meeting was fixed for 1916 in Berlin.

The Government Whip entrusted with the special duty of shepherding Scottish Members into the lobbies of the House of Commons was in a state of grave anxiety as the year 1912 reached its close.

By all the treasured traditions of the North, New Year's Eve belongs exclusively to the family, but the desire to proceed with parliamentary business was so pressing that Ministers were planning a resumption of duty on the 30th December after a short Christmas holiday.

Loyal Liberals from the hills and the glens declared that no power on earth would induce them to "see the New Year in" at Westminster; there would be no luck in any good resolutions recorded in such a controversial atmosphere.

Ministers declared that business was pressing and the House must meet. The Government could not afford to do without its Scottish supporters. The double emergency had to be faced, and work was so arranged that the main division was taken at ten twenty-five. A brief discussion, restricted by the Rules to half-an-hour, followed on the Motion for the adjournment, and the records of Parliament bear this reassuring statement:

"Adjourned at five minutes before eleven of the clock." A good hour was thus assured in which company more congenial to New Year festivities might be sought.

New Year's Day found the House of Commons in turmoil once more. There had been rumours, some vague, some professedly circumstantial, of threats from Ulster men that the historic appeal of the Protestants to William of Orange might be repeated in another direction, and the name of the Emperor of Germany as the head of a great Protestant Dynasty had been mentioned. In a Debate on the Irish Bill Mr. Bonar Law, dealing specially with the case of Ulster, said:

> These people in the north-east of Ireland, from old prejudices perhaps more than from anything else, from the whole of their past history, would prefer, I believe, to accept the government of a foreign country rather than submit to be governed by honourable Gentlemen below the gangway. [The Irish Nationalist Members].

Mr. Churchill, who rose to reply on behalf of the Government, seizing upon this passage said:

> I refer to the statement which he quoted with approval that the Loyalists of Ulster would rather be annexed to a foreign country—
>
> Sir EDWARD CARSON: Than under moonlighters.

Mr. Churchill tried to continue his remarks but he was assailed with angry interruptions. Shrugging his shoulders, he observed "If you do not listen to me it is a matter of total indifference".

"We listened to your Leader", said Mr. (afterwards Sir) Stephen Collins, a popular Liberal Member, addressing the excited men on the Conservative Benches.

For a moment there was a lull, and Mr. Churchill went on:

> Ulster would rather be annexed to a foreign country than continue in her allegiance to the Crown—

"No, no!", "Withdraw!", "Scandalous!", cried Members opposite.

Mr. Churchill waited with reproachfully irritating patience till the force of the fierce resentment was spent, and then shot his shaft:

> This, then, is the latest Tory threat. Ulster will secede to Germany.

The storm now burst forth afresh.

"Germany? Who said Germany?" cried several of the Conservative Members.

"What will they say about that in Berlin?" shouted Lord Winterton.

Requested by the Speaker not to interrupt, the noble Lord asked on a point of order if the reference to Germany by the right honourable Gentleman was not deliberately provocative and calculated to cause ill feeling between this country and Germany.

Mr. Churchill said he felt bound to call the attention of the House to a statement indicating what the Leader of the Conservative Party considered proper conduct in the Loyalist population in the North of Ireland.

When Mr. Bonar Law rose once more people who had missed the significance of his words till the passage had been extracted and emphasised by Mr. Churchill possibly expected a sweeping denial of the whole of Mr. Churchill's interpretation. The correction by the Opposition Leader was, however, purely personal. Mr. Churchill had said that he quoted the statement as to the intentions of the Ulster people "with approval". Mr. Bonar Law said this was inaccurate, and added:

> I deliberately and carefully stated I believed it to be the fact but I quoted it neither with approval nor disapproval.

Political attention was soon diverted once more from Home Rule to other matters. The Doctors were still agitating over the new Insurance Act. They held a public meeting in the Queen's Hall, denounced Mr. Lloyd George and called Panel Doctors "black-legs", but the Panel was growing. Better terms as to the capitation grant were given by the Government and eventually the British Medical Association, by one-hundred-and-fifteen to thirty-five, released their members from their pledge not to serve on the Panel.

Possibilities also arose of another crisis and further change of leadership in the Conservative Party. Some stalwarts demanded a full-blooded policy of Preference, including a

tax on foreign foodstuffs for the next Election, come when
it might; others memorialised the Leaders against this.
Mr. Bonar Law and Lord Lansdowne talked of resigning,
and ultimately a temporary compromise was arrived at by a
pronouncement that they would retain the joint leadership
on condition that if when a Unionist Government had been
returned to power it should be found desirable, after consultation with the Colonies, to impose new duties on any
articles of food, such duties should not be imposed until
they had been submitted to the people at a General Election.

With this domestic matter out of the way, the Unionist
Party in the House of Commons threw all their power of
attack into the Debate on the Third Reading of the Home
Rule Bill.

Member after Member on both sides reviewed yet once
again the history of the subject. Mr. John Redmond, in a
tone of mingled pathos and prophecy said:

> The present Leaders of the Irish Nationalist Party in this
> House are war-worn in this struggle, and in the ordinary
> course of nature speedily their places must be taken by younger
> men.

After recalling the fact that the struggle had been carried
on by their fathers before them, he continued:

> This Bill has behind it the passionate enthusiasm of the
> great masses of the Irish people. It has centred on it the
> hopes and prayers of millions of loyal Irish subjects of the
> Empire wherever the flag of the Empire flies. At this moment
> when we are actually speaking here, amidst the snows of
> Canada and under the scathing sun of Australia there are
> millions of people of Irish blood who are eagerly waiting for
> the message this country is to send them. The fate of this
> Bill is also eagerly awaited by millions of people of Irish blood
> in America. My own belief is that there is not a people or
> a country in the civilised world who will not welcome as glad
> tidings of great joy the announcement that this powerful
> British nation has at last been magnanimous enough to undo
> an old national wrong and that in the words of Mr. Gladstone

the long periodic time has once more run out and again the
star of Ireland has mounted in the Heavens.

Mr. Bonar Law, again asserting that Ulster would resist,
declared:

> They have a right to rebel against such treatment if they
> think they can succeed. There is no question of their succeed-
> ing. They are bound to succeed. It does not mean that
> they must be in a position to defeat British soldiers. Nothing
> of the kind. It means this, and this only : that they should
> be ready in this case to give up their lives at the hands of
> British soldiers and they are ready. If you shot down a
> hundred of them in Belfast to-morrow a thousand would
> be ready the next day to share the same fate.

Every available man in all Parties was in the Division.
One Irish Nationalist Member, bedridden with sickness, was
brought over, attended by a nurse, who waited for him
within the precincts whilst his colleagues carried him in to
vote. The confident predictions of a substantial Liberal
defection were not fulfilled: two Liberal Members only voted
against the Bill. Some of the Members were paired, and
some on both sides who were away had been unable to
arrange pairs. In the end, the Third Reading passed by
three hundred and sixty-seven to two hundred and
fifty-seven.

Supporters of the Government were cheered on their way
to their Clubs. A demonstration was held outside the
Constitutional Club, at which the Home Rule Bill was burnt,
and there was some rioting in Belfast but the excitement
did not extend to the general public. The British man in
the street was still philosophically inclined to let the
politicians settle this matter among themselves.

There was really more animated argument between men
and women on the question of Franchise Reform. The
Government brought in a measure for dealing with some of
the grievances of male voters, but the main interest in the
Bill centred upon the part which was not there. Mr. Asquith

had already given an undertaking that if any Amendment
for including women among the future voters was put down,
the Government would not oppose it and would abide by
the decision of the majority on a free vote of the House.
The Speaker, however, on the matter being referred to him
as a point of order, ruled that if such a change in the principle
of the measure were made it would be a new Bill and would
therefore have to be withdrawn.

The militant Suffragists, who had been quiet for a while
in anticipation of this Bill, declared the truce at an end and
set out upon another window-breaking campaign. The
non-militants, while exonerating the Prime Minister from any
suspicion of having made the original promise well knowing
that it would be ruled out, pressed for a fulfilment of the
pledge in some other form and were not satisfied with his
further undertaking to give facilities in the next Session of
Parliament for a Private Member's Bill.

Meantime the House of Lords rejected the Home Rule
Bill on the Second Reading by three hundred and twenty-
six to sixty-nine, and politicians prepared for a two years'
campaign under the new Parliament Act.

By a coincidence, a bye-election occurred in Londonderry,
the traditional stronghold of Ulster Unionism. Lord Hamilton, the Unionist Member, succeeded to the Dukedom of
Abercorn, and the seat thus became vacant. Mr. D. C.
Hogge, a Liberal Home Ruler, was put forward in opposition
to the Unionist Candidate. Every available vote was registered on both sides; sick men were brought to the polling
stations; some instances were quoted of voters attended by
priests ready to administer Extreme Unction should they
expire on the way. In the end, Mr. Hogge was returned
by a majority of fifty-seven on a ninety-five per cent. poll.

At a complimentary luncheon to Mr. Hogge, Mr. John
Redmond declared that any scheme to safeguard the interests
and liberties of Ulster, even if it involved her over-repre-
sentation in the Irish Parliament, would readily be accepted
by his Party.

The industrial districts of England, Scotland and Wales were more keenly interested in the fate of the Bill which had been introduced and re-introduced in consequence of the Osborne Judgment. On the Third Reading, after a long fight in the Standing Committee, Mr. Bonar Law said:

> I think everyone in all quarters of the House recognises that the Osborne Judgment left trade unions in an invidious and, I think, an unfair position. They ought to have been able, if they wished, to carry on political action under fair conditions.

Controversy had centred on the protection of Trade Unionists who objected to contribute to political funds. Mr. Bonar Law intimated that in view of the provisions now inserted, under which Trade Unionists might refrain from contributing to the political funds, he would not vote against the Third Reading. Repudiating the view that the Conservative and Unionist Party were hostile to Trade Unionists, he said:

> The last thing I should personally desire would be a return to the position before the first Trade Unions Act, when the individual workman would have to make his bargain with the individual employer. I think that is too unfair and unequal, and I thoroughly approve of a combination for workmen to improve the conditions of their labour, and, what is more, to whatever extent they could succeed in doing it without destroying industry itself, to take their share of the profits.

The Bill passed its Third Reading without a division, and was ultimately passed by the House of Lords.

Chapter 48

HEROIC MEN
INTERNATIONAL AND DOMESTIC QUESTIONS

ALL controversy, political or social, was stilled by the news which reached London on the 10th February, 1913, of wonderful heroism in the Antarctic regions.

An expedition had set out from London in June 1910 on the "Terra Nova", which went first to New Zealand and in November of that year sailed from Port Chalmers under the command of Captain Robert Falcon Scott, R.N.   Captain Scott, who had commanded a previous expedition in 1901 came from the land of Drake and Raleigh.   He was the son of a Devon gentleman, and entered the Navy very young as a Cadet.   His expedition reached McMurdo Sound in the Antarctic in January 1911, and after various inevitable delays a small party, including Captain Scott, Dr. E. A. Wilson, Commander Evans, Captain Oates of the Inniskilling Dragoons, Lieutenant Bowers, R.N., and Petty Officer Evans, started for the South Pole on the 2nd November, 1911.   On the 3rd January, 1912, Captain Scott sent back his last despatch by Commander Evans, from a point 150 miles from the Pole and the remaining five pushed forward, reaching the Pole on the 18th January, where they found the tent and records of Captain Amundsen, the Norwegian Polar explorer who had reached there on the 14th December, 1911.

The details of the successful journey to the goal and the tragic story of the attempt to return are preserved through the records found in a tent by a search party beside the dead bodies of Captain Scott, Dr. E. A. Wilson and Lieutenant Bowers.

One misfortune followed upon another, and fearful weather was encountered.   The first of the party to succumb was Petty Officer Evans, who fell while travelling over rough ice and sustained concussion of the brain.   He struggled on for some time and died on the 17th February at the foot of the Beardmore Glacier.

The party still pushed forward through terrible difficulties. Captain Scott, in his diary, wrote:

I do not think human beings ever came through such a month as we have come through.

With the shadow of despair hovering over him he continued:

We should have got through in spite of the weather but for the sickening of a second companion (Captain Oates) and a shortage of fuel in our depots for which I cannot account —finally, but for the storm which has fallen on us within eleven miles of this depot at which we hoped to secure final supplies. Surely misfortune could scarcely have exceeded this last blow. We arrived within eleven miles of our old One Ton Camp with fuel for one hot meal and food for two days. For four days we have been unable to leave the tent, the gale blowing about us—we are weak—writing is difficult.

One of the great classic examples of self-sacrifice in the world's history was recorded in the action of Captain Oates. His feet and hands were badly frost-bitten. He had borne intense suffering for weeks without complaint. Describing what followed, Captain Scott wrote:

He was a brave soul, he slept through the night hoping not to wake, but he awoke in the morning. It was blowing a blizzard. Oates said " I'm just going outside and I may be some time." He went out into the blizzard and we have not seen him since.

We knew that Oates was walking to his death, but although we tried to dissuade him we knew it was the act of a brave man and an English gentleman.

It was obvious from all the surrounding circumstances that this great-hearted man recognised he was quite unfit to travel but knew the others would not leave him, and he went out into the blizzard to give his comrades a chance.

After relating the circumstances of the expedition Captain Scott, in his last records, wrote:

I do not regret this journey. We have shown that Englishmen can endure hardship, help one another and meet death with as great a fortitude as ever in the past. We took risks —we knew we took them. Things have come out against us. Therefore we have no cause for complaint but bow to the will of Providence, determined still to do our best to the last.

But if we have been willing to give our lives to this enterprise which is for the honour of our country, I appeal to our countrymen to see that those who depend upon us are properly cared for. Had we lived I should have had a tale to tell of the hardihood, endurance and courage of my companions which would have stirred the heart of every Englishman.

These rough notes and our dead bodies must tell the tale, but surely a great rich country like ours will see that those dependent upon us are properly cared for.

In the House of Commons on the 11th February Mr. Austen Chamberlain asked whether the Prime Minister had seen Captain Scott's last request and whether the Government would give favourable consideration to the appeal made by Captain Scott on behalf of those who, in his own words, had been willing to give their lives to this enterprise which was for the honour of our country.

When Mr. Asquith rose to reply all those Members who still observed the custom of wearing their hats during ordinary Debates "uncovered" as a mark of respect. The Prime Minister, speaking in a tone of deep reverence said:

We are all, at this moment, under the deep impression produced by reading the last message of Captain Scott—one of the most moving and pathetic utterances in the annals of discovery and of a brave and enduring man face to face with a tragic but noble end to a career of self-devoted service. I can only say that his appeal will not fall on deaf ears.

A corresponding assurance on behalf of the Government was given in the House of Lords by Lord Emmott, who said:

The splendid example which these men have set will be, I am sure, an inspiration to Englishmen for all time. Their last thoughts were for others and not for themselves.

The Lords of the Admiralty announced that the two naval men would be regarded as "killed in action" and that their story would long be remembered with honour by the Navy. Funds were also opened by the Lord Mayor of London, the British Antarctic Exploration Committee and the "Daily Telegraph".

From the original in the National Portrait Gallery

CAPTAIN SCOTT

A Memorial Service at St. Paul's was attended by the King, the Prime Minister, the Leader of the Opposition, Ambassadors and Ministers of Foreign States, the Lord Mayor and Sheriffs of London, members of learned Societies and representatives of Civic Authorities throughout the country. The Service was conducted by the Archbishop of Canterbury and the Bishop of London. The huge Cathedral was filled to its utmost capacity, and a crowd of some ten thousand people lingered outside though unable, for sheer lack of space, to gain admission.

*   *   *   *   *

When Parliament was reopened after the 1912 Session had overflowed for several weeks into 1913 the most interesting feature of the ceremony was the fact that the King wore his Crown.

Since the days of William IV the Crown had been borne in front of the Sovereign on these occasions. The resumption of the ancient custom was appreciated as adding to the picturesque dignity of the proceedings.

In the early part of the debate on the Address one of those points arose which passed without any special notice at the time but was afterwards quoted as a link in the chain of circumstances leading to the matters of graver importance. Lord Hugh Cecil referred to the possible military necessities of the country and this dialogue ensued:—

LORD HUGH CECIL : There is a very general belief that this country is under an obligation, not a treaty obligation but an obligation arising out of an assurance given by the Ministry in the course of diplomatic negotiations, to send a very large armed force out of this country to operate in Europe. That is the general belief. It would be very presumptuous of anyone who has not access to all the facts in the possession of the Government——

The PRIME MINISTER : I ought to say that it is not true.

A little later in the Session further questions were put to the Prime Minister as to whether by our Treaties we were

under any obligation to send a British Army to the Continent
to support France in the event of European hostilities. To
these questions the following reply was given:

> The PRIME MINISTER : As has been repeatedly stated this
> country is not under any obligation not public and known
> to Parliament which compels it to take part in any war. In
> other words, if war arises between European Powers there
> are no unpublished agreements which will restrict or hamper
> the freedom of the Government or of Parliament to decide
> whether or not Great Britain should participate in a war.
> The use that would be made of the naval or military forces
> if the Government and Parliament decided to take part in
> a war is, for obvious reasons, not a matter about which public
> statements can be made beforehand.

Just about this time public attention was excited—to the
exclusion of other matters—by rumours and by statements
in some newspapers as to the relations of certain members of
the Government with companies interested in wireless telegraphy.

The term "Marconi" ceased for a while to suggest a new
and marvellous stage of scientific progress. It was the
topic of countless arguments. Far reaching and far fetched
assertions were made by persons who professed to have
special information. Journalists filled columns upon columns
with "Marconi". Conversationalists kept social circles silent
on all topics save "Marconi". Clubs, morning trains, and
houses of refreshment of all kinds rang with "Marconi".

In view of the contemplated contract between the Government and the Marconi Company it was decided that a careful
inquiry should be held into the whole situation.

A Committee was accordingly appointed by the Government and Parliament, and their proceedings were followed
with more excitement than was devoted to discussions on any
other question of national—or international—importance.

It may be convenient to mention at this point that the
particular contract then under consideration was not completed. The Marconi Company in the exercise of their right

preferred to withdraw from further negotiations on the basis of the original proposals, and this fact was duly announced. A different agreement was made at a later date.

Eventually the Committee of Inquiry presented a series of Reports all of which declared the charges in certain sections of the press to be unfounded, but differences of opinion arose upon the purchase of a number of shares in the Marconi Company of America, by the Attorney General, some of which he had resold to the Chancellor of the Exchequer and the then Chief Liberal Whip. The American Marconi Company was a different concern from the English Company, but in a Minority Report some members of the Committee contended it was materially though indirectly interested in the movements of the English Company.

A debate in the House of Commons on the result of the Inquiry was initiated by a resolution moved from the Conservative side to the effect that:

> This House regrets the transactions of certain of His Majesty's Ministers in the shares of the Marconi Company of America and the want of frankness displayed by Ministers in their communications on the subject to this House.

The main point of criticism thus was that the fact of the purchase of the shares was not stated earlier instead of being placed before the Committee of Inquiry. Both the Ministers concerned agreed that in the light of subsequent discussions it would have been better if they had acted differently in this respect. After they had addressed the House an amendment to the original resolution was moved from the Liberal side to the effect that:

> This House after hearing the statements of the Attorney-General and the Chancellor of the Exchequer in reference to their purchases of shares in the Marconi Company in America, accepts their expressions of regret that such purchases were made, and that they were not mentioned in the debate of 11th October last, acquits them of acting otherwise than in good faith, and reprobates the charges of

S

corruption brought against Ministers which have been proved to be wholly false.

Mr. Bonar Law in the course of discussion said there was a clause acquitting Ministers of corruption in the original draft of the resolution moved from his side of the House, but it was pointed out by one of his hon. friends that they never made any such charge. He now intimated that he was willing to accept a motion in the following terms:

> That this House, having heard the statements made by the Attorney General and the Chancellor of the Exchequer, acquits them of acting otherwise than in good faith and reprobates the charges of corruption which have been proved to be wholly false, but regrets their transactions in shares of the Marconi Company of America and the want of frankness displayed by them in their communications with the House.

Ultimately the Liberal amendment was carried and the subject passed into history.

Chapter 49

SOUND AND FURY

PRINCE LOUIS of Battenberg, the First Sea Lord of the Admiralty, sat in the Distinguished Strangers' Gallery of the House of Commons on the afternoon of the 26th March, 1913. Admirals, Captains, and sea experts, eager and intent, occupied places in the ordinary Gallery usually filled by casual visitors. The scene was set for a full-dress Naval day, with an important speech from the First Lord of the Admiralty.

As a preliminary the House went into Committee on the Consolidated Fund (No. 1) Bill—a gathering of the various items on account discussed and voted in Committee for carrying on the Services till the full financial programme of the Session was presented.

The Chairman, formally putting the question that Clause I authorising the Treasury to issue the money "stand part of the Bill" said: "As many as are of that opinion say 'Aye'!" whereupon some Members on the Government side shouted "Aye".

The Chairman then said: "To the contrary 'No'" and a number of Members on the Opposition side cried "No".

"I think the 'Ayes' have it" announced the Chairman, in due form.

It was, of course, open to the Opposition to challenge this, which they did, by shouting "The 'Noes' have it!" They repeated the challenge when the Chairman repeated "I think the ayes have it".

While the formalities preceding a division were thus proceeding general attention was directed to Mr. Handel Booth, the Liberal Member for Pontefract, who was making vigorous efforts to attract the attention of the Chair. He said he had risen to speak, and desired to make a few observations upon the subject before the question was decided by the House.

A triangular discussion followed as to the precise moment at which Mr. Booth rose. Upon this the Chairman after deliberation said:

> It has been pointed out to me that although I had called for the Ayes and the Noes, I had not declared which of the two had it. Therefore, I have not completely put the Question, and the hon. Member is entitled to address me on the Question, "That the Clause stand part of the Bill".

Sir Frederick Banbury from the Opposition side asserted that Mr. Booth did not rise till after the Chairman had twice said "I think the 'Ayes' have it" and the ruling had twice been challenged. On the other hand, Mr. Leif Jones, who was sitting on the same side as the Member for Pontefract, said Mr. Booth, to his certain knowledge, rose just after the Chairman had collected the "Ayes" and just before he had collected the "Noes".

The Chairman in his final decision said:

> As the challenge was so unexpected I have thought it my
> duty to consult my advisers at my side, and their opinion was
> that I had not completed putting the question.

The advisers referred to were two of the senior officials
of the House who sit beside the Chairman when the
House is in Committee and act as assessors on technical
matters.

After this conclusive pronouncement from the Chair, Mr.
Booth was entitled to proceed with his remarks. When he
had been speaking for some time an ironical shout from the
Opposition side "Your majority is safe" revealed the inner
meaning of the excitement.

The supporters of the Government, expecting that the
Consolidated Fund Bill would go through without a division,
had not hurried down to the House. While the Opposition
Benches showed no preponderance of Conservatives and
Unionists and their voices when collected did not outweigh
the "Ayes", suspicions of a "snap" were aroused and it was
assumed that more Conservatives would have arrived while
the bells were ringing if a division had taken place at once.
While Mr. Booth was speaking panting Liberal Members
were hurrying into the precincts one by one, and the chances
of a Government defeat dwindled minute by minute.

Mr. Masterman, the Secretary to the Treasury, ostensibly
speaking more in sorrow than in anger, severely lectured the
Opposition on their tactics. He asserted that if the clause
had been defeated there would be no money after the 31st
March—the end of the financial year—for the Civil Service,
the Navy, or the Army. His reproof had a stormy reception.
When he proceeded to say "There are some things too
discreditable even for a discredited Opposition to propose"
the storm became a hurricane.

Shouts of "Withdraw" and other more pungent observations drowned each other. Points of order were thrust
forth so quickly that they trod upon each other's heels.

The calm, even tones of the Chairman succeeded in restoring order, whereupon some of the Members of the Opposition asserted that Mr. Masterman had used the word "disgraceful". Was this in order? The Chairman said the word he heard at the Table was "discreditable". That word he ruled to be strong but not unparliamentary. If the word "disgraceful" had been used, it would have been out of order. Mr. Masterman asserted that the word he used was "discreditable". This word was within the bounds of order. Old Parliamentarians recalled the fact that a few years before a ruling to that effect had been given when on one occasion Mr. Balfour described a speech by Mr. Lloyd George as "discreditable".

A walk through the Lobbies for a division failed to calm the perturbed spirits. The figures, showing only a comparatively small majority for the Government, served to emphasise what might have been.

The Opposition now began to vent their wrath upon Mr. Winston Churchill by holding up his big effort. They debated the Consolidated Fund Bill point by point. At one of these points Mr. Mitchell-Thomson, a rising young Unionist, called the action of the Government "disgraceful". The Chairman pointed out that he had ruled that this expression would have been unparliamentary if used by a Member of the Government.

"If the honourable Member withdraws it, I will repeat it" promptly shouted Mr. William Moore (afterwards Lord Chief Justice Moore) a leading Conservative Member from the North of Ireland.

Again points of order burst forth from every quarter like the rattle of artillery. Some Members tried to show that there were precedents for the word "disgraceful". Mr. Moore wanted no ruling in his favour, and lest there should be any doubt about his position after Mr. Mitchell-Thomson had conformed to the traditions of the House, he carried the matter farther by declaring that the action of the Secretary to the Treasury was a "piece of disgraceful trickery".

This expression he was called upon to withdraw. "I absolutely refuse to do so" he replied. The Chairman, under the Rules of the House, ordered him to "withdraw from this day's proceedings".

A division then proceeded on an amendment ostensibly under discussion. While it was in progress another point of order was raised. Upon this such a confusing torrent of protests and challenges poured from the Opposition Benches that not even the voice of the Chairman could be heard.

"Don't make the House of Commons into a pot-house" shouted Sir Arthur Markham, the Liberal Mining engineer and mine-owner from the Midlands, whose penetrating voice, developed in the long tunnels and roadways, made itself heard above the deafening roar.

When the division was over attention was called to the fact that Mr. Moore was still in the House, and a further scene is thus recorded:

THE CHAIRMAN : I have to remind him of the Rules of the House, under which I am bound to act, when an hon. Member declines to have regard to the authority of the Chair, and that is to order that he withdraw from the remainder of this day's Sitting. Do I understand that he declines to do so ?

MR. MOORE : I will take the opinion of the House on it. I do not think it is a fair ruling.

CAPTAIN CRAIG : Will you turn out Masterman at the same time ?

SIR A. MARKHAM : Turn out the pothouse crowd.

THE CHAIRMAN : I must report the hon. Member to the House for having disregarded the authority of the Chair.

MR. MOORE : Was it the Clerk or the Chair ?

THE CHAIRMAN : I have to name the hon. and learned Member for North Armagh for disregarding the authority of the Chair, and the Sitting will be suspended pending the arrival of Mr. Speaker.

MR. SPEAKER having taken the Chair,

THE CHAIRMAN : Mr. Speaker, I regret that I have to report to you that it has been my duty to name the hon.

and learned Member for North Armagh for having disregarded the authority of the Chair.

THE PRIME MINISTER (Mr. Asquith) : I beg to move, ' that the hon. and learned Member for North Armagh be suspended from the service of this House.'

Question proposed, ' That Mr. William Moore be suspended from the service of the House.'

CAPTAIN CRAIG : Are we permitted to discuss this question ? It seems to me a gross scandal.

MR. SPEAKER : Standing Order 18 says—

' and the Speaker shall on a Motion being made thereupon put the same Question without amendment, adjournment, or debate.'

CAPTAIN CRAIG : Then I should not be in order in including two or three hon. Members opposite who have behaved in a most abominable manner ?

A division was challenged and the Motion ordering the House to be suspended was carried by 263 to 150.

When the result of the division was announced yet another lively passage occurred which is thus officially recorded :

MR. SPEAKER : If the hon. Member is in the House I must ask him to observe the Resolution of the House and to withdraw.

MR. MOORE : I have always obeyed your ruling with pleasure, and will do so on the present occasion.

AN HON. MEMBER : Do not make a speech.

CAPTAIN CRAIG : That interrupter also is entitled to be suspended from the House.

MR. SPEAKER : It was certainly a very improper observation.

CAPTAIN CRAIG : A dirty cad !

The hon. and learned Member for North Armagh then withdrew.

When the House got back into Committee Sir C. Kinloch-Cooke had another point of order in re the matter of the "pot-house". Sir Arthur Markham admitted that he used the expression, but added that he did so "when hon. Members opposite were disgracing the House of Commons". The Chairman pointed out that the word "disgraceful" had already been ruled a disorderly expression, and he called upon Sir Arthur Markham to withdraw the word "disgracing".

"I have never disobeyed an order of the Chair" said Sir Arthur Markham, "but I regret very much, feeling as I do the disgraceful scene, that I cannot withdraw the expression". This meant that the hon. Baronet was ordered to withdraw from the House "for the remainder of this day's proceedings", which he did.

The evening was wearing on, but the resources of the Opposition were by no means exhausted. Points of order, amendments and divisions, filled up the precious hours, and, finally the leader of the Opposition asked Mr. Churchill did he remember what happened in 1905? So many things have happened in 1905 in which Mr. Churchill figured that for a while the allusion seemed vague. Mr. Bonar Law went on to say that ill-doing was apt to bring its revenge. Mr. Churchill inconvenienced Cabinet Ministers in those far-off days. He was being inconvenienced to-day.

"Inconvenienced! Oh dear, no!" Mr. Churchill did not admit anything of the kind. "I have had the privilege", he said with a bland smile, "of listening to a very interesting and amusing debate".

This was rather disappointing, but what Mr. Bonar Law wished to make clear on behalf of his friends was that while he did not deny there had been obstruction that evening, Mr. Churchill was the ringleader in the very great obstruction which, the Leader of the Opposition asserted, took place on a similar occasion in 1905. When shortly after eight o'clock, at the end of a four hours' wait, Mr. Churchill was permitted to make his statement on the Navy he said he did not complain because:

What has happened illustrates a very important naval and strategic truth which I have several times endeavoured to impress upon the House—I mean the difficulty under which the strongest naval Power lies of being ready to meet at its average moment the attack of the next strongest naval Power at its selected moment.

Out of the episode came a ruling on the interesting question as to whether, since no period had been settled for a suspension in case of disorder, it would be constitutional to invite the disorderly Member back to the House. The point was raised by a question as to when Mr. Moore's suspension would terminate. Mr. Pringle, who had come into the House since the debates on the reconstruction of the rules asked if it was not usual for an hon. Member to give some apology to the House before he was reinstated. Captain Craig promptly intervened with a further question:

> Is the right hon. Gentleman aware that my hon. and learned friend refuses to give any apology for that which he considers was quite right.

A few days later Mr. Asquith, acting, he said, with the concurrence and at the request of the Chairman of Ways and Means, moved that the period of Mr. Moore's suspension should terminate. Mr. Charles Fenwick, a Liberal Labour Member and one of the representatives of the Northumberland Miners, intimated that he felt it his duty to divide the House against the motion, as the hon. Member was reported to have publicly stated in Ireland that he deliberately resisted the authority of the Chair and that he would neither withdraw nor apologise.

Mr. John Redmond urged Mr. Fenwick not to oppose the motion. The Irish Nationalist Leader said he was glad of the opportunity of saying that he made this appeal for a Member from Ireland, although they differed politically. The Chairman of Ways and Means made a similar appeal, and Mr. Fenwick, in deference to the desire that the motion should pass unanimously, withdrew his opposition. He protested, however, against the conduct of the hon. and learned Member, adding:

> I have heard it said again and again that his conduct was such as you might expect from Members of the Labour Party. I thank goodness that in my experience not a single Member of the Labour Party has ever been guilty of such open defiance to the authority of the Chair.

The motion was then passed, and Mr. Moore came back after three weeks absence.

Chapter 50

THE CINEMA "ARRIVES.' SUFFRAGIST TRAGEDY

THE Cinematograph had now established itself firmly as a source of pleasure and also as the foundation of an extensive industry. Moving pictures portraying public men in current incidents and depicting passing events had been thrown upon the screen in the 'nineties as "turns" in Variety theatre performances. Considerable improvements were taking place when the New Century opened but at that time it was never assumed that the possibilities would go very much beyond the "side show" Exhibition. When a greater degree of perfection in producing the film had been obtained the pictures began to represent dramatic scenes. Actors with strong powers of facial expression were employed. Still the general public in this country took a somewhat passive interest in the new form of entertainment. The boom may be said to have come somewhere in the second half of the first ten years of the century. Many people thought the cinemas would be like the skating rinks which were exceedingly popular for a few years only. Others more optimistic saw a profitable investment. Acting for the cinema became a serious profession. It dawned upon investors—or rather came as a revelation to them—that people would continue to come in large numbers to a full performance consisting entirely of the production of pictures on the screen. Classic plays were adapted to film production. Buildings were erected or purchased. The pessimist looked on and awaited the changing mood of the fickle public, but the public in all countries demanded more "pictures." Skilled producers and expert actors supplied their needs.

Excited discussions on Hunger Strikes diverted public attention temporarily from Tariffs, Home Rule and other parliamentary topics.

The newspapers devoted columns to a controversy on the desirability or the efficacy of forcible feeding for the Suffragists in gaol who, as a protest, still refused food. Picturesque details of the process were published, and the public were favoured with learned disquisitions from scientific persons in support of and opposed to this method of imparting nourishment.

The Home Secretary advised other steps in order that the dignity of the law might be maintained. The Government therefore introduced and carried the measure which still remains on the Statute Book enabling the Authorities to release prisoners undergoing sentence for misdemeanour whose health is endangered by their retention in prison.

Licence under the Act is granted with certain conditions and the person may be rearrested without warning if these conditions are broken.

Under the plan adopted to deal with Suffragists "hunger strikers" were let out at the point when self-imposed starvation became dangerous to life and rearrested if they took further part in violent agitation. The Suffragists thus extended the volume of legal enactments, and they also enriched the colloquial vocabulary of the law. The new measure was officially called the "Prisoners (Temporary Discharge) Act". The "Militants" christened it the "Cat and Mouse Act", and as such it has ever since been popularly designated.

Mr. Keir Hardie got eight votes for an amendment declaring that no law directed against hunger strikers should be passed until a Woman Suffrage measure, if passed on Second Reading by a free vote of the House of Commons, had been taken up by the Government.

The "Cat and Mouse" Bill became an Act, and the agitation still went on. Buildings were burnt and other violent methods adopted. Mrs. Pankhurst, released after a hunger strike, was sentenced at the Central Criminal Court to three years' penal servitude for inciting an explosion at Walton-on-Sea. Shouts of "Shame" greeted the sentence from people in Court, who sang "For She's a Jolly Good Fellow" and the "Marseillaise" as they were being escorted from the building.

It is interesting to note here that the first woman magistrate Miss Emily Duncan—a West Ham guardian—was appointed in May 1913.

Public controversy gradually centred on another topic, which was considered by the Authorities as "outside the range of practical politics".

In railway carriages and in smokerooms innumerable, the protagonists of compulsory military service did not hesitate to use the word "conscription". It was on this blunt declaration in support of the adoption of the continental system of calling up every man for a period of direct military training and service that the every day argument was conducted. In the press and on the platform the term "National Service" was employed by public men. Leaders of the Conservative Party were not very pronounced in their declarations on the subject. The Territorial Force was slowly making headway: it had incorporated the old Volunteers, who were working hard under their new conditions, but in many quarters the support for it was very lukewarm. The out-and-out advocates of compulsion regarded it as a stumbling block to the real thing: some on the other hand, thought it would help recruiting for the Regular Army. An attempt to "put Members to the fence" on the question of compulsion was made by a few enthusiasts through the medium of a private Member's Bill brought in one Friday afternoon in April, 1913, called the "Territorial Forces" Bill.

This measure proposed to make the four years' service in the Territorial Army compulsory on all male British subjects at the age of eighteen, under penalty of fine and loss of civil rights. Even at this early stage provision was made for exempting "conscientious objectors". The Bill was moved by Captain Sandys, a Somerset Unionist, and seconded by Sir C. Rose, the Liberal member for Newmarket.

Colonel (afterwards General) Seely, Minister for War opposed the Bill as a passionate supporter of the voluntary system, but appealed for greater support for the Territorial

Force. He hinted that compulsion might be necessary eventually, and expressed the hope that the opponents of this Bill would realise the importance of using all their efforts to make the voluntary system a success. Mr. Bonar Law expressed great disappointment with Colonel Seely's speech, but gave no direct lead as to compulsion, maintaining that it was the duty of the Government to deal with the situation. He suggested that it was too big a subject for a Friday afternoon, and, acting apparently on this same belief, Major Archer Shee from the Unionist Benches, despite attempts on the part of private Members to move the Closure, talked the Bill out.

Thus Members were not called upon to commit themselves in the Division lists for or against the principle of compulsion.

The controversy still went on outside the House of Commons. The House of Lords took it up in a general Debate, in the course of which Lord Haldane, now Lord Chancellor but speaking from the side of the Woolsack, defended his Army Scheme generally, and the Territorials especially. He referred to an observation of Lord Lovatt on the Opposition Benches that there were two sections of the Conservative Party on this question, and, throwing up his hands, he cried :

> Good heavens, my lords, are we to have, in addition to Food Taxes, controversies over the Budget and the situation under the Parliament Act, a controversy over Army policy ? If so, Heaven help the country when the Opposition come into power.

There was a shortage in the numbers of the Territorial Force and the responsibility Lord Haldane declared, rested with those who, instead of co-operating and assisting in making it a success, put difficulties and discouragement in the way. In saying this he added that many prominent Members of the Conservative and Unionist Party had done noble work and had applied themselves with energy to the task of making the Force a success. As to Home defence generally, he said, Great Britain would not be in real peril so long as the Navy was unbeaten. The Territorial Force was necessary in order that if need arose the Expeditionary Force might be free to go abroad—to the Continent or elsewhere.

Lord Curzon retorted that if the Territorial Army had attained a certain measure of success it was due to the political opponents of the Government—the County magnates who had been so freely denounced but who had spent their time and labour in advancing the plans. He expressed the opinion that the voluntary system in connection with the Territorial Army had shot its last bolt and called for a conference of the two great political Parties on the question as to whether some form of compulsion was necessary. In one passage of his speech he said:

> The people look to the two Parties at home, and what do they see ? They see the Party opposite destitute of any plan, hoping that things will go well, trying to meet the shortage in the Territorial Army by promising ranges and drill halls and a few petty things of that description, and seeking to force on our Party the unpopular label of Conscription. On the other hand, they see our Party not having made up its mind in the matter, holding out views but steadily moving in the direction of a belief that some form of compulsion is required.

Meantime Earl Roberts, backed by the National Service League, was addressing large meetings in the big industrial centres and elsewhere in support of National Service.

Argument generally proceeded on the assumption that a force of seventy thousand men was the lowest number by which an enemy would care to invade this country with a view to conquest. It was urged that the Navy would intercept such an invasion. Lord Roberts said that while the figure of seventy thousand was originally mentioned by him as a minimum, he would have put it at seven hundred thousand if he had thought it would become historical or be treated as a maximum. So the argument continued— based entirely on individual opinions without any definite declarations from either side of Party policy.

Another Suffrage Bill brought in by a Private Member, opposed by Mr. Asquith and supported by Sir Edward Grey, was defeated in May by a majority of two hundred and sixty-seven to two hundred and nineteen. As fifty-four Irish Nationalists voted in the majority it was evident that they still held the scales, a fact which again occasioned comment. The militants became increasingly active and made a point—in which they received a measure of support from people who disapproved of their tactics—of demanding that measures taken against them should also be taken against those who were inciting Ulster to resist Home Rule by force.

Sir Edward Carson declared that the right of Ulstermen to remain citizens of the Empire gave them a moral right to use force and accepted full responsibility for whatever measures were taken to resist Home Rule.

A Suffragette created a sensation at the Derby. When the horses came round Tattenham Corner Miss Emily Wilding Davison, an M.A. of London and a resident of Northumberland, a hunger striker who had been imprisoned several times, threw herself in front of the King's horse. The horse fell down and the jockey was thrown, but neither was very much hurt. Miss Davison, however, was fatally injured and died the following Sunday without regaining consciousness. Her body was sent to Morpeth (Northumberland) for burial.

A procession, headed by a woman bearing a cross, escorted the coffin through London from Victoria Station to King's Cross; young girls dressed in white and carrying laurel leaves followed immediately behind the cross, and after them came thousands of women, some dressed in white, some in black and some in purple, and carrying Madonna lilies, red peonies and purple irises. Purple banners preceded each section of the procession, which was accompanied by bands playing the "Marseillaise" and the "Dead March".

Memorial services were held in London on the way and also at Newcastle-on-Tyne, when the remains arrived there on the journey to Morpeth.

Chapter 51

CROWDED POLITICAL EPISODES

THE Welsh Church and Irish Bills were once more carried by the Commons; rejected by the House of Lords and automatically went forward on their career through the further stages provided under the Parliament Act. The most interesting incident in the discussions at this stage was a conspicuous speech made by Mr. Gladstone, the grandson of the illustrious Victorian Statesman, on the Welsh Bill.

As a Liberal Churchman Mr. Gladstone had taken a strong independent line during the 1912 Debates in favour of amendments rendering the Bill less inacceptable to the Church, some of which he succeeded in carrying. He now appealed to the Bishops to make peace on lines which were inevitable.

High hopes were formed of a great future for this young politician but, like many other brilliant men, he was destined to make the supreme sacrifice in the world tragedy now slowly approaching.

Public excitement was again switched back to the evergreen Suffrage question. Debates on the treatment of the women in prison, more burning of buildings, more arrests, releases and rearrests under the "Cat and Mouse" Act followed each other in rapid succession. Women from all ranks—daughters of peers, wives of professional men, members of manufacturing families and mill girls were to be found in the militant movement. Onlookers were sharply divided in opinion. Some derided the methods; others denounced them and took part in hostile demonstrations against the militants. The general trend of thought was strongly opposed to the tactics, but the sincerity of people who were prepared to suffer was widely admitted.

The non-militant suffragettes created a distinct impression by a march to London organised through the National Union of Woman's Suffrage Societies. In a gradually increasing procession they linked up the towns and villages

of England, holding meetings as they went. Their ranks
included Town Councillors, Poor Law Guardians, nurses,
actresses and women employed in all kinds of local movements. Setting out from four main points in the country
they joined up for a monster demonstration in Hyde Park,
at which a Resolution in favour of Woman Suffrage was
carried from nineteen platforms. The non-militants saw
the Prime Minister and urged that the Government should
bring in a Franchise measure containing a Woman Suffrage
clause. Mr. Asquith was courteous but unconvinced.

For a short period the everyday public aroused itself to
another stage of interest in the Irish question. The statesmen and politicians had been discussing procedure and
possible conferences. The Ulster Unionist Council produced
something more picturesque. They formed a "Provisional
Government" consisting of a Central Authority of seventy-six
Members with a Military Council. Sir Edward Carson gave
ten thousand pounds himself and got other large subscriptions
towards a fund to indemnify members of the Ulster Volunteer
Force from personal injury or loss of life in the service of
the Provisional Government.

Sir Edward Carson was popularly dubbed "King Carson";
Ministers were asked why they did not take action against
him, and Mr. J. M. Robertson (the Secretary of the Board
of Trade) one of the most effective public debaters of the
day, speaking at Newcastle, said they did not want to make
"King Carson" "Saint Carson".

With his 1909 Budget now a matter of history, Doctors
on the panel in thousands, National Health Insurance in
working order, and the Welsh Disestablishment Bill on its
way to the Statute Book, Mr. Lloyd George looked for other
worlds to conquer. Claiming to be a son of the soil who,
as Mr. Winston Churchill expressed it, had "marched from
his mountain home to the heights of fame", the Chancellor
of the Exchequer declared himself at one with the landless
villager. Years ago, when he was a boy, Mr. Jesse Collings,
a Devonian living at Birmingham, with the strong support

T

of Mr. Joseph Chamberlain, had thrilled the countryside with a demand for allotments and smallholdings. The British faculty for coining popular phrases summarised that agitation into the saying "Three acres and a cow". The cry rang through the British Isles and was quoted in lands beyond the sea. It contributed in a very large degree to the Liberal victory of 1885. After the Liberal split on Home Rule in 1886 and the alliance of Mr. Chamberlain and his friends with the Conservatives other subjects intervened.

The Chancellor of the Exchequer decided that the time had come round for a revival of the Birmingham policy of some thirty years ago. "Far from the madding crowd" Mr. Percy Illingworth, a member of an influential family of Yorkshire Liberals was dwelling amid rugged beauty off the coast of Ayrshire at Brodick Castle on the Isle of Arran. His house party included the Prime Minister, Mr. Lloyd George, Colonel Seely, Sir Rufus Isaacs, and Mr. Runciman. Here during the rest and calm of the Recess the western waves heralded the reincarnation of the land campaign.

Mr. Lloyd George, armed with credentials from his colleagues, went forth from the Gaelic castle bearing the fiery cross. His crusade, he explained, was not against landlords individually nor as a class, but the land system which he declared to be the greatest and least controlled of all monopolies. No class, he said, could be trusted with such sweeping powers.

The campaign opened with two meetings at Bedford in the heart of what might be described as Saxon England. The Celtic fire of the Chancellor found a welcome but not a vehemently demonstrative response. Some well-known people were present; the audience listened attentively, but they were not visibly moved by the picture of pheasants destroying the farmers' crops and pecking the mangold wurzels.

They did not rise and shout as Welshmen would, nor cheer as men of the West and North might when, with Cymric emotion, Mr. Lloyd George pictured a happy, contented people in a new British countryside where "the valleys stand so thick with corn that they shall laugh and sing".

Rumours that the militant suffragettes were planning devices to break up the meeting led to such extreme precautions that an artificial atmosphere of restraint pervaded the proceedings. The Unionist press declared that the meetings had fallen flat. Merry sport was made of the idea that pheasants pecked at mangolds, but Mr. Lloyd George's statement on this point was declared to be specially verified.

The campaign got powerful support from a careful enquiry into wages and conditions of labour and housing. Mr. A. H. Dyke Acland, a former Head of the Education Department, since retired from active politics, was Chairman of the Committee which undertook this for England and part of Wales. He had with him Mr. E. R. Cross, well-known in the public life of the North of England, Mr. B. Seebohm Rowntree whose writings founded upon investigations of social problems were universally appreciated, and five Liberal Members of Parliament. In their Report which ran to nearly six hundred pages they asserted that over sixty per cent. of ordinary adult agricultural labourers received less than eighteen shillings a week from all sources, that in only a few counties was the wage of a farm worker adequate to keep a normal family efficient.

Broadly the campaign concentrated on greater facilities for small holdings and allotments; reasonable security of tenure, and fair rent for the farmer in order that better conditions might be secured for the agricultural labourer.

The platform crusade aroused more enthusiasm at Swindon, where Mr. Lloyd George touched the fringe of the western counties and at Middlesbrough where the men of the north-east welcomed him with a full-throated rendering of "The Land Song". This anthem of the campaign was set to the inspiring music of the American Civil War song "Marching to Georgie". Each verse ended with the line "God gave the land for the people".

Attention was directed for a while from home affairs to the question of national armaments. The First Lord of the Admiralty proposed a twelve-months' naval holiday during which all Powers should cease building war ships. The suggestion was politely but emphatically declined in Germany, and again the whole force of naval energy and science resumed the growing competition in armaments.

Efforts to avoid domestic strife were meanwhile made by various public men. The most significant meeting at this moment was held in a small wayside hall in East Fife. It was Mr. Asquith's custom to give an annual address to his constituents on the general political situation. Anticipating something of importance representatives of the Press arrived from all parts of the country and the delegates of the local Liberal associations courteously gave up a large part of the little building for the accommodation of these expectant visitors. In the light from a cottage paraffin lamp placed on a small table the Prime Minister reviewed the history of Home Rule and, while declaring that the Government could not and would not be intimidated by threats of force, invited an interchange of views. On behalf of his colleagues and himself he said he was prepared to consider schemes for the adjustment of the position of the minority in Ireland.

The speech was telegraphed to the ends of the earth. It was followed by other speeches from both sides in an autumnal stream of oratory. At some moments a settlement appeared possible, at others defiant speeches from Unionists were characterised by Liberals as incitements to anarchy.

At a meeting in London Mr. Lloyd George said the most thoughtful Conservatives who possessed the sagacity to see they had everything to lose by accustoming people to a defiance of the law regarded Sir Edward Carson as "a wet dog in a drawing-room". The Chancellor of the Exchequer further declared that Protestantism would be safer in Ireland under Home Rule than Non-conformity was in the English villages, and went on to say:

> To those who are sincerely anxious to seek peace in Ulster
> or elsewhere we extend the right hand of goodwill and fellow-
> ship; but to those who are simply using Ulster's legitimate
> fears for the purpose of fiighting their own selfish battles in

this country, I guarantee that if the fighting begins it will not be all on one side.

* * * * *

Our opponents are out to catch gulls. We are out to feed the hungry.

And so with clashing argument on the platform, labour troubles arising out of strikes in Ireland and in Great Britain, and more violent attacks on property by militant suffragists, 1913 bequeathed a portentous legacy of sensations, fated to be overwhelmed and absorbed by the vast inheritance of the years to follow.

Chapter 52

FATEFUL 1914

OF all the newer industries the construction of motor cars had made the greatest progress. People who scoffed at the beginning of the century were enthusiasts. Here and there a genuine Conservative was still to be found who boasted that he had never been in a car and had no intention of riding in one. Improvements in construction attracted the general user. The early cars were built for locomotion. As time went on the newer type became more convenient, more graceful—or, as the loyal admirers of the carriage and pair would say, less ugly. By more convenient arrangements for the protection of those who rode in the cars, it was no longer necessary to get into an outfit resembling that of a diver before undertaking a journey in a motor car. The weird figures with their leather coats and "goggles" had disappeared from the country side. In the towns professional men wearing immaculate tall hats and frock coats were to be seen driving their own cars. Ladies were not compelled as formerly to wear unsightly costumes. The motor car had become a source of pleasure—not merely an engine for getting from one place to the other as quickly as possible, with probable stoppages on the way during which the driver spent a considerable time on his back under the car.

Naturally there grew up around the industry a number of ancillary trades with the usual result—sad in some individua instances—that an old style of labour was replaced by a new. The adaptable person found employment; the unadaptable drifted wherever sanctuary for an unwanted could be found. Where there had been sheer manual labour, mechanics sprang into action. The habits and customs and the domestic arrangements of people were changing with the new conditions. The sedate coachman gave way to a dapper chauffeur.

In the manufacture of cars France took the lead, but Great Britain was a bigger user. Needless to say the industry made rapid progress in America where Mr. Henry Ford had established his factories for standardising and quickly assembling the various units. His object was to provide cars within the range of practical economics for the million.

The adaptation of the motor to commercial purposes proceeded rather slowly at first. The car began as a hobby, then as a sport. Its general use for all purposes was a matter of time. The motor omnibus which preceded the taxi-cab entirely superseded the horse bus and its supporters predicted that it would soon supersede the tramcar. The last horse omnibus ran in Paris in January 1913 amid mock funeral ceremonies. The char-a-banc, like the commercial motor van, was coming into more general use. As in the case of many another department of inventive genius, what seemed like huge progress was destined to be dwarfed in the stupendous development influenced by events as yet unforeseen.

The fateful year 1914 opened in an atmosphere of general anxiety. The labour unrest in England grew more acute. In moving the second reading of the Home Rule Bill for the third time of asking Mr. Asquith referred to unsuccessful conversations that had taken place between Mr. Bonar Law, Sir Edward Carson, and himself upon possible proposals towards agreement.

Mr. Lloyd George in the course of a reference to Anglo-German relations was able to declare that at the moment they were more friendly than had been the case for some years past. There were, however, direct indications that the world at large was not in the mood for relinquishing activity with respect to armaments.

In our Army Estimates there was a substantial increase. Colonel Seely explained that this was due partly to increased pay and also to the increased needs of aviation. A million pounds was included in the Estimate for this young and growing branch of the Service.

It fell to the lot of Mr. Churchill to introduce the largest Estimates for Naval expenditure ever presented to Parliament up to this date. The figure reached fifty-one and a half millions as compared with just under thirty-one millions in the first year of the present century.

After explaining his programme in detail Mr. Churchill concluded:

> The world is armed as it was never armed before. Every suggestion of arrest or limitation has so far been ineffectual. From time to time awkward things happen, and situations occur which make it necessary that the Naval force at our immediate disposal, now in this quarter, now in that, should be rapidly counted up. On such occasions the responsibilities which rest on the Admiralty come home with brutal reality to those who are responsible; and unless our Naval strength were solidly, amply, and unswervingly maintained, the Government could not feel that they were doing their duty to the country.

Shortly after this Mr. Churchill was the central figure in a stormy Parliamentary scene arising out of the ubiquitous Irish problem. In the course of a speech at Bradford he had said if Ulstermen extended the hand of friendship it would be clasped by Liberal and by their Nationalist countrymen in all good faith and in all goodwill, but, he continued:

> If all the loose wanton and reckless chatter we have been forced to listen to these many months is in the end to disclose a sinister and revolutionary purpose, then I can only say to you: Let us go forward together and put these grave matters to the proof.

This was the text of many a vehement speech from the other side, and it formed subject matter for spirited discussion in the course of a debate upon a vote of censure moved against the Government in the House of Commons. Speaking on that motion Mr. Bonar Law again demanded the referendum, and referring to the possible consequences if this step were not taken the Leader of the Opposition went on to say:

And what about the Army? We really now have got to a stage when we must face facts. What about the Army? If it is only a question of disorder, the Army, I am sure, will obey you, and I am sure that it ought to obey you; but if it really is a question of civil war, soldiers are citizens like the rest of us. [Hon. Members: " No! "] It never has been otherwise in any country at any time. If it is civil war, whether it is right or wrong—and I say nothing about it, whether it is right or wrong—the Army will be divided, and you will have destroyed the force, such as it is, on which we depend for the defence of this country.

The Prime Minister gratefully acknowledged that upon the general question the speech of the Leader of the Opposition was couched in mild and moderate terms, and he heartily assented to the proposition that in dealing with this grave and momentous question no door should finally be closed, if it could be avoided, to a settlement. Proceeding, he said:

I cannot give the same, or, indeed, any degree of assent to a proposition advanced by the right hon. Gentleman towards the close of his speech in regard to the duties and functions of the Army in case of civil war? Who is to be the judge whether any particular contest in which the armed forces of the Crown are called upon to intervene does or does not fall within the category of civil war?

I very much deprecate the laying down by a responsible Statesman of the right hon. Gentleman's position of any such doctrine—that it lies in the discretion of those in the service of the King to determine whether or not any particular contingency justifies them in acting as the right hon. Gentleman would seem to suggest.

Mr. Bonar Law : The question, surely, whether a contest is or is not civil war is generally decided by both combatants. For instance, in the American War the South were regarded not as rebels but as combatants. That is the distinction.

The Prime Minister : The South, as a matter of fact, were always described as rebels. I do not want to go into that. I only wanted to enter my protest against what I thought was a dangerous and unwise proposition.

Mr. Asquith returning to the general question repeated a proposal which he had made at the beginning of the Session that counties in Ulster, including the county boroughs of Belfast and Londonderry, might vote themselves out of the scope of the Bill for six years at the request of one-tenth of the Parliamentary electors. At the end of that time they would come in unless the Imperial Parliament otherwise determined.

At a later stage in the debate Sir Edward Carson referred to Mr. Churchill's Bradford speech and thus initiated this lively triangular combat :

Sir E. Carson : The right hon. Gentleman (Mr. Churchill) says I am wrong on the merits or something or other and that I shall be handed down to history as being so, as if I care twopence whether I was or was not. I am not on the make.

*   *   *   *   *

Mr. Devlin : I do not know what a great lawyer means by a politician on the make, but I will tell the House what an untutored layman means by it. When a young lawyer becomes an Irish Home Ruler, and subscribes to the principles of Home Rule, and when the forces of honour and justice are beaten, joins the forces of a powerful enemy— that is what I call a man on the make.

Sir E. Carson : I wish to say that the observation of the hon. Member is an infamous lie, and he knows it.

White with passion, Sir Edward Carson stood by the table : his tall figure swung round towards the Nationalist benches. "Joe", as his Nationalist colleagues affectionately called Mr. Joseph Devlin, was the centre of a cheering crowd who shouted across the gangway at the protesting men behind Sir Edward Carson. Very soon Members in all parts of the

House were shouting indiscriminately at the two Irishmen and at one another. Rising impressively the Speaker quelled the storm. He reminded Sir Edward Carson that the expression he had used was not a proper one, however strong his feelings might be.

"I should be sorry, Sir, to offend the dignity of the Chair by any expression I used" said Sir Edward. "This is a statement which has been repeated and contradicted many times. At the same time, I would ask leave to withdraw 'infamous lie' and to say 'wilful falsehood'".

Mr. Devlin endeavoured to pursue his point. The fact that Sir Edward Carson was once a Member of the National Liberal Club had been discussed quite recently in the press. It was asserted that membership of this institution was often broadly interpreted. Mr. Devlin was proceeding to quote the form signed on admission in which each member declared himself a Liberal in politics when the Speaker asked whether it was desirable to introduce personal matters which they had heard several times before. Speaking in very solemn tones he added:

We are now approaching a very serious climax in the affairs of this country, and I would appeal to hon. Members to drop these personal remarks.

Mr. Churchill here asked to be allowed to say, as his name had been brought in, that he had not the slightest personal resentment in respect of any comments made about him, and he certainly did not desire that anyone should take up the cudgels on his behalf. Mr. Devlin, passing to the broad issues, delivered an eloquent speech on the general principle of Irish self-government. As an Ulsterman he represented the Home Rule aspirations of that considerable portion of the population in the North-eastern counties who were opposed to the Orangemen and Unionists. He observed that it had been inferred in Conservative speeches that the Irish Home Rulers were "skulking behind British troops". On this he declared:

I have stated on platforms, and I repeat it now, that if this were to be determined by the arbitrament of the sword,

and if you took your British troops and British police out
of Ireland we, who hold passionately to the conviction that
Ireland ought to have Home Rule upon logical, upon democratic, upon reasonable, upon historical, and upon traditional
lines, are prepared to have the issue fought out in that way.

The next incident followed upon wild rumours in London
as to the movement of troops in Ireland and alleged disaffec-
tion in the Army.

Chapter 53

WILD RUMOURS. THE SPEAKER DEFIED

MARCH hares were chasing each other madly round
all the circles of political gossip.

There was little doubt that arms had been landed in the
North of Ireland and leading men in Ulster still asserted they
would fight against Home Rule even if passed by Parliament.
Picturesque stories of active preparations for armed resistance; vague references to elaborate military measures by
the Government; sensational predictions of impending
violence kept the political world ablaze.

Questions, interjections in debate, and scenes followed
each other in the House of Commons with such turbulent
persistence that the ordinary onlooker found a difficulty in
disentangling a connective narrative from the maze of
assertions and contradictions.

According to the Minister for War information had reached
the Authorities which led them to assume that hotheaded
persons under no discipline might try to capture certain
stores of arms and ammunition. It was resolved that steps
should be taken for guarding military supplies against any
such attempt, and reinforcements were moved into this
particular district. As there was a suggestion that there
might be a difficulty in carrying the troops by train,
preparations were made to send them by sea. It was also
decided that a battle squadron and a flotilla should be

moved from Arosa Bay, where they were cruising, to Lamlash, whence they could rapidly reach Belfast.

Mr. Churchill, summing up the situation in the light of history, says in his realistic book "The World Crisis":

> Beyond this nothing was authorised; but the Military Commanders, seeing themselves confronted with what might well be the opening movements in a civil war, began to study plans of a much more serious character on what was the inherently improbable assumption that the British troops would be forcibly resisted and fired upon by the Orange Army.

An impression arose that these activities were intended as a demonstration of force against Ulster. It was suggested that there was a plan to treat Ulster as an enemy's country and to overwhelm the province with a surprise attack. Hypothetical questions as to what might be their attitude in certain circumstances were put to some officers. They offered their resignations in protest and hysterical statements appeared in some of the London papers as to the state of feeling in the army.

The officers concerned were summoned to come at once to London. After investigations the Army Council satisfied themselves that there had been a misunderstanding and the officers returned to their duties expressing their full willingness to discharge their duty of supporting the civil power in the maintenance of order and the preservation of peace.

A memorandum was given to the senior officer to the effect that this was all that would be demanded of them.

As to the naval position, Mr. Churchill was asked in the House of Commons by Mr. Amery whether he "expected and hoped that purely precautionary measures to look after stores would lead to fighting and bloodshed".

Mr. Churchill asked leave to "repudiate that hellish suggestion".

The Speaker pointed out that whatever indignation the First Lord of the Admiralty might feel, an expression of that sort could not be permitted.

Later in the evening during a debate upon the same subject the storm still raged round the First Lord of the

Admiralty. When Mr. Churchill rose to continue the discussion he was assailed with cries of "Resign". In a fighting speech he contended that nothing had been done which the circumstances did not warrant.

In the course of the evening the Leaders of the Conservative Party in response to challenges from the Labour Members had drawn a distinction between soldiers called upon to take part in an expedition to enforce Home Rule in Ulster, and soldiers brought into action to quell disorder during a strike. Mr. Churchill thus took up this point:

> Every effort has been made with the greatest dialectical skill by the right hon. Gentleman the Senior Member for the City of London (Mr. Balfour) and by the Leader of the Opposition who emulates his dialectical force without his dialectical subtlety, to show that it is always right for soldiers to shoot down a Radical or a Labour man—[hon. Members: "Liar!" "Withdraw" and Interruption]—and always wrong—[Interruption and Hon. Members: "Rub it in!" and "Withdraw!"].

> * * * * *

> As I say, great efforts have been made to show that when it is a Tory quarrel then the Army ought to act. But in any matter where Liberals are concerned, then, of course, no gentleman would demean himself by doing his duty to the Crown and Parliament.

In this temperature that debate concluded. Two days later the Prime Minister produced a special Army Order under the heading of "Discipline" which had been issued by the Army Council to the effect that no officer or soldier should in future be questioned by his superior officer as to his attitude in hypothetical contingencies; nor should any officer or soldier ask for assurances as to the orders which he might be required to carry out; and further that it was the duty of every officer and soldier to obey all lawful commands given through the proper channel.

The feature of the very brief discussion on this was an indignant speech by Captain Morrison-Bell, every word of which was that of a man speaking from the depths of his heart and soul. On behalf of the officers and men in the Army he declared that the statements read by the Prime Minister were the grossest insult to the whole of the Army. There never was, and there never would be, he asserted, a single doubt as to the possibility of the officers or the men obeying the orders of their superior officers.

This incident occurred on Friday afternoon. On the following Monday Colonel Seely arrived during Question Time. When he reached the centre of the House it was observed that instead of taking his place on the Treasury Bench he walked up the gangway. From this it was evident that his resignation, which he tendered the previous week, had now been accepted. It was also intimated that other resignations of the permanent staff had been handed in. The short reason was that the Memorandum given to the officers after the interview in London had gone farther than the Cabinet authorised.

It should here be mentioned that several prominent Conservatives had all along asserted that there could be no question as to the duty of soldiers to obey orders given by the proper authority in any circumstances.

Mr. Asquith announced that, after much consideration, he felt it his duty, for the time being at any rate, to assume the office of Secretary of State for War. At a later period he observed that while he was at the War Office his Department would hear no politics from him and he would expect to hear none from them.

The matter was not disposed of by changes at the War Office. Mr. Austen Chamberlain, on behalf of the Opposition, put down a motion that in view of the serious nature of the naval and military movements and the continued failure of the Government to deal frankly with the situation, there should be a full and impartial inquiry into all the circumstances.

Mr. Churchill described the motion as "the most audacious Vote and the most impudent demand for a judicial inquiry of which our records can provide a parallel". He observed that the first maxim of English jurisprudence was that complainer's should come into court with clean hands. And then occurred this enlivening passage:

> Mr. Churchill : Here we get the right hon. Gentleman the Member for Dublin University (Sir E. Carson) and the Hon. Member who sits behind him, fresh from their gun-running exploits——
>
> Sir E. Carson made an observation which was inaudible in the Gallery.
>
> Hon. Members : Behave like a king !
>
> Sir E. Carson : You behave like a cad !

Next came the inevitable point of order. The Speaker ruled the expression used by Sir Edward Carson improper, but also rebuked other hon. Members for their "taunting and offensive" observations.

Out of these volcanic debates, strangely enough, arose a general movement in the direction of concord.

Towards the end of his speech Mr. Churchill adopted a conciliatory attitude, and appealed for some agreed settlement on the lines of safeguarding the dignity and interests of Protestant Ulster. Mr. Balfour took a similar line. He declined to admit that there were no circumstances in which it was justifiable for a population to resist the Government. Such cases, he added, were rare:

> The coercion of Ulster, in the sense of compelling Ulster to leave a free Government under which she is happy, and put her under a Government which she detests, is one of those cases. I hold now, and I held nearly thirty years ago, that if Home Rule was forced upon Ulster, Ulster would fight and Ulster would be right.

Then followed one of the most affecting and impressive passages of persuasive oratory ever delivered in the House of Commons. Accepting Home Rule with the exclusion of Ulster as a possible solution Mr. Balfour in a tone of deep emotion that fascinated the House continued:

> There was a time, and it is not so very long ago, when I cherished the dream that . . . ancient memories would gradually soften, men would look forward as well as backward,

and there would grow up what there ought to be as between these two islands, a common hope, a common loyalty, confidence in the common heritage, and all this might be accomplished under one Parliament. . . . If in order that civil war may be avoided, with all its incalculable horrors, there is yet to be established in Dublin a separate Parliament to the injury, as I personally think, of the British people, then I, for my part, may be an object of pity to the right hon. Gentleman (Mr. Churchill); but he need not think that I shall regard such a consummation as a triumph over my political enemies. On the contrary, it is the mark of the failure of a life's work; it is the admission that the causes for which I have most striven, which I have most earnestly sought to accomplish, are fated to break down, and that long labours spent in this House, and out of this House, in political work have not borne the fruit that I once hoped they might.

With such an example before them Statesmen in the forefront of the conflict were encouraged to make another effort towards mutual concessions, but when the House met for the Third Reading of the Home Rule Bill on the 21st of May there was a thrilling demonstration of the fact that no agreement had yet been reached.

Lord Robert Cecil opened the attack with a motion that the debate be adjourned. When the Prime Minister rose in response to this motion he was met with a running fire of interjections.

The Speaker appealed to hon. Members to continue the discussion in the ordinary parliamentary way, and later on called Mr. Amery to order for referring to the Prime Minister as "an old gentleman who cannot make up his mind".

Eventually the motion to adjourn the debate was defeated and then the crescendo note was struck.

Mr. J. H. Campbell rose from the Front Opposition Bench ostensibly to continue the debate.

"Adjourn! Adjourn!" shouted the Conservative Members below the gangway. The cry was taken up by the back Bench Members of the official Opposition above the gangway. If Mr. Campbell was addressing the House no syllable could be heard. He stood at the Box complacently surveying the

Government Benches opposite outwardly unmindful of the continuous roars of "Adjourn! Adjourn!" from his own side.

Some two years before Members of the Opposition had been advised in certain quarters to shout "Dissolve! Dissolve!" continuously and thus prevent the House of Commons from proceeding with its business. The fact that a Member of the Conservative Party—a vehement anti-Home Ruler—happened to be on his feet was incidental. The demonstration had no reference to his presence at the Table: Either the advice formerly given was being followed or this was a spontaneous outburst of violent protest against the policy of the Government.

Mr. Bonar Law sat in the middle of the Front Opposition Bench with folded arms looking straight over the heads of the men on the Government Bench. The other Conservative Leaders sitting beside him, while taking no active part in the commotion, indicated by their attitude that they had no subduing advice to offer their followers.

The shouts consolidated into a deafening chant. Any attempt at ordered debate was impossible. The Speaker rose and the turmoil subsided for a moment. What followed is thus officially recorded:

MR. SPEAKER: Hon. Members seem determined not to hear their Leader. I would ask the Leader of the Opposition whether that is with his assent and approval——

EARL WINTERTON: Do not answer!

MR. BONAR LAW: I would not presume to criticise what you consider your duty, Sir, but I know mine, and that is not to answer any such question.

MR. SPEAKER: Having invited the right hon. Gentleman to assist me in obtaining order, I have been disappointed in that—[An Hon. Member: " Hurrah! "]—and there is nothing open to me except, under Standing Order 21, to suspend the sitting of the House, which I do until to-morrow.

The Conservative Members wildly cheered their Leader. One of them walked over to the Front Bench and stood in front of the Prime Minister shouting abuse at him as the

U

Speaker left the House. They then crowded into the Lobby jeering and gesticulating as they passed the Government supporters who complacently remained in their seats.

A Private Member's day intervened, and when the House met again for Government business a more conciliatory atmosphere all round prevailed, in which the Speaker with judicial tact took the lead. He remarked that Mr. Bonar Law seemed to think that his request conveyed some imputation of responsibility for the demonstration which had taken place. "I wish to say frankly" added Mr. Speaker "that no such idea was in my mind, and if I conveyed such an imputation by the question which I put to him, I am extremely sorry."

Dealing with the strained situation generally, the Speaker suggested that the Prime Minister, if he could see his way to do it, should give some further information to the House with regard to the amending Bill which it was understood would be introduced with a view to a settlement by agreement. Mr. Bonar Law expressed his personal gratitude to the Speaker for the generous statement which he had just made, adding "Such a statement could only be made, if I may venture respectfully to say so, by one who is conscious of his strength".

Mr. Asquith, also responding to the Speaker's suggestion, said he had not abandoned hope of agreement, and he assured the House it was the intention of the Government to introduce an amending Bill embodying the substance of the proposals which had already been outlined by him with respect to the position of Ulster. Mr. Bonar Law admitted the conciliatory nature of the Prime Minister's speech.

After a little "sniping" across the floor from below the gangway the Bill was read a third time by a big majority, and another stage was reached in the controversy which at that moment appeared to be monopolising public life.

*　　*　　*　　*　　*

In a year of unexampled excitement, it might be mentioned at this point, another step was taken towards bringing justice to the doors of the poor. Measures had already been adopted to provide for the defence of poor prisoners, but there was

no recognised machinery up to this point for assisting persons
of small means who desired to bring or were called upon to
answer claims in the Civil Courts. Accordingly "Poor
Persons Rules" were formed and a "Prescribed Officer for
Poor Persons" established. Solicitors and Barristers were
invited to put their names on a Rota to undertake cases
within the rules. If a person could satisfy the Prescribed
Officer that there was a prima facie case for a Civil Court
or for the Divorce Court, and that he or she possessed only
limited financial resources, Court fees would be remitted and
legal aid assigned. The Solicitors undertook to act without
remuneration beyond out of pocket expenses and the Barristers
without fees.

Chapter 54

THE ENTENTE CORDIALE—POLITICS AND COMMERCE

KEEN public interest was aroused by a pleasing
international incident.

The King and Queen returned the visit paid by President
Poincare to this country in 1913. On their arrival at Paris
they were met by the President of the Republic and Madame
Poincare and were cheered by enthusiastic crowds as they drove
from the railway station. The State functions in their honour
were, as "The Times" remarked, "conducted with a dignified
splendour which no Court in Europe could excel". At one of
the banquets the President observed that this was the tenth
anniversary of the conclusion of the Anglo-French Entente.

The decade had brought its changes, but the friendship
remained firm. King George was as welcome in Paris as
King Edward.

Meantime Sir Edward Grey held conferences with the
French Premier as to various questions of interest to both
countries. It was suggested in some quarters that matters
had progressed so far that the Entente might now develop
into an Alliance. The British Government made no movement

that warranted this expectation, but the neighbourly feeling between the two countries was undoubtedly strengthened.

The death of the Rev. Silvester Horne during a visit to America deprived the English Free Churches of a popular preacher and the Liberal Party in the House of Commons of a Member who in a comparatively short period had become a Parliamentary influence. Under the constitution a clergyman of the Established Church may not sit in Parliament. There is no rule which prevents a Nonconformist Minister being elected, but very few had become Members, and Mr. Horne's position was thus somewhat singular. The experiment promised success.

The bye-election at Ipswich rendered necessary by Mr. Horne's death was keenly contested and resulted in the loss of a seat for the Government. The victory coming just while the Home Rule Bill was going through its third reading, together with another win for the Opposition in North-east Derbyshire in a three-cornered contest, led the Conservatives to the belief that though the Government were still able to secure majorities in the House of Commons they were losing ground in the country. Various causes were suggested for the defeats of Government candidates. It was evident that the tacit and unofficial understanding by which Labour Members in the House of Commons were giving a general support to the Government was weakening in the country. Mr. Lloyd George declared that the "rock ahead" was "not the trumpery little trouble in Ulster" but the division between Labour and Liberalism. Both bye-elections, he said, had been lost owing to dissentions between Liberals and Members of the Labour Party in the constituencies.

The suffragettes claimed some share in the defeat of the Government candidates. Apart from the militants, a number of women who had been ardent Liberal workers were either less enthusiastic or had ceased to render active support. The fact that the organisers of big meetings were compelled in self-defence to restrict the audiences to men had a depressing effect upon some of their best supporters.

The militant suffragettes meantime were growing more turbulent. At a special matinee of "The Silver King" attended by the King and Queen a woman stood up and addressed His Majesty as a Russian Tsar. There were more burnings of buildings; more arrests; an attempt was made to force a way into Buckingham Palace to present a petition to the King, and Mrs. Pankhurst, who was out of prison under the "Cat and Mouse Act" was rearrested at the head of the procession.

All these political events were overshadowed at Whitsuntide by the greatest disaster since the "Titanic". The Canadian Pacific Liner "The Empress of Ireland" was run down in a fog off Father Point, and of the fourteen hundred and sixty-seven persons aboard, one thousand and twenty-three were lost, including Mr. Laurence Irving—the son of Sir Henry Irving—and his wife, both of whom were gifted and highly popular actors.

When attention reverted to political matters, suffragettes obtruded the question of forcible feeding upon worshippers at service in the Cathedrals. At the King's Court Miss Mary Blomfield, daughter of an eminent architect and a descendent of a famous Bishop of London, fell on her knees when passing the King and Queen and cried out "Your Majesty, wont you stop torturing women?" The campaign of violence up and down the country went on with redoubled fury. Lord Robert Cecil, as a consistent supporter of woman suffrage, protested in Parliament against this "anarchy". He remarked that public irritation was increasing and was venting itself upon peaceful suffragists. Lord Robert expressed a strong opinion that while the followers might be sincere, the leaders of the militant movement were more interested in their party than in the success of woman suffrage. A joint protest against militancy was also issued by the National Union of Woman Suffrage Societies and the Conservative and Liberal Unionist Women's Franchise Association, declaring militant methods to be "a negation of the very principles for which we stand" as making physical force the ultimate basis of government.

Lord Robert Cecil very shortly afterwards showed anxiety about disorder in another direction. He moved the adjournment of the House in order to call attention to "the growing danger caused by the existence of the Volunteer Forces in Ireland and the failure of the Government to deal with the matter". There was no doubt that as a counter to the Ulster forces the Irishmen in the South and West were drilling. It was estimated that the Ulstermen had some one-hundred-and-ten-thousand men, while the Irish volunteers representing the Home Rule forces were already estimated at eighty to one hundred thousand, and it was said that they were increasing at the rate of some fifteen thousand a week. This was generally accepted in the debate as a correct summary of the position. Mr. John Dillon on behalf of the Irish Nationalist Party asked if Lord Robert Cecil had ever remonstrated with his own Front Bench who went over to review the Ulster Volunteers. Mr. Birrell the Chief Secretary for Ireland remarked that he had recently spent some days in Ulster and the one thing brought home to him very much indeed was the genius of the Irish people for admiring each other. He went on to say:

> The recent gun-running expedition by Ulster Volunteers excited almost as much admiration amongst the Roman Catholic Nationalists as it did even in the highest councils of the Ulster Volunteers. There are a great many people, I find, strongly opposed to Home Rule who also entertain, I will not say a sneaking, but a really genuine feeling of pride in the fact that amongst the Irish National Volunteers are so many old soldiers ready for action, and so many of the very finest and best of the young men in the South and West of Ireland.

From this Mr. Birrell drew the moral that self-respect might spring even out of these somewhat strange methods, and that it might still be possible to find a solution of the difficulties. He intimated in effect that he saw no useful purpose in prosecuting either side. A voice from the Liberal benches was raised against this attitude by a son of Lord Rosebery—Mr. Neil Primrose, whose ability and sincerity in

debate predicted a distinguished future, but who was destined, like others, to complete his service to his country
while yet in the full glow of youth and hope.   Mr. Primrose
declared that it was "impossible to conceive a more farcical
motion being brought forward by a prominent member of a
party which has aided and abetted and organised armed force
in Ulster," but he nevertheless urged upon the Government
the importance of administering the law without any respect
for persons on either side.   Otherwise, he went on to say,
they would lose the moral right to enforce law elsewhere.

Mr. Bonar Law's remedy was that the Government should
have a General Election and seek the sanction of the people
for their policy, in which case he said he and his friends
would not support resistance in Ulster.

The motion for the adjournment was defeated and attention
drifted to other subjects.

The Commercial world looking upon the prospects of
business was realising that a process of evolution was now
maturing in the general trend of business methods.   Most
people in business had in their day dealt with the private
banks.   These institutions belonged to well known families.
Some of them were the property of the ruling territorial
Houses.   In the agricultural districts the banker was part
country gentleman and part business man.   In many cases
the country gentlemen predominated and the business was
conducted by efficient junior partners.   In the towns small
companies, the shares in which were held by well known
local men, owned most of the banks.   The private banks
and the company banks operated in their own areas.   The
heads of the concerns were known personally to most of
their customers and the condition in life of each individual
customer was approximately known to the banker.

Gradually—indeed almost imperceptibly so far as the
man in the street observed things—the private families had
thrown in their lot with the companies.   Then the companies
combined and the movement began towards amalgamations.
Large joint stock banks carrying on big business and operating

over wide areas began to acquire the smaller banks with results to be discussed hereafter.

The tendency in banking was the index to commercial life. The rumoured combinations at the beginning of the Century had taken practical form. In every branch of human activity—save in those particular professions where the personal element was paramount—amalgamations extended year by year. The old form of private partnership was disappearing. When partners shared the same office—often the same room—with daily consultations concerning every department of their business it was quite reasonable to assume—as the law did—that each partner acted by and with the consent of the others and was in consequence their responsible agent to the full extent of their individual assets if need should arise for calling upon them. A Limited Partnerships Act was passed in 1907 under which a passive or sleeping partner might invest his money without being liable beyond the extent of his investment. This was taken advantage of to some extent but it did not meet the case of the bigger syndicates with business premises at different spots—often in different towns and in different parts of the country. For these undertakings the Public Limited Liability Company was obviously the only system. One concern after another was reported first to be in alliance with and then incorporated by a bigger undertaking.

The expansion of international trade encouraged the "big business" method. Capital was growing more mobile. Investments were assuming a cosmopolitan character. Private investors as well as business men placed their money out in the market most favourable at the moment irrespective of geographical limit. In speculations such as these the large corporation necessarily had an advantageous position. It was inevitable that there should also be alliances between companies in different countries. This was especially so between British and American Companies but it was also true of other countries. Inter-trading was conducted on a scale almost undreamt of a few years earlier. Little wonder the matter of fact person, leaving out of account human passions, ambitions and frailties, began to assume that the civilised world was becoming one vast community with interests so interdependent that a disintegration of these intimate business relations was unthinkable.

The debates in Parliament and the speeches in the country as to the unsettled condition of affairs did not disturb these commercial calculations.   Politicians talked of civil war; the ordinary person went about his daily affairs.   There was a general notion that something was going on behind the scenes and that some sort of agreement would be arrived at between the political leaders.   Some people in other lands who did not understand the psychology of British politics or the Irish temperament, drew a different conclusion.

Simultaneous British naval visits to Kronstadt and Kiel took place at the end of June.   For the first time in several years British and German vessels were moored side by side; yachts and passenger ships carrying spectators were also there to mark the festive character of the occasion.   Mr. Churchill thus describes the scene:

> Undue curiosity in technical matters was banned by mutual agreement.   There were races, there were banquets, there were speeches.   There was sunshine.   There was the Emperor.   Officers and men fraternised and entertained each other afloat and ashore.   Together they strolled arm in arm through the hospitable town, or dined with all goodwill in mess and wardroom.   Together they stood bareheaded at the funeral of a German officer killed in flying an English seaplane.

Did any mortal imagine that a tragedy was in the mint of fate at the other end of Europe moulding all these hopes of friendship into the bitterness of relentless conflict?

Chapter 55

THE SERAJEVO MURDER AND AFTER

ON the evening of Sunday June 28th, 1914, in the midst of the Kiel festivities, news arrived that the Archduke

Ferdinand, nephew of the Emperor of Austria and heir presumptive to the Austro-Hungarian throne, and his Consort, had been murdered in the streets of Serajevo the capital of Bosnia, while on their way from a State ceremony.

The German Emperor was out sailing when he received the message. Mr. Churchill records that he came on shore in noticeable agitation, and that same evening, cancelling his other arrangements, quitted Kiel.

The tragedy revived memories of the annexation in 1908 by Austria of Bosnia-Hertzogovinia, the country where adherents of the orthodox Eastern Church known as Serbs; Catholics calling themselves Croats; and Moslems described as Turks, dwelt in religious discord, but all belonged to the Serbo-Croatian branch of the Slavonic race and were therefore of the same family as the Serbians and Russians.

Austria with the acquiescence of the Powers under the Berlin Treaty of 1878 had exercised supervision in the interest of the restoration of peace and order. When the presumably temporary occupation became annexation Serbia was naturally displeased at the prospect of this Balkan State being swallowed up in the Austrian Empire. Russia might have protested, but Germany "rattled the sabre in the scabbard" warning all whom it might concern that Austria was her ally; and Russia, then still weak from the war with Japan, acquiesced in the inevitable.

Outside diplomatic circles that affair was almost forgotten by 1914. "Trouble in the Balkans", once a hardy annual, had often been the initial spark of conflagration in Eastern Europe, but more often the flame had faded to a localised flicker.

Under the shadow of the latest tragedy the deepest sympathy was felt with the Austrian Royal family. In the British House of Commons the Prime Minister moved that an humble Address be presented to His Majesty the King expressing the indignation and concern with which the House learned of the assassination and praying that His Majesty would be graciously pleased to express to the Emperor of Austria on behalf of the House of Commons their abhorrence of the crime. This was seconded by Mr. Bonar Law and carried unanimously. A similar motion was passed by the House of Lords.

Communications and "Notes" now began to pass between diplomatists. Austrian opinion, expressed through the press and other channels, clearly indicated that the Austrian Government attributed the crime to Serbian fanatics who were alleged to have plotted and planned the murder on Serbian soil, and that official assurances of some kind might be asked from the Serbian Government.

So far as the general public were concerned, matters rested there for some weeks. Meantime home affairs engaged the attention of the British people.

On the 2nd July Mr. Joseph Chamberlain who had lived in virtual retirement since he appeared in the House of Commons to take the Oath after the second 1910 Election, passed peacefully away at a ripe age. At his funeral at the Key Hill Cemetery, Birmingham, the Church was filled with representatives of the City Council, local and political associations. Vast crowds lined the streets; messages of sympathy were received from the King, the King of Spain, the President of the French Republic, from the Dominions, and all parts of the world.

A Memorial Service in Westminster Abbey was attended by representatives of the King, Foreign Powers and the Dominions, and by many Members of both Houses, including Ministers. In the House of Lords the Marquis of Crewe from the Liberal side spoke of Mr. Chamberlain as "the greatest civic figure ever engaged in British politics". The Marquis of Lansdowne paid a sincere tribute to Mr. Chamberlain's merits as a colleague and leader, and Viscount Milner referred to him as "an incomparable Chief".

It was natural that the most impressive token of gratitude for Mr. Chamberlain's long services should come from the House of Commons, where he had been in the forefront of Parliamentary life for thirty years. The Prime Minister recalled the fact that Mr. Chamberlain's name was and would be imperishably associated with all the great public controversies of his day. Neutrality was impossible to a man of his temperament and of his convictions. Mr. Asquith continued:

> In that striking personality—vivid, masterful, resolute, tenacious—there were no blurred or nebulous outlines, there were no relaxed fibres, there were no pauses of lethargy. . . . . He and I have exchanged many blows, particularly in the latest enterprise of his active career. Though he was an unsparing, he was always a generous antagonist, and I rejoice to remember that we never ceased to be friends. . . . . It is fitting that within these walls—where the echoes of his voice seem to many of us still to linger—we should suspend for a few hours the clash of controversy, while we all join in acknowledging our common debt to the life and the example of a great Englishman. I beg to move that the House do now adjourn.

Mr. Bonar Law expressed his thanks to the Prime Minister on behalf of Members of his side of the House for the reverence he had shown to the Leader whom they admired and loved. Mr. Balfour, who spoke with a memory of Mr. Chamberlain's entry into the House of Commons and with a close knowledge of him as a colleague, paid a touching tribute to "a great Statesman, a great friend, a great orator, and a great man ".

The House of Commons unanimously accepted Mr. Asquith's proposal to adjourn at once.

When the ordinary controversies of political life were renewed, Ireland was still an unsolved problem. It was agreed on all hands that the Leaders of political parties should make an approach to each other, and the King clearly interpreted the wish of the nation in a summons inviting Conservative, Liberal, and Irish Party leaders to meet in conference at Buckingham Palace.

Meantime the general public were deeply interested in a Naval Review at Spithead on the 17th and 18th July. The most powerful Fleet ever assembled, numbering two hundred vessels in all, was manned by some seventy-thousand officers and men. There were also squadrons of seaplanes and aeroplanes. The King was to have gone down in the early morning, but waited in London to make arrangements for the conference, and left in the afternoon, when he inspected the ships of every class.

In the morning of the 19th the whole Fleet put to sea for exercises. Decked with flags and crowded with Bluejackets and Marines, they sailed past the Royal Yacht with seaplanes and aeroplanes circling above them. The whole ceremony occupied over six hours.

The Speaker of the House of Commons presided over the Buckingham Palace conference, and, as afterwards became known, the two sections of Irishmen were unable to agree, mainly upon the boundaries of the counties of Fermanagh and Tyrone. The question at issue was whether these counties or parts of them, and which parts respectively, belonged to the South of Ireland, or to that part of Ulster which should be excluded from the Home Rule Bill. On Friday 24th July the House of Commons had been discussing a Housing Bill brought in by Mr. Runciman the President of the Board of Agriculture, designed to do something for the housing problem in the agricultural districts. Just before five o'clock information circulated through the usual channels that the Cabinet were sitting, and an important announcement on the Irish question would be made on the motion for the adjournment.

Onlookers who were privileged to be in a position to watch the Members of the Cabinet filing in from behind the Speaker's chair were struck with the look of deep solemnity on the face of each individual Minister.

It had already been rumoured that the Buckingham Palace conference had broken down. That was serious enough, but Statesmen had been living with that problem for so long at high tension that the failure of another attempt at a settlement was hardly sufficient reason for such profound gravity.

When the Speaker put the motion "This House do now adjourn" the Prime Minister briefly announced that the conference summoned by His Majesty the King held meetings on the 21st, 22nd, 23rd and 24th July respectively, and being unable to agree either in principle or in detail upon the

possibility of defining an area for exclusion from the operation
of the Government of Ireland Bill, it had brought its meetings
to a conclusion. Mr. Asquith further announced that the
Government's amending Bill embodying his own proposals
would be taken the following week.

Mr. Bonar Law, who rose after Mr. Asquith sat down,
merely said "I propose to follow the example set by the
Prime Minister and make no comment on the report".

He agreed to the suggestion that the amending Bill should
be discussed the following week. In reply to a question as
to whether the House could be informed of the exact difference of
opinion, the Prime Minister said with the brevity of a man who
is thinking of deeper matters that he would rather make no
statement.

The House gradually emptied. As people wandered from
the precincts for the week-end they asked each other what
really was in the minds of those preoccupied men sitting
rigidly on the Front Bench while the Prime Minister made
his brief announcement.

The explanation has been supplied in vivid language by
Mr. Winston Churchill in "The World Crisis":

> The discussion [on Ireland] had reached its conclusive
> end, and the Cabinet was about to separate, when the quiet
> grave tones of Sir Edward Grey's voice were heard reading
> a document which had just been brought to him from the
> Foreign Office. It was the Austrian note to Serbia. He
> had been reading or speaking for several minutes before I
> could disengage my mind from the tedious and bewildering
> debate which had just closed. We were all very tired, but
> gradually as the phrases and sentences followed one another,
> impressions of a wholly different character began to form in
> my mind. This note was clearly an ultimatum ; but it was
> an ultimatum such as had never been penned in modern times.
> As the reading proceeded, it seemed absolutely impossible that
> any State in the world could accept it, or that any acceptance,
> however abject, would satisfy the aggressor. The parishes of
> Fermanagh and Tyrone faded back into the mists and squalls of
> Ireland, and a strange light began immediately, but by per-
> ceptible gradations, to fall and grow upon the map of Europe.

Mr. Churchill's book was published years afterwards. At the moment people outside the Cabinet little knew what the anxious faces of the Ministers portended.

Chapter 56

VITAL NEGOTIATIONS

IN his Memoirs Viscount Grey (then Sir Edward Grey) says: "The world will presumably never be told all that was behind the murder of the Archduke Ferdinand". Lord Grey observes further: "Probably there is not and never was any one person who knew all that there was to know. There was more than one quarter in which the Archduke's succession to the great position of his uncle might be supposed to be unwelcome".

There had been an attempt to murder him on his way to the ceremony and the inference to be drawn from all the circumstances was that if the second attempt had failed there would still have been others.

The theory advanced by the Austrian Government—unsupported, as Viscount Grey points out, by direct evidence —was that the Serbian Government was responsible for the assassination; and about a month after the tragedy the ultimatum read to the British Cabinet, as mentioned by Mr. Winston Churchill and referred to in the last chapter, was delivered.

In this fateful document the Austrian Government, after asserting that there was in Serbia a subversive movement with the object of detaching a part of the territories of Austria-Hungary from the dual monarchy, and after alleging that the Serajevo crimes were planned in Belgrade, went on to demand that the Serbian Government should publish on the front page of its official journal a declaration condemning propaganda directed against Austro-Hungary. The "Royal Government of Serbia" was also called upon to dissolve certain societies which were alleged to be engaged in propaganda against the Austro-Hungarian monarchy. Then followed these further demands:

(5) To remove from the military service and from the administration in general all officers guilty of propaganda against the Austro-Hungarian Monarchy whose names and deeds the Austro-Hungarian Government reserves to itself the right of communicating to the Royal Government:

To accept the collaboration in Serbia of representatives of the Austro-Hungarian Government in the suppression of the subversive movement directed against the territorial integrity of the Monarchy;

(6) To take judicial proceedings against accessories to the plot of the 28th June who are on Serbian territory. Delegates of the Austro-Hungarian Government will take part in the investigation relating thereto.

After insisting upon the arrest of certain persons and calling for explanations of reported utterances by individual officials, the Austrian note concluded:

The Austro-Hungarian Government expects the reply from the Royal Government by six o'clock on Saturday evening the 25th July.

For the sake of the peace of Europe, Great Britain and France—also it was understood Russia—urged conciliation on Serbia notwithstanding the drastic nature of the demands.

A reply was sent to Austria in which the Serbian Government, while expressing pain and surprise that members of the Kingdom of Serbia were supposed to have participated in the crime, agreed to issue an official declaration condemning propaganda; undertaking to pass a Press law against it and to suppress the societies of which Austria complained, though no proof existed of any criminal act. In point of fact all the conditions of the Austrian ultimatum were accepted with the following reservations on articles (5) and (6):

(5) The Royal Government must confess that they did not clearly grasp the meaning or the scope of the demand made by the Imperial and Royal Government that Serbia shall undertake to accept a collaboration of the Organs of the

Imperial and Royal Government upon their Territory but they declare that they will admit such collaboration as agrees with the principle of international law and criminal procedure and good neighbourly relations ;

(6) It goes without saying that the Royal Government consider it their duty to open an enquiry against all such persons as are or eventually may be implicated in the plot of the 28th June who happen to be within the territory of the Kingdom. As regards the participation in this enquiry of Austro-Hungarian agents or authorities appointed for this purpose by the Imperial and Royal Government the Royal Government cannot accept such an arrangement as it would be a violation of the constitution and of the law of criminal procedure ; nevertheless in concrete cases communications as to the results of the investigation in question might be given to the Austro-Hungarian agents.

Summing up the two documents Viscount Grey observes: "The Austrian ultimatum had gone even further than we had feared in the way of peremptory severity. The Serbian answer went further than we had ventured to hope in the way of submission."

Austria however declared the Serbian reply to be unsatisfactory. Sir Edward Grey and allied diplomatists entered into active communication. The British Foreign Minister asked the French, German and British Governments to meet in conference with a view to negotiating a settlement. Italy and France promptly accepted the invitation; Germany declined it. Still Sir Edward Grey and those who thought and worked with him in the Councils of Europe, as the records show, strenuously endeavoured to promote an understanding, but the Austrian Government declared war on Serbia, and Russia then formally announced the mobilisation of troops in the defence of the sister Slavonic race.

The public of Europe now began to realise that war was upon us. The vital question was how far would it extend? It was common knowledge that Austria was the protégé and virtually the instrument of the bigger Germanic power dominated by the old Prussian oligarchy. France would come

x

to the aid of Russia in recognition of the alliance between the two countries.

The decision of Great Britain was in the balance. The Government announced to the House of Commons that they were doing their best to "circumscribe the area of possible conflict". Lord Grey chronicles the fact that there was a difference of opinion among Members of the Cabinet as well as among Members of Parliament and the public outside as to whether and in what circumstances Great Britain ought to intervene.

The neutrality of Belgium was the all important factor. By Treaty in which certain other conditions were imposed on Belgium the great Powers of Europe pledged themselves to respect and preserve the neutrality of Belgium. When France and Germany were at war in 1870 the British Government declared its intention to maintain the Treaty and induced the two belligerent Powers not to violate it. A glance at the map showed that the speedy way to the heart of France from Germany was through Belgium, but there was a strong belief in many quarters that the German Government would refrain from violating the neutrality of a Power whom they were pledged by their predecessors to protect.

When the House of Commons separated for the week-end the spectre of war hovered over the land. The King as a last personal effort sent a direct telegram to the Tsar offering mediation. Meanwhile a German Ultimatum had been presented demanding the demobilisation of the Russian forces; and before the British Monarch's message reached the Tsar, Germany had declared war on Russia.

Sunday, August 2nd, found the British people calmly but seriously watching the swift progress of events. Prayers for the preservation of peace were offered in the places of worship. A London War Protest Meeting was held in Trafalgar Square, but a large element moved across the road to the Admiralty Arch and held a meeting in favour of supporting the Authorities in any eventuality.

In the evening a crowd of several thousands marched to Buckingham Palace singing the British and French National Anthems. The King and Queen came on the balcony and were greeted with enthusiastic cheers.

The following letter was handed to the Prime Minister:

> DEAR MR. ASQUITH,
>
> Lord Lansdowne and I feel it our duty to inform you that in our opinion as well as in that of all the colleagues whom we have been able to consult, it would be fatal to the honour and security of the British Empire to hesitate in supporting France and Russia at the present juncture; and we offer our unhesitating support to the Government in any measures they may consider necessary for that object.
>
> Yours very truly,
>
> A. BONAR LAW.

In some parts of the country where the rapidly developing movements at home and abroad were at the moment unrevealed, there was still a vague feeling that "it might blow over". People in touch with the London clubs and other resorts where news came through continuously from the Exchange Telegraph Company on their tape machines realised as the night advanced that the Germans were taking decisive steps for the invasion of France.

German troops seized the capital and railway bridges of Luxembourg the independent little Grand Duchy which slopes down into the Moselle valley. This was obviously a movement to obtain a strategic advantage. It was entirely contrary to the rights of little States, but when the Grand Duchess at the head of her Government protested she was told by the German Commander to "go away home".

Chapter 57

WAR

THE long green benches and the balconies of the House of Commons were crowded to the last inch on August Bank Holiday.

x*

Rows of chairs were placed on that stretch of floor between the Bar and Table rigorously marked out upon ordinary occasions as neutral territory.

Eager men listened with tense interest when Sir Edward Grey—his clear-cut, handsome face set and determined—advanced to the Table. Speaking slowly and deliberately the Foreign Minister reviewed the history of recent years down to the crisis in which as he pointed out France had become involved because of an obligation of honour under a definite alliance with Russia.

"We are not" he said "parties to the Franco-Russian alliance. We do not even know the terms of that alliance". He went on to speak of our friendship with France and the sense of security which that friendship had engendered in French minds. Even to the lay mind the significance of the following statement was plain:

> The French Fleet is now in the Mediterranean, and the Northern and Western coasts of France are absolutely undefended.

The House was prepared for, and with shouts of acclamation approved, the announcement:

> Yesterday afternoon I gave to the French Ambassador the following statement:

> ' I am authorised to give an assurance that if the German Fleet comes into the Channel or through the North Sea to undertake hostile operations against the French coasts or shipping, the British Fleet will give all the protection in its power. This assurance is, of course, subject to the policy of His Majesty's Government receiving the support of Parliament, and must not be taken as binding His Majesty's Government to take any action until the above contingency of action by the German Fleet takes place.'

News had arrived since that assurance was given that if Great Britain would pledge herself to neutrality the German Government would be prepared to agree not to attack the Northern coast of France. "It is far too narrow an engagement for us" said Sir Edward, and again cheers burst from different parts of the House.

The situation grew more and more dramatic as the quiet, profoundly earnest man unravelled the tangled skein of diplomatic negotiations. The gulf between the prospects of peace and war grew wider and wider. The serious consideration—becoming more serious every hour—of the neutrality of Belgium had yet to be determined. The Foreign Minister recited the circumstances of the Treaty of 1839. On this he said:

> We were sounded in the course of last week as to whether if a guarantee were given that, after the war, Belgium integrity would be preserved that would content us.

His voice hardened in dignified contempt as he went on to say:

> We replied that we could not bargain away whatever interests or obligations we had in Belgian neutrality.

Ringing cheers greeted this pronouncement. Memories of old-world oratory were revived as Sir Edward Grey quoted Mr. Gladstone's declaration upon our duty towards Belgian neutrality when the possibility of its violation in the war of 1870 was in issue:

> We have an interest in the independence of Belgium which is wider than that which we may have in the literal operation of the guarantee. It is found in answer to the question whether under the circumstances of the case, this country, endowed as it is with influence and power, would quietly stand by and witness the perpetration of the direst crime that ever stained the pages of history, and thus become participators in the sin.

Members leapt to their feet. Waving their Order Papers they cheered and cheered again. The grave spokesman for the Government was carrying the overwhelming majority of the crowded assembly with him at every step; though there were some sincere and silent men who heard and withheld assent.

When the Foreign Minister sat down the last word had yet

to be spoken. So quickly had events rushed upon each other that it was not quite certain at that moment whether war really existed between Germany and France. Ostensibly Western Europe still stood on the brink contemplating the torrent and listening to the roar of the distant cataract.

Speaking of possibilities Mr. Bonar Law as Leader of the Opposition had the enthusiastic concurrence of his party in his pronouncement:

> The Government already know, but I give them now the assurance on behalf of the Party of which I am Leader in this House, that in whatever steps they think it necessary to take for the honour and security of this country, they can rely on the unhesitating support of the Opposition.

In the course of his speech Sir Edward Grey had observed that the one bright spot was Ireland. He said he would like it to be clearly understood abroad that the general feeling throughout Ireland now did not make the Irish question a consideration which had to be taken into account in influencing the Government policy upon this crisis. From the corner seat below the gangway Mr. John Redmond rose. The full-toned cultured voice—heard so often of late in passionate appeals for Nationalist Ireland—ringing through the Chamber in a few eloquent sentences dispelled all calculations that might have been based upon civil disturbance at this critical moment in the British Isles:

> To-day there are in Ireland two large bodies of Volunteers. One of them sprang into existence in the North. Another has sprung into existence in the South. I say to the Government that they may to-morrow withdraw every one of their troops from Ireland. I say that the coast of Ireland will be defended from foreign invasion by her armed sons, and for this purpose armed Nationalist Catholics in the South will be only too glad to join arms with the armed Protestant Ulstermen in the North.

Mr. Ramsay Macdonald remained unconvinced that intervention by Great Britain was necessary or wise. He admitted that the feeling of the House was against those who thought with him. But speaking for this minority he declared:

> If the right hon. Gentleman had come here to-day and told us that our country is in danger, I do not care what Party he appealed to, or to what class he appealed, we would be with him and behind him. If this is so, we will vote him what money he wants. Yes, and we will go further. We will offer him ourselves if the country is in danger. But he has not persuaded me that it is.

Mr. Macdonald went on to assert that if he and his friends were convinced that the conflict was confined to protecting a small European nationality like Belgium, or if there was a danger of the power, civilisation and genius of France being removed from European history, they would support the Government. As matters stood they were not so assured, and in the deepest part of their hearts they believed this country should remain neutral.

The Leaders of Parties had spoken. There was no motion before the House, but Members were loath to leave the subject at this stage. The sitting was suspended for two hours. During that two hours news vital and decisive arrived. When the House reassembled the Foreign Minister, with an abstention from comment more forcible than words, reported that he had received the following intimation from the Belgian Legation in London:

> Germany sent yesterday evening at seven o'clock a Note proposing to Belgium friendly neutrality, covering free passage on Belgian territory, and promising maintenance of independence of the kingdom and possession at the conclusion of peace, and threatening, in case of refusal, to treat Belgium as an enemy. A time limit of twelve hours was fixed for the reply. The Belgians have answered that an attack on their neutrality would be a flagrant violation of the rights of nations, and that to accept the German proposal would be to sacrifice the honour of a nation. Conscious of its duty, Belgium is firmly resolved to repel aggression by all possible means.

The sentiments in the concluding sentences of this chivalrous declaration were re-echoed in vehement cheers from all parts of the House. Earnest speeches were made by Mr. Edmund Harvey, Mr. Arnold Rowntree—two members of the Society of Friends—and others urging a final effort for peace, but the sunshine of peace was fast fading into twilight. Before nightfall Germany formally declared war on France. The French Government had already given an assurance that in the event of war they would respect the neutrality of Belgium. A British Ultimatum was presented to the German Government demanding a similar undertaking by eleven p.m. (Midnight German time). The reply was a summary refusal. There could be but one interpretation.

Science, Art, Literature, Learning, Commerce, Law, gave place to force of arms.

The Temple of Janus was open. As Ancient Rome thus symbolised the end of peace, and by this mythological inspiration contemplated the destinies of battle, so cultured Europe now gazed beyond the Shrine of Western civilisation into the mists of an illimitable wilderness.

At eleven o'clock on the night of the fourth of August nineteen hundred and fourteen the old world passed away.

END OF VOL. I.

5|7|31

INDEX

329

PRINTED BY PURNELL AND SONS
PAULTON, SOMERSET, ENGLAND